BIM and Integrated Design

STRATEGIES FOR ARCHITECTURAL PRACTICE

Randy Deutsch, AIA, LEED AP

AIA

WILEY

John Wiley & Sons, Inc.

Copyright © 2011 by Randy Deutsch. All rights reserved.

Published by John Wiley & Sons, Inc., Hoboken, New Jersey.

Published simultaneously in Canada.

Library of Congress Cataloging-in-Publication Data:

Deutsch, Randy.
    BIM and integrated design : strategies for architectural practice / Randy Deutsch. — 1st ed.
       p. cm.
    Includes index.
    Summary: "Building Information Modeling (BIM) software combines 3-D elements and information in all aspects of the design of a building. While many books are published on BIM related to technology and computer programs, this one focuses on the practice-related information needs of architects, showing them how BIM and integrated practice can transform their practices. It features: Methods for addressing the obstacles and challenges to implementing BIM How to implement it in an efficient and effective manner How to use BIM as a tool to transform the role of architects "—Provided by publisher.
    ISBN 978-0-470-57251-1 (hardback); ISBN 978-1-118-08644-5 (ebk); ISBN 978-1-118-08647-6 (ebk); ISBN 978-1-118-08649-0 (ebk);
    ISBN 978-1-118-13018-6 (ebk); ISBN 978-1-118-13019-3 (ebk)
  1. Architectural practice. 2. Building information modeling. I. Title.
  NA1996.D475 2011
  720.285—dc23

                                     2011022703

Printed in the United States of America
10 9 8 7 6 5 4 3 2 1

BIM and Integrated Design

CONTENTS

INTRODUCTORY STATEMENT BY THE AMERICAN INSTITUTE OF ARCHITECTS

In this book, Randy Deutsch describes building information modeling (BIM) as a means of coordinating project information. Like the American Institute of Architects (AIA), Deutsch recognizes that while these methods and tools play a vital role in integrated practice, the collaboration essential to integration can be used with any type of project delivery.

As stated in the *Primer on Project Delivery* by the AIA and the Associated General Contractors of America, "At the present, there are no industry-wide accepted definitions of project delivery methods, and many groups, organizations, and individuals have developed their own. In so doing, they have often used different characteristics to define the delivery methods. The result has been a multiplicity of definitions, none of which is either entirely right or entirely wrong." Groups may use the same term to articulate different organizational concepts for project delivery as well as the tools used to bring about a successful project.

Deutsch's text describes the BIM process to be a dynamic, continuously evolving strategy for designing and making buildings. Because it is an emerging form of practice technology, the AIA acknowledges that other definitions of BIM may appear over time. The term *building information modeling* as used within the following pages may also be used to describe other operational arrangements by different groups. This book is an important step forward in the definition and discussion of a BIM-enabled project delivery approach that holds great promise.

PREFACE

This is not another technology book on Building Information Modeling (BIM), the software tool and process for generating and managing building data during its complete lifecycle, from conceptual design through fabrication, construction, maintenance, and operation of the building. While there are several excellent resources at your disposal that can answer many of your most pressing software-related questions concerning BIM, this is not one of them.

Nor is this a business BIM book that measures your return on investment (ROI) or provides business models or value propositions.

While these subjects are discussed in these pages, this is a different sort of BIM book.

That's because his book addresses *you*.

BIM and Integrated Design addresses obstacles faced by design professionals and their organizations in their use of technology, offering strategies—and in doing so—clearing a path toward success, however defined, for yourself, your firm, the profession, or industry.

Figure A   Building Information Modeling (BIM) platforms can be used to design just about anything. *Zach Kron, www.buildz.info*

Until BIM use is ubiquitous, until BIM permanently enters the lexicon and design professionals start thinking in terms of BIM's impact on all trades—until that day comes—you have this book to guide you.

This book originated with something I overheard. Charles Hardy, director of the General Services Administration's (GSA) Office of Project Delivery, put it bluntly when he said that "BIM is about 10 percent technology and 90 percent sociology." And yet to date 90 percent of the focus in training, education, and media has been on the innovative and admittedly visually appealing technology, or equally on the business model and value proposition of BIM. (See Figure B.)

Think about it. If the difference between a successful BIM implementation and a failed or even potentially catastrophic one has as much or even more to do with the mindsets and attitudes of those who use it as it does the technologies and work process the technologies enable and require, how will these necessary practical, attitudinal, and behavioral changes come about? (See Figure C.)

But 90 percent sociology? If that's the case, why are we spending 90 percent of our time attending webinars, seminars, and conferences on the technology? Why are 90 percent of the websites, user groups, and blogs devoted to the software? If true, we're perhaps asking the right questions but focused on the wrong outcomes. That's because it's mastering the process—not the technology—that leads to exceptional results, both aesthetically and financially. (See Figure D.)

There is a gap in our research and in our understanding. This book seeks to fill that gap by asking questions of and gathering insights from those who have worked in the BIM environment, used the software, adopted and implemented the programs and work processes in their organizations, taught the subject in a university setting, and struggled and watched the tools and process evolve over time.

Of the triumvirate of business, technology, and culture, culture is by far the least studied, analyzed, and, frankly, exploited. It is also the least understood. Human habits, social relations, social interaction, and intelligence—these are taken for granted and are the last frontier for garnering the greatest gains from the technology and work processes. The business and technology cases for BIM have already been made and largely accepted. It is about time that somebody made the cultural case for BIM. That is what this book sets out to do. (See Figure E.)

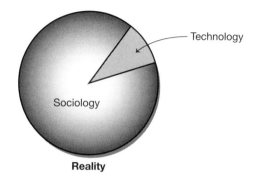

Reality

Figure B   "BIM is about 10 percent technology and 90 percent sociology." Charles Hardy, Director, Office of Project Delivery at U.S. General Services Administration (GSA).

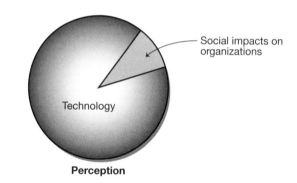

Perception

Figure C   The misperception is that BIM is about 90 percent technology and 10 percent sociology.

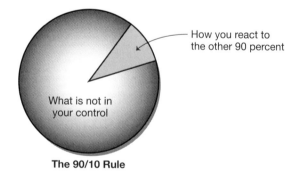

The 90/10 Rule

Figure D   Alternatively, 10 percent is what happens to us as a profession and industry, while 90 percent is decided by how you react to it.

Where were the answers to my questions concerning what it is like to be someone in the design professions or construction industry that works in a BIM environment? How is it different from the way we used to practice? How is the workflow changed—and what exactly is meant by "workflow"? What's with all those large screens and monitors? What exactly is a Big Room or iRoom, and do I need to have one? What's the difference between a BIM manager, an IT manager, and a CAD manager, or between a BIM operator and a BIM coordinator? Whom do I hire, whom do I mentor, and exactly whom do I select to work in BIM? Is it necessarily the employee who excelled at CAD, or is CAD expertise a potential impediment? Is it true that BIM takes as much social intelligence as technical competence? What changes to the workplace should I expect? How will we share data among the parties involved?

Figure E   The business and technology cases for BIM and integrated design have already been made. It is time to make the social case for firm culture, including working relationships, interactions, and intelligence.

Figure F   The one element propelling you and your organization today toward achieving your goals in the future is people—people with the right attitudes and mindset to benefit the most from using the new tools and collaborative work processes.

Everyone says you need to work collaboratively, but no one tells you how that's supposed to come about. All of a sudden, with a long history of confrontation, we're supposed to hold hands and sing "Kumbaya"? As soon as I started to seek out answers to these questions, other questions arose. (See Figure F.)

The book you hold in your hands is the result of having asked these questions. Like integrated design itself, there may be one author listed, but, as in the best of collaborative efforts, the book is informed by many. In this sense, the book less expounds the theory of one than shares the collective, unified wisdom of multitudes. I hope you find the responses I received and the answers I've uncovered insightful, informative, and ultimately invaluable.

ACKNOWLEDGMENTS

The fact that there is but one name on the cover of this book has not been lost on the author. Writing a book—much less one that promotes and fosters collaboration—always involves the work and thinking of many people. This book is no exception.

I would like to acknowledge Wiley vice president and publisher Amanda Miller; senior editor John Czarnecki, Assoc. AIA; editorial assistant Michael New; production editor David Sassian; marketing manager Penny Makras, and Sadie Abuhoff for their guidance and assistance in helping bring this book into being.

Thanks to Phil Bernstein, Charles Hardy, Jonathan Cohen, Rich Nitzsche, Yanni Loukassis, Kristine Fallon, Paul Durand, Allison Scott, Andy Stapleton, Peter Rumpf, Aaron Greven, Jack Hungerford, Bill Worn, and David Waligora, all of whom made significant contributions to the building of this book through the generous sharing of their time, resources, and hard-earned insights.

Thanks to Paul Teicholz, James Vandezande, Zach Kron, Markku Allison, Howard Ashcraft, Gregory Arkin, Paul Aubin, John Boecker, Laura Handler, Brad Hardin, Dan Klancnik, Steve Stafford, Phil Read, Tatjana Dzambazova, Lachmi Khemlani, Christopher Parsons, Deke Smith, Kimon Onuma, Michael Tardiff, Sam Spata, Dean Mueller, Mark Kiker, Barry LaPatner, Jerry Yudelson, Professor Bryan Lawson, Andrew Pressman, James Salmon, Howard Roman, and James Cramer for their thought leadership and continued inspiration throughout the writing of this book.

Thanks to Dan Wheeler, FAIA, an exceptional role model to countless architects and a tireless integrator. To Brad Beck for once again going beyond the call of duty, his modus operandi; and to Marcus Colonna for his unrivaled enthusiasm, persistence, and guidance.

And thanks to my wife Sharon and kids, Simeon and Michol, for the sacrifices they have made in providing me with the freedom to write this book.

To my parents, Irene and Manny, for their belief and encouragement, I dedicate this book.

INTRODUCTION:

Rethinking Our Work Processes, Roles, and Identities

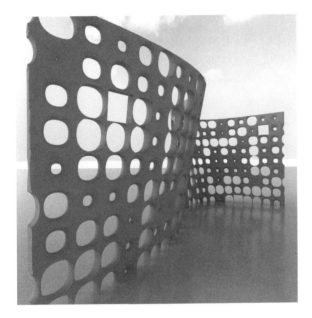

Figure G   Collaboration: one person writes the plug-in, another compiles the source code, and a third writes the installer, resulting in a generative design curtain panel with a divided surface. *Zach Kron, www.buildz.info*

This book addresses something that most firms don't even consider when implementing and working in BIM—and such firms are at risk for not giving this factor their full consideration.

What is the one element that stands between where you and your organization are today and achieving increased success, leadership opportunities, and increased commissions?

Looking Ahead

Business issues such as value proposition and ROI will work themselves out, as will legal issues, ownership issues, issues of responsibility, standards of care, and insurance.

Technology will become easier to use, software will become more or less interoperable, and file sizes will become easier to manage.

The fact is that none of these things are up to you. There is, however, one seminal element that will determine your success—and your organization's—while working in a BIM and integrated design environment.

And that element is *people* (see Figure H).

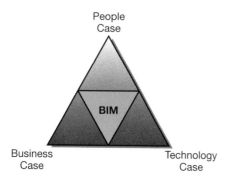

People
Case

BIM

Business
Case

Technology
Case

Figure H   The case for BIM is incomplete without the people case.

A Focus on People

This book addresses the number one problem of BIM implementation in the workplace: not technology or business value propositions, or even ROI, but rather *people*.

People are the crux—the key—to advancing BIM and integrated design. You—your organization's people—are the one remaining question mark that needs addressing. Your firm culture will not work itself out. Issues of playing well with others cannot continue to be addressed on a piecemeal basis. Human factors such as personal initiative, mutual respect and trust, human nature, ownership and authorship, comfort with work processes, workflow, impact of technology on design, work habits, preferences, identity and role, personality, legacy, collaboration and communication—all of these impact the efficiency and effectiveness of your BIM efforts. Moving ahead, it will be increasingly necessary to align people's attitudes, mindsets, and work habits in order to continue to not only survive but excel in this new BIM environment. Helping you and your firm to do so is the purpose for, and focus of, this book.

How, you ask, can something as obvious as *people* be overlooked and underrepresented in the vast literature on BIM and integrated design?

Severely underaddressed and currently seemingly unresolved people issues brought about by the introduction and adoption of BIM represent a crisis in the implementation of this exciting and potentially revolutionary technology and integrated design process.

The focus needs to be on people and the strategies they use to manage and cope with the transition to the new digital technology and the collaborative work processes it enables, as they adopt, implement, and then take the technology and process to a higher plane.

Where can you find these firm culture issues addressed thoroughly, convincingly, and effectively in a way that is universally applicable?

Human-Centered BIM

This is where *BIM and Integrated Design* can help to address these pertinent questions and rectify this situation, putting implementation of the new technologies back on track by making them manageable, understandable, and approachable in people terms.

Up until now the focus has been on the business case for BIM, on ROI, on software and technology—but not on the one factor we can do something about. For an organization built on human values—client service, trust, and relations—suddenly introducing a project on a 54-inch flat screen TV monitor, holding or "attending" meetings via satellite, challenges and changes that situation and relationship. Too often, people are left out of the equation. This is such an important theme throughout this book that the book's first part is entitled "BIM as though People Mattered."

If you and your organization haven't yet benefitted from all of the promises of working with BIM, it's the contention of this book that *when people issues are addressed, all of the other issues will work themselves out.*

Despite articles and books having been written on the subject of BIM, the problem—the *people* problem—persists. Very little has been written specifically on which elements from the traditional design process change with BIM and which stay the same, or on what knowledge, methods, and strategies must be let go of with BIM and what is critical to keep. What, in the learning process, needs to be *unlearned*?

Unlike other BIM guides, *BIM and Integrated Design* is less focused on the mechanics of the implementation than the "sociology" that makes a smooth adoption and implementation possible—the difference between an aborted or abandoned effort and one that sticks.

The vast majority of BIM-related literature has been focused on the technology, not on the people who use it. This is a problem, given that people issues and people's thought processes, mindsets, and attitudes are the main impediment to widespread adoption and implementation of the technology and, as importantly, of the integrated design work processes enabled by the technology (see Figure I).

People problems, human issues, issues of communication and collaboration, firm-culture issues, issues of motivation and workflow: all brought about or exacerbated by the advent of BIM into the workplace, profession, and industry, these people-oriented factors are a greater challenge than solving the considerable software, business, and technical problems this approach requires. This is the subject addressed in this book.

Social Implications of BIM for Firm Culture

For years the software resellers and for-profit educators, beating the *technical/business* drum, have been

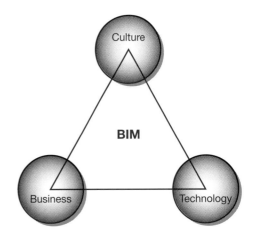

Figure I   Three drivers of change factor into the industry's implementation of BIM.

pushing BIM as a way to increase the output of junior staff, improve document accuracy, and reduce the number of change orders. All well and good. Senior management would listen to the sales pitch and consider the cost of implementation in terms of dollar value, learning curve, and perceptions of the track record of these tools and software programs.

This book looks at these benefits and results as well, but it considers the costs and gains in terms of the social and firm-culture factors of implementing and working in BIM.

Dealing with Change in an Environment of Change

What design professionals do—what they produce—is neither just facilities nor documents but *change*. Yet, ironically, when it comes time for them to confront it they seem to have such a hard time swallowing change themselves.

It is the difference between technical and systematic companywide change, as indicated in this report: "In its haste to introduce a BIM capability Company X

Within the context of this book, BIM refers to **Building Information Modeling** *as a process—as opposed to software, technology, or tool—of generating and managing building data during its complete lifecycle, from conceptual design though maintenance and operation of the building.*

    Integrated design *here is a collaborative approach—inclusive of delivery methods such as integrated project delivery (IPD)—to building design marked by the qualities of early participation by all team members, sharing risk and reward, among other benefits that attempt to resolve efficiency and waste concerns and overcome historically adverse relations while creating the most value for the owner in the resulting completed project. Integrated design also implies "integration," connoting a sense of acceptance, even transparency, within the user environment. Together, BIM and integrated design support and reinforce each other to mutually beneficial results.*

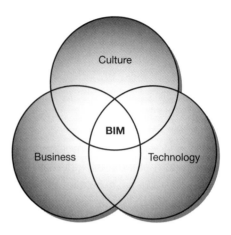

Figure J   Your success and progress with BIM occurs where the three drivers of change overlap.

purchased software, but did not factor in the process changes/training required to implement new workflow and design processes that would optimise the way the BIM system fitted with current and future business needs."[1]

What is that factor and how does it work? This book seeks to explain just what that missing factor is—and how best to utilize it for you and your organization to work more fluidly and effectively. With the social impacts of BIM addressed and mastered, ROI should come more naturally, and more effective use of the tools come more easily (see Figure J).

The Situation Today

BIM adoption and implementation are no longer the main challenge most firms are currently grappling with, as they were a few years back. Today, the challenge is the social implications of the technology and associated work processes on firm culture and workflow brought about by implementing BIM. Firms want to know how best to optimize their work processes to become more efficient at what they do best, to remain competitive by utilizing the competitive advantage of BIM and integrated design.

Today, most organizations face economic uncertainty, greater competition for projects, and clients demanding less waste, more efficient use of labor and resources, shorter schedules, projects on budget, fewer unpleasant surprises, and less finger-pointing and litigation—the very issues that have brought BIM and integrated design to the fore.

The movement to BIM and integrated design, though largely driven by owners and government, can take place only when design professionals and others in the construction industry have a compelling reason to change. Together, the technology and work processes enabled by new technology are seen as one of the drivers of change in the industry to help keep construction lean and achieve these goals.

About the Book

BIM and Integrated Design is an implementation book from a firm-culture standpoint, addressing Building Information Modeling as a cultural process with a focus on the technology's impact and transformative effect—both potentially disruptive and liberating—on the social, psychological, and practical aspects of the workplace.

Neither a technology nor software book per se, *BIM and Integrated Design* addresses the questions that implementing BIM poses to the firm that adopts it. Through thorough research and a series of case study interviews with industry leaders—and leaders in the making, out from behind the monitor—and with a focus on real-world practice, process, and people, *BIM and Integrated Design* is the first book devoted to the subject of the social impact BIM has had on individuals and organizations within the ever-changing construction industry.

This book presents multiple snapshots from varied viewpoints of the state of BIM implementation and of what's holding back design professionals and keeping them from reaching a widespread leadership role in the AECO industry, as well as offering recommendations and strategies for regaining a leadership position.

Who ought to read this book? *BIM and Integrated Design* is for those who want to be prepared with the right attitudes, mindsets, skill sets, and aptitudes for when they adopt BIM and the collaborative work process of integrated design throughout

their organization, as well as for who seek to attain a solution that leverages the skills, experience, and insights—as well as prevailing attitudes and mindsets—already present in your organization.

BIM and Integrated Design is for you if you

- Are curious about BIM but would like the facts and know what impacts are involved—the full picture.

- Have the software but feel that you are not completely utilizing it—or are utilizing it less satisfactorily than you had hoped.

- Find yourself in transition between the old way of doing things and things to come.

- Are already running with the technology, but have run into roadblocks—unexpected issues that you would like to resolve effectively, once and for all.

- Have mastered BIM but would like to learn more about how others use this knowledge to leverage integrated design in practice.

While the book assumes vendor software neutrality—I was trained and work in Revit but have also worked in ArchiCAD and am familiar with other programs—"BIM" is used generically throughout. And while the book does not promote any one proprietary BIM program, the interviewees frequently mention design data created in an authoring application such as Revit or ArchiCAD.

Research Methodology

Because the focus of this book is on the sociological impacts of the various new technologies and work processes, besides the stated and cited data a good amount of the information is empirical, garnered from a variety of reliable sources including in-depth interviews with individuals immersed in the technology and the industry, including industry leaders and technology experts revealing actionable strategies through their insights and experiences. These interviews provide a balance of qualitative as well as quantitative research and evidence.

As important, in this book I write from the perspective of having served for twenty-five years as a lead design architect working on the design of large, complex projects; on the front lines in BIM and IPD environments where BIM was used both alone and collaboratively; having run my own design practice and served in senior management in organizations both large and small; having helped inaugurate and teach an integrated building science/design studio for a number of years in one of the finest graduate architecture programs in the country; and having served on the board of AIA–Chicago chapter for many years. In other words, I write as one of you—immersed in a profession and industry that I want to see not only survive but flourish in the years to come.

How To Use This Book

BIM and Integrated Design is organized into three parts: "BIM as though People Mattered," "Leading Integrated Design," and "Leading and Learning."

Chapter 1—What You Adopt When Adopting BIM

Chapter 1 introduces the human factors in BIM and integrated design; discusses owning the process and managing change and transition; covers the biggest myths and misconceptions regarding BIM and introduces the many co-benefits of working in BIM. Questions this chapter will attempt to answer include: Firms intend to start every new project in BIM, but do so in actuality only a fraction of the time. Why is this?

Why does BIM take so long to implement? And why it's not BIM that you implement, but rather your decision, your choice, to adopt BIM?

Chapter 2—The Social Implications of Implementing BIM

Chapter 2 addresses social implications of working in a BIM environment, including work processes and workflow; makes suggestions for how to overcome barriers to successful BIM implementation and how to conduct a BIM self-assessment for individuals as well as for your organization. It concludes with two interviews. The first is a case study interview with leaders of a successful design firm that, through the creative and bold use of BIM, has not only been able to hold its own but grew during the recent economic downturn. They share what worked, what didn't, and what they believe is necessary to accomplish similar results for yourself and your organization. The second, a conversation with a BIM and integrated design consultant who has extensive experience working in BIM with designers, a design/build firm, and constructors, explains how his peers and clients went about successfully implementing BIM.

> Interview with Paul Durand and Allison Scott, Winter Street Architects
>
> Interview with Aaron Greven, BIM Consultant

Chapter 3—Working with Others in BIM

Chapter 3 describes the ten most commonly encountered obstacles to successful collaboration; suggests strategies to overcome these obstacles and for making collaboration work; and follows with an in-depth interview with a clinical and organizational psychologist, executive coach, and organizational consultant working with architectural firms—and in the construction industry himself—for over thirty-five years.

The chapter concludes with a conversation with a pioneer in applying information technology to architecture, engineering, and facility management in the design and construction industry and in helping AEC firms and government and corporate facilities groups evaluate and implement technology systems.

Interview with Jack Hungerford, PhD

Interview with Kristine K. Fallon, FAIA, Kristine Fallon Associates

Chapter 4—Who Works in BIM and Who Doesn't

Chapter 4 describes the new roles design professionals play on teams, in organizations, and in the profession and industry, as well as what happens to former roles (such as project designer, project architect, and project manager) in the transition to BIM. The chapter culminates in a conversation with one of the industry's most well-informed and strategic CIOs, a registered architect and LEED AP who is responsible for the strategy, supervision, coordination, and delivery of all information systems and services for his top-tier firm.

Interview with Rich Nitzsche, CIO, Perkins+Will

Chapter 5—BIM and Integrated Design

Professionals in the building and construction industry have been slow to jump on the integrated design bandwagon. One goal of this book is to rectify this situation.

Before one can suggest and promote the integrated design process to owners, we need to thoroughly understand what it entails. If the best way to learn is by trial and error, this book aims to keep the mistakes—and associated pain—to a minimum. Chapter 5 serves as a brief but incisive overview of integrated design and closes with two interviews: the first with two construction professionals who are helping lead their organization's efforts in the development of Virtual Design and Construction (VDC) and BIM for the advancement of technology in construction; and closing with a discussion with an architect, development advisor, past-chair of the Integrated Practice Steering Committee of the AIA California Council and author of *Integrated Project Delivery: Six Case Studies,* published by AIA, AGC, and Mc-Graw-Hill.

Interview with Andy Stapleton and Peter Rumpf, Mortenson Construction

Interview with Jonathan Cohen, FAIA

Chapter 6—Leading from the Model

Leading at any time is hard. Leading during turbulent times is even more difficult. Due to disruptive technologies and new ways of working together—the introduction of collaborative work processes—learning how to shift into the mindset essential to leading the BIM and integrated design process has become especially critical. Chapter 6 will help you—working in a BIM and Integrated Design environment—to become more effective leaders no matter where you find yourself in the firm hierarchy or on the project team. The chapter concludes with a conversation with a project architect/BIM manager for the highly ambitious Canadian Museum for Human Rights (CMHR). He was charged with the transforming of 2D Design Development documents into a complete 3D Building Information Model that is currently being utilized as an aid in construction. A second interview is with the director, Office of Project Delivery, at the U.S. General Services Administration (GSA) Public Buildings Service National Capital Region.

Interview with Brad Beck, BIM Manager, Architect

Interview with Charles Hardy, GSA

Chapter 7—Learning BIM and Integrated Design

The introduction of BIM into the workforce has education and training implications as well—factors that impact firms and practices, especially those that hire directly out of school. This impacts HR, hiring practices, recruitment, and ultimately the makeup of the firm—its organization, if not its organizational chart. The ultimate goal for the architect is to lead the process and create the ultimate BIM and Integrated Design experience for all involved. It is not a question of learning software. It is a question of becoming familiar with the process and how this awareness is learned and acquired. Chapter 7 features two interviews with exceptional educators, authors and thinkers: The first with a postdoctoral associate in the Program in Science, Technology, and Society at MIT, where he studies human-machine-environment interaction, having served as visiting lecturer at Cornell University, bringing an interdisciplinary background in architecture, computing, and ethnography to his work.

The second is a candid interview with a vice president at Autodesk who is responsible for the company's future vision and strategy for technology serving the building industry. He is a former principal with Pelli Clarke Pelli Architects; educator of Professional Practice at Yale where he received both his B.A. and his M. Arch.; coeditor of *Building (In) The Future: Recasting Labor in Architecture,* published in 2010 (MIT); a senior fellow of the Design Futures Council; and former chair of the AIA National Contract Documents Committee.

Interview with Yanni Loukassis, PhD, MIT

Interview with Phil Bernstein, FAIA, Autodesk VP, Yale University

Do You Have What It Takes?

Perhaps Phil Bernstein, FAIA, explains it best when describing what he personally went through in his first well-publicized and documented IPD project:

> Our project involved a certain amount of me just going around and saying, "I'm just going to jump off the cliff." I cannot in good conscience be running around the world talking about this process revolution and technology and we're going to run another one of these jobs as a CM at risk. And everyone is saying, "Are you sure this is going to work?" And, "Do you have any way of demonstrating that this is going to work?" And I said, "No, except go read our marketing materials." Since we're talking about this we need to have the intestinal fortitude to actually go and try it. That's not a learned thing. I don't know how to convince people to do that. We just did it ourselves. We just jumped off the edge of the cliff.[2]

Whether or not you have the intestinal fortitude to "jump off the cliff," reading the book is a much safer—and more enjoyable—way to learn.

Notes

Note: Unless otherwise noted, interviews refer to those conducted for this book.

1. "BIM Implementation: Learning from the mistakes of others," *BIM Journal*, August 1, 2009, http://bimjournal.com.
2. Phil Bernstein, interviewed by the author, October 15, 2009.

part **|** # BIM As Though People Mattered

In Part I, you will uncover mistaken beliefs surrounding BIM and its social benefits. Here you will explore the most commonly encountered obstacles to successful collaboration, as well as the challenges this technology and process create for individuals and organizations in their initiatives toward a comprehensive, successful adoption and implementation. You will discover the social implications of working in BIM for individuals and firms and how to overcome real and perceived barriers to its use.

Read these chapters to discover proven strategies for managing the disruptive change brought about by BIM, how to assess your team's progress, and how to own not only the software but also the process. You will learn about the recent proliferation of BIM-related professional titles and roles, the current state of transition of the industry from CAD to BIM, and what the real distinctions are between BIM-, CAD-, and IT-related roles, including distinctions between BIM managers, CAD managers, and IT managers. In this part, you will read about a design firm that struggled with adopting BIM, only to find itself growing through the recent downturn, thanks in large part to its attitudes and approach to BIM. You will also learn how firms have successfully implemented BIM, from the varying perspectives of a consultant with extensive experience working in BIM with designers, a clinical and organizational psychologist who works with design and construction professionals who are contending with constant change, and a firm owner who has strategically and successfully worked with BIM since the application's inception.

chapter **1** What You Adopt When
Adopting BIM

Figure 1.1   Whether the project is a wall sconce or a city hall, the workflow that results from working in BIM is as fascinating as the imagery and as vital to its success. *Zach Kron, www.buildz.info*

Adopting BIM. Good or bad idea? Is there even a choice? Should you wait until they work out all the kinks and it becomes easier to learn and less cumbersome to use? Should you hold out until it becomes a more intuitive design tool?

Your firm is considering BIM or has already acquired the 3D software, perhaps is even using it to some degree and making strides. Why read a chapter on BIM adoption? Why refamiliarize yourself with BIM's many benefits? *We're sold*, you say. *Can't we finally move on?* Why read about the challenges, roadblocks, impediments, and hurdles that stand in the way of a full, successful BIM adoption for you and your organization? Anyone working in BIM must be well aware of these. *Right*?

It all depends on what is meant by BIM *adoption*. Too often it just means purchasing software, implementing, and moving on.

Read this chapter first—even if you are already working in BIM—because you need to understand the full implications and impacts on the people you work with and for, or who work for you, as well as those impacts on the profession and industry you are an important part of—not only in business and technology terms, but also in terms of how you and your organization have been impacted socially and culturally by the new

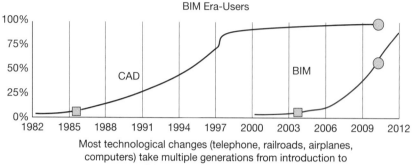

Figure 1.2   CAD versus BIM adoption chart. BIM has been adopted twice as quickly as CAD. *Dennis Neeley, AIA*

Design professionals are moving to BIM [at least two] times faster than the transition from hand drawing to CAD, which took about fifteen years. BIM will be the predominant tool of choice throughout the professions by 2011.

—Dennis Neeley, AIA Convention, 2009

work processes the industry is currently absorbing in response to the latest software (see Figure 1.2).

There is a larger impediment to the full, speedy, and widespread adoption of BIM by the design professions, and that has to do with the social impacts of the technology on individuals, organizations, and even the profession. You can be assured of a much smoother entry to this new technological process by understanding the social—communication, collaboration, and culture—impacts on your firm. As Autodesk's Phil Bernstein asks, "The productivity and economic benefits of building information modeling (BIM) to the global building industry are widely acknowledged and increasingly well understood.

Further, the technology to implement BIM is readily available and rapidly maturing. Yet despite the obvious benefits and readiness of BIM software, BIM adoption has been slower than anticipated. Why?"[1]

In this chapter we will take a look at a design firm that struggled with adopting BIM—only to find itself *growing* through the recent downturn, in large part due to its attitudes and approach to BIM adoption. We'll cover not only BIM's technical and business benefits but also its *social* benefits, as well as the challenges to individuals and organizations that this process creates. This chapter closes with proven strategies for managing this disruptive change. Whether you are new to the BIM world or have been working in BIM for some time, you may not be getting the best and highest use—and return on investment (ROI)—of this phenomenon unless you consider the concepts described and explained in this chapter.

Bogged Down in Detail

BIM adoption and implementation are often used interchangeably, but they are not interchangeable—and

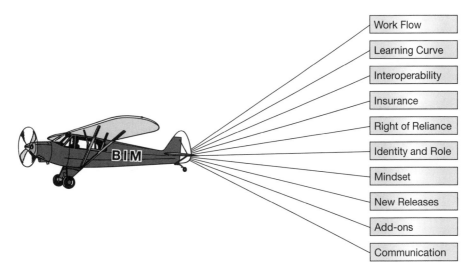

Figure 1.3   Adopting BIM without a plan can be like taking a trip unaware of all the baggage that can slow you down.

part of the reason for failure by firms to fully embrace BIM is because they mistakenly confuse the two concepts.

It is not enough to say BIM was adopted. How was it adopted? By what approach? Top-down or bottom-up? Enthusiastically or begrudgingly? All at once or slow and drawn-out? By a select team, then gradually spread out? Or on all projects from "go"?

Firms that have purchased the software have been getting frustrated with it, bogged down in detail, or have abandoned it altogether after initial pilot projects or efforts. Why is that? (See Figure 1.3.)

Although uptake has occurred quickly, BIM adoption is not widespread among all design professionals, and where adoption does occur it is not sticking in all cases. The big picture—beyond industry announcements to the contrary—indicates that BIM adoption is sporadic, incomplete, and prohibitively shallow. Technological and business adoption has occurred or is currently occurring at the majority of larger firms, but social

adoption, and a full understanding of BIM's impacts on the firm and the individuals that make up the firm, is not. Impacts to the profession—thought to be game-changing—are understood by few and being watched closely by many. Deep, meaningful, and lasting BIM adoption has stalled not because of technological or business factors but because of *human* factors.

Owning the Process

Where are you and your firm in the adoption process right now? Where do you find yourself along the continuum? You may

- Not have gotten some initial traction—you may have given the software a test run or even ventured into a pilot project.

- Be wondering how to get BIM to stick and become a competitive part of your firm's future.

- Have installed it and are running with it—but have run into roadblocks, unexpected issues that you would like to resolve effectively.

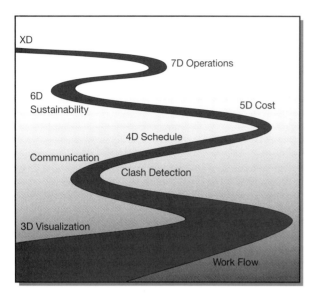

Figure 1.4 BIM as process: Where on the path are you? How far will you take it?

- Be looking for a clearheaded explanation of what is involved and what impact this technology will have on your practice.

- Be in search of an objective explanation that separates the facts from the marketing hype.

- Own the software but perhaps are not completely utilizing it or are utilizing it less satisfactorily than you had hoped—not for its highest and best use, or to its full advantage. (See Figure 1.4.)

Though BIM use reached the 50 percent mark among design professionals, business leader and author Rex Miller has taken announcements of BIM adoption rates to task. "It is an accurate number," Miller notes, "if counting the number of architectural firms who have bought BIM software." Miller continues,

> However, this is where the mirage comes in. My take is by no means scientific but I have probably visited close to 100 firms in the last two plus years and I always probe how firms are using BIM. Here is what I hear. Most use BIM for visualization and some for clash detection. The clash detection is again a derivative of the visualization. Both of these applications only require "dumb objects." A dumb object is a door, a run of ductwork or any part of a building that includes the geometric information but none of the objects properties or rules for how it behaves in relation to other objects. In other words these have the "M" or modeling part of BIM but none of the "I" part that provides analytics. . . . Half of the architectural firms are now out telling their clients that they "do BIM" when less than 10 percent are fully using analytics.[2]

The message is clear. Firms may own the software but not yet own the process. What firms are looking for is some sense of control and assurance that they are utilizing the technology to the fullest advantage. For true adoption to take place—and be counted—other criteria must be considered. There are almost as many definitions as there are practitioners. What does BIM adoption involve? (See Figure 1.5.)

To some, BIM adoption means acquiring software. To others it implies embracing BIM, which is not just a matter of buying seats. To what extent in your organization is BIM adopted? What are the scope and scale of the adoption? Although there remain some significant and surprising BIM holdouts, it would be hard to find a leading AEC firm today that is not using BIM in some form or capacity; however, the breadth and depth of the implementation can vary widely. One thing is certain: acquiring and adopting BIM

Firms may own the software but not yet own the process.

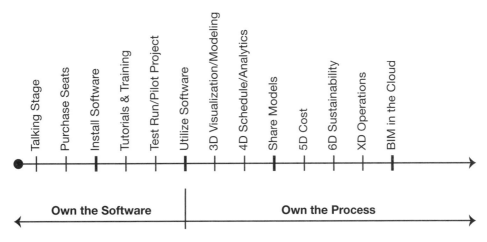

Figure 1.5   Where are you—and your organization—on the BIM adoption continuum?

tools are not the same thing. As trainer and blogger Gregory Arkin wrote, "Just because a firm has seats of Revit doesn't necessarily mean they're using Revit actively."[3]

It is a contention of this book that buying seats does not constitute adoption because despite having the right tools, many BIM efforts have failed as a result of having the wrong people in place, the wrong attitudes ("We paid for the software—use it!"), and the wrong mindset ("Everybody else is doing it—we'd better get up to speed and fast!"). As Arkin predicts, "People investing heavily in a product *will* eventually demand that their employees use that product and deliver a return on that investment."[4]

Four Rules from the Start

Rule 1: Adopt first. *Then* implement.

Rule 2: What you adopt when you adopt BIM is *change*.

Rule 3: Change is inevitable. Transition is a choice.

Rule 4: BIM is both a tool *and* a process.

Tradition and the New Technology

What role does tradition play in this process? Do we just adopt this technology and throw away all we've worked on and built up over the years to get to where we are today? In addition to being known for design, business practices, or delivery, your firm has a tradition of taking in and taking on technology as it has been introduced. You may not talk about it or even recognize it, but how you have reacted to new technologies over the years is also part of your firm tradition (see Figure 1.6).

You don't want to just break with the past altogether. Legacy software and projects can be referenced and in many cases adapted or incorporated into BIM projects. The important thing is to see your work as part of a continuum. You are not throwing it all away. Your values, ethics, and focus continue. You recognize that in order to continue you need to remain relevant, and it is for *that* reason that you have agreed to enquire into this new technology and adopt—and adapt. Tradition isn't a staid and static thing—it is a process. It changes, however slowly. Take it at your own pace—but do change. (See Figure 1.7.)

Then	Now
Hand Rendering	BIM
2D Drafting	
Hand Drafting	
Lettering	
Sketching	
Coordinating	
Red Lining	
Scaling	
CAD Skills	
Memorizing Macros	
Linear Thinking	

Figure 1.6   No longer drafting, today we model. BIM changes everything.

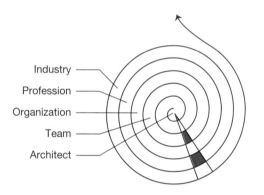

Figure 1.7   BIM impacts and changes all levels, from the individual to the industry.

Architects don't want to give up the traditional ways of doing things. In part, they are held back by their identification with drawing and being artists and ideators, combined with their fear—however mistaken—of becoming information inputters, slaves to technology.

Tradition is a powerful force—almost as powerful as the technologies and processes that seek to overcome it. A large, internationally recognized architecture firm in the Midwest refuses to adopt BIM because, they say, it is *too convoluted*. In the midst of the technological maelstrom around them, they're waiting until BIM software and processes become simpler, easier, less complicated before embarking on a new path. That's tradition talking.

Managing Change and Transition

What if a well-informed, trusted authority figure said you had to make difficult and enduring changes in the way you think, feel, and act? If you didn't, your time would end soon. Could you change when change mattered most?
—Alan Deutschman, *Change or Die*

So, you want to change? What works and what does not work?

Give people a better story to believe, Alan Deutschman tells us, and their actions will be consistent with the new story. He encourages them to practice the story line even if they don't yet fully believe in it. One goal of this book is to help you create a better story to tell.

Tradition is in transition. Architects who are not convinced that their time—that is, the world as they've known it—will soon end are living in denial. We have heard this before, they say—with CAD, with design-build, even with green design. But this time is different.

BIM and IPD yield an eight-in-ten chance of completing a project on schedule and within budget, a notable improvement from design-bid-build project statistics.
—Jacqueline Pezzillo, LEED-AP, communications manager at Davis Brody Bond Aedas, "AIA Navigates the Future of BIM and IPD," e-Oculus, April 28, 2009

BIM as Though People Mattered

None of this would be a concern if BIM were designed primarily with people in mind. Building information modeling is often explained as a business process supported by technology—or as a technological phenomenon resulting in business outcomes.

We are all by now familiar with the many technological and business benefits offered by the adoption of BIM, the specific practical benefits and computer program innovations that make BIM and integrated design appealing options. These opportunities and changes in thinking are often put forth to promote the benefits of the tools, but lack insights concerning workflow and communication that are essential to successful teams and projects. This book was written in part to rectify this situation and decrease this disparity.

What we are less familiar with—but need to recognize—are the benefits to human behavior that BIM and integrated design bring about, the sociological factors that can make or break an outcome and experience for you and your firm. What are the sociological and cultural benefits that integrated design and BIM bring to a firm utilizing these practices?

It is the human factor that makes a smooth adoption and implementation possible and makes the difference between an aborted or abandoned effort and a successful one that sticks. You and your firm are looking for a solution that has legs—that leverages skills and insights but also considers prevailing attitudes and mindsets already present in individuals in your firm (see Figure 1.8).

The Missing Human Factor

The vast majority of BIM-related presentations, articles, and books are focused on the technology—not

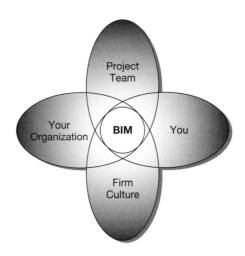

Figure 1.8 You, your team, and your organization continuously revolve around the BIM experience.

on the people who use it. This is a problem, given that people's thought processes and issues—people problems, human issues, issues of communication and collaboration, firm-culture issues—are the main impediments to widespread adoption and implementation of the technology. People-oriented factors are a greater challenge than solving the software, business, and technical problems of BIM implementation. What are these human factors?

Human Factors in BIM and Integrated Design

Communication

Collaboration

Trust

Respect

Firm culture

Workflow and work processes

Identity

Roles

Working across generations

Mindset

Attitude

Control

Managing change

Transition

BIM etiquette

Leadership

Training

Learning and education

The number one problem of BIM implementation is not technology or business value propositions but rather behavioral, temperamental, emotional, and mental attributes: the sociocultural impact of BIM and integrated design on the design professions and construction industry. This means addressing a situation that many design professionals and their firms don't even think of when considering BIM—people, *you*—the social impacts, benefits, and challenges brought on and about by this still relatively new technology currently being introduced into the workforce. Understanding this concept will help you put BIM adoption and implementation back on track by making it manageable, understandable and approachable in people terms.

Yes, clash detection is a low-hanging fruit. Anyone with all trades modeled and a license to NavisWorks can do it. But here's the thing about it—it's really, really satisfying.

— Laura Handler, Tocci Construction, (bim)x, October 2, 2008

Adopt First, *Then* Implement

BIM adoption and implementation are often used interchangeably—but they are not exchangeable, and part of the reason for failure by firms to fully embrace BIM is because they merge the two concepts, if they consider them at all. It is critical for the successful launch of the process that each is addressed separately. Neither step can be skipped.

BIM adoption has to do with familiarizing yourself—as you are doing right now by reading this book—*and* informing others. Gathering information *and* seeking out sources; making a decision *and* making a commitment; changing your mindset *and* attitudes about the technology for the long haul (see Figure 1.9).

BIM implementation of the technology is critical—we'll be covering it in the next chapter—but BIM adoption is its own first step. And unless it is addressed directly and experienced head-on, the likelihood for success of your BIM implementation will lessen. Why is this?

The challenges one faces in trying to learn a new technology while serving clients and turning a profit

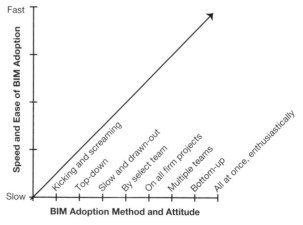

Figure 1.9   The speed and ease of BIM adoption is dependent on approach and attitudes.

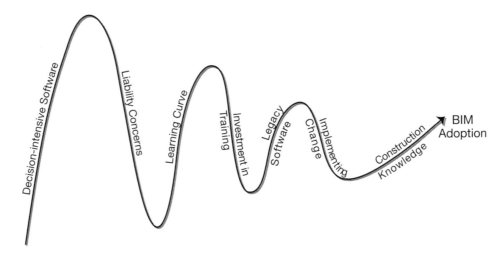

Figure 1.10 The most widely cited challenges to a smooth, firm-wide BIM adoption.

can be daunting. We'll cover some of the steepest challenges later in this chapter. First, it must be acknowledged that working in and with BIM can be difficult. Many new skills and habits are introduced and must be learned, understood, and mastered to make the most effective use of the work process and technology. Another important reason is because inevitably you will hit a snag, a technical difficulty, and you will feel like giving up; senior management will be dismissive of—or discouraged by—the meager ROI of the firm's initial attempt; or you will make it through your first project but will have no clear way to determine whether it was an improvement over previous pre-BIM processes (see Figure 1.10).

BIM Adoption in Context

BIM adoption refers here to the stage in which a technology is selected for use by an individual or an organization. Why adopt a new technology? While we'll soon cover the benefits and co-benefits of BIM, here suffice it to say that past adoptions of a new technology for architecture and other fields have "indicated confidence in its potential to alleviate a particular problem or to make a job easier or more efficient."[5] Problem solving, ease of use, and efficiency: if it were only so easy. Why does BIM have to be so hard to adopt and implement?

Mistaken Beliefs Surrounding BIM

Even with a working definition of BIM, it is easy to confuse the BIM process with others. In this section we will look at some of the most common BIM misconceptions—those that can serve to undermine your team's progress, efforts, and success.

If your firm has existing problems, adopting new technology will either exacerbate the problems or mask them. It won't solve the problems. Of course, architecture is not the only profession facing this situation. Health care, for example, has also found that throwing new technology at every problem won't solve it.[6]

Five Misconceptions Regarding BIM

1. Productivity suffers during the transition to BIM.
2. BIM applications are difficult to learn.
3. BIM disrupts established workflows.
4. Owners and contractors benefit most from BIM—not the designer.
5. BIM increases risk.

BIMManager, "Five Fallacies Surrounding BIM—an Autodesk White Paper," July 1, 2009, http://www.bimmanager .com/2009/07/01/five-fallacies-surrounding-bim-from-autodesk/.

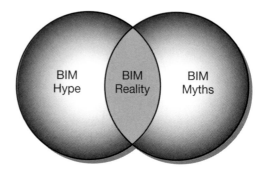

Figure 1.11   Make it your goal to separate BIM facts from BIM fiction by learning to recognize the hype and myths.

BIM Myths

- BIM requires a different project delivery method.
- When using BIM, you cannot tell who is responsible for what or who owns the model.
- When using BIM, anyone can change anyone else's model.
- BIM blurs the distinction between design and construction.
- The architect is not in "responsible charge" of the design.
- You cannot have some information in the model and some only in 2D details.
- The model cannot be a contract document.
- You cannot rely on the dimensions of the model.
- The architect is subject to more lawsuits from contractors and subs because now there are direct privities of contract.

Douglas C. Green, New York City Revit User Group.

Some say that you can't design in BIM (you can.) Others will tell you that you can't detail and complete CDs in BIM (you can.) Still others will contend that BIM will completely replace CAD right away (they're wrong.) CAD will be around a long time, and firms using BIM ought to maintain at least one copy.

It's a misconception to think BIM is a panacea that will solve everything. The model is only as good as the information or data put into it; the program is only as good as the competence, design, and construction experience of the modeler. "A key misconception that many make about BIM is that it is a product. Wrong. It is not a product it is a process, a process made up of sharing intelligent data and reducing repetitious user input."[7] (See Figure 1.11.)

Misconceptions are rampant and all over the board—especially for those who are not intimately familiar with the software. As indicated in this discussion, "BIM will destroy our ability to produce good-looking drawings. The argument, or concern, here is that 'extracting drawings' or re-symbolizing a 3D model to represent 2D information produces substandard results."[8]

BIM is often presented as the cure-all for whatever ails the construction industry. And although it has the potential to address and resolve many owner concerns, the tool itself is only as robust as the data fed into the model. When one considers using the BIM model for energy analysis, for example,

Contrary to the popular notion that BIM makes energy analysis a snap, it turns out that BIM, in fact, does not actually help that much. This is because building geometry is only one of the inputs needed for analysis, and a relatively easy one at that, as it is completely objective. Much more effort is involved in defining the conditions and assumptions for the analysis, as those are very subjective. Also, analysis tools need the building geometry to be specified only at a certain level of detail, while BIM provides the complete detailed model, which is usually overkill for the tools. For BIM to become really useful for analysis, what is needed is for BIM tools to have filters so that the required information can be abstracted out for input to analysis tools.[9]

In presenting the positive attributes and capabilities of the BIM program, setting and managing client expectations from the start is one of the design professional's most important tasks.

There is another somewhat common belief that architects bring ego and visions of grandeur to a project and not true value to building design, leaving the client to pay for monuments to one's perceived greatness. Undoubtedly, this belief is based in fact and a few true instances, the exception rather than the norm. But is also a burgeoning belief that I've witnessed that B.I.M. applications will "solve" this perceived problem by distilling the design process down to a couple of "buttons" that when pressed in the correct sequence will produce a building meeting all the requirements of a client's program, compliant with all state and local building regulations, free from errors and omissions, and completely describing the construction process; and by pressing the desired "style" button, details will be applied to the building design to make it look like the desired style.

Providing all the value without the "cost" of ego (you just disable the "ego" button.)[10]

What is BIM, and why is the industry so confused? To answer that question it is probably easier to first define what BIM is not. As Nigel Davies posits, "BIM is not 3D. There is no added intelligence to give you any 'data' about the project. BIM is not Revit. The terms BIM and Revit are becoming interchangeable. BIM is not a single database or 'single building model.'"[11] It just may be that backing into a definition is the best approach.

Social Benefits of Adopting BIM

So why restate the obvious? Why is it important to be familiar with—or to refamiliarize yourself with—BIM's many benefits? Here are a few reasons:

- To remain motivated

- For encouragement and refueling

- As a selling tool to owners

As Autodesk VP Phil Bernstein says, "The productivity and economic benefits of Building Information Modeling (BIM) to the global building industry are widely acknowledged and increasingly well understood." Benefits, whether described as competitive advantages, opportunities, strengths, or even reasons to adopt BIM, don't seem to bear repeating.

Who Benefits?

Who benefits? Who are BIM's beneficiaries? Architect, contractor, and owner, facility operations, subcontractors, manufacturers, all benefit—in different ways. Often overlooked is the realization that when the owner benefits, the architect benefits—unintentionally—from a happy and engaged client. (See Figure 1.12.)

Figure 1.12   Sake diagram: reasons for working in BIM. After Martin Fischer, *For BIM's Sake.*

If the benefits are legion and well known (*"Enough with BIM's benefits—aren't these a given? Let's move on!"*), why bother to reiterate them here? Whereas the technical and business benefits may be numerous and widely understood, BIM's equally critical social benefits are perhaps less so. We reiterate BIM's benefits because

- When frustrated—and you will get frustrated at times—it is good to remember why you are using it.

- You will need to repeat these benefits when marketing your services or explaining BIM to others.

- They serve as context for the main discussion of this book.

By "social benefits," we mean the sociological, behavioral, collaborative, psychological, and motivational benefits of adopting BIM. The focus here is less on the benefits themselves than on the change that comes about due to BIM's many benefits. Here we will explore two types of social benefits: co-benefits and qualitative benefits.

With BIM, as with bidirectional associativity, a change anywhere is a change everywhere.

In an *ArchDaily* interview, Phil Bernstein of Autodesk mentioned the *clarity of the design* as a benefit—and then went on to explain the benefit as "the ability to interact with the description of the building in numerous ways so people from various perspectives can understand it."[12] That is a *co-benefit,* where a benefit for one entity positively impacts others, serving to dissolve silos while ostensibly paving the way toward collaboration and integrated design.

Why Co-Benefits?

Too often, BIM's many benefits are presented as a seemingly unending list. In order to organize the list, several sources have divided BIM's benefits by category—or in other cases by entity: this one is a benefit to the owner, this to the contractor, and this to the architect, engineer, or consultant. There have been attempts to create a definitive list of BIM's benefits,[13] but none exhaustive, thoroughly categorized, or ordered.

Despite the apparent orderliness of these lists, it is not helpful to organize benefits in terms of trades. Why? Because it reinforces the notion that each is separate, when the team ought to be emphasized. Instead of focusing on the constituent part, the whole must be kept in mind: what benefits the owner also benefits the architect and contractor, and so on. Some benefit directly—or the most—while others benefit indirectly. Take for example the case of clash detection: the contractor benefits directly, and the architect indirectly in that she is now working on a building where the risks are a bit better known.

Also, it is disingenuous—and shortsighted—to assume, for example, that modeling helps the contractor and only the contractor with clash detection and, if done properly, provides accurate piece and quantity counts. In this instance, where there is little direct benefit to the architect, what helps one must necessarily help the other.

So, who benefits from BIM? Owners? Architects? Contractors? Benefits by trades only serve to reinforce silos—the opposite of what we're trying to achieve with integrated design.

The Co-Benefit Statement

A co-benefit statement looks something like this: technological and/or business attributes of BIM *that* benefit ROI or the bottom line *as well as* encourage team collaboration *can also* result in a more integrated design. These linkages (*that, as well as, can also*) are referred to as "co-effects" or "co-benefits."

The following section explores some of the less apparent co-benefits that can help your team to collaborate more efficiently and effectively, ultimately resulting in an improved integrated design experience for all. It asks how these very benefits impact the employee, the designer, and the architect; what change comes about due to these benefits; and what, if any, are the negative social impacts of otherwise positive technical and/or business benefits.

Focused on advanced technology in the building industry, I don't seek the typical benefits of BIM, such as increased coordination of drawing sets. I look for large-scale societal benefits of reduced errors, improved energy performance, and higher quality at lower costs.

—Mike Bordenaro, co-founder, BIM Education Co-op

Sociological Benefits of BIM

Table 1.1 illustrates the typical relationship between software features and benefits to individual team members. *It does x, y, and z.* On the left are listed the benefits; in the middle are bonus benefits—that is, indirect benefit, practice culture benefit, social benefit, team-building benefit—based on the original benefit. On the far right are summaries of the various impacts of these social benefits. An example of this might serve to illustrate: clash detection (*benefit*), where the key issue is to determine major conflicts such as ducting/piping and ducting/structural—which makes collaboration easier (*co-benefit*), so that these conflicts are removed in the model when still relatively easy and cost-effective to contend with (social or sociocultural impact, regarding the sociological and cultural benefits that BIM and integrated design bring to any individual or organization utilizing these practices.) An offshoot—or indirect benefit—of clash detection: you avoid pointing fingers and laying blame later in the project—you are all in this together. "Clash detection makes collaboration easier so that these problems are identified and rectified digitally in the design, rather than during construction."[14]

BIM's Qualitative Benefits

Of the many ways of organizing benefits, organizing in terms of qualitative and quantitative benefits can be of great use to teams:

- **Quantitative** benefits are—just as they sound—measurable using metrics, numerical comparisons, or tracking, resulting in a measurable quantity.
- **Qualitative** benefits cut across disciplines and subject matter, taking into consideration an in-depth understanding of firm culture, human behavior, and the reasons that govern such behavior.

Table 1.1   The Benefits, Social Benefits, and Implications of Adopting BIM

Benefit	Co-benefit	Sociocultural Impact
Interference checking and avoidance, clash detection, conflict resolution	Avoids headaches of rework, paybacks to subs; results in fewer callbacks, lower warranty costs	Results in smoother sailing for the schedule, creates fewer issues, helps in relationships
Team members start earlier in the process	Fosters a greater sense of involvement, input, being "at the table"	Provides greater opportunity to contribute
Clash detection	Makes collaboration easier	Eases tensions during construction
Takes less time overall	Allows more time to design	Allows architects to use their core competency vs. putting out fires
Requires one to be more involved as a contributing architect	Makes one more of a collaborator	Makes architects more balanced, well-rounded
Increases productivity; cuts man-hours and manpower by reducing team size	Reduces length of documentation phase	Increases design phase; emphasizes design
Increases coordination	Gives rise to professionals who think more globally; reduces need for field coordination by subcontractors	Leads to more successful projects and dramatically increased profits
Fewer RFIs and change orders	Smoother construction phase	Less conflict and stress
Improved cost control	Aligns budget and building	Designers perceived as fiscally responsible
Recent graduates work alongside experienced designers and train younger team members	Emerging architects just starting out learn how buildings come together earlier in career	Emerging architects avoid the drudgery of picking up redlines, are involved with the whole process
Robust modeling tool changes the playing field	Small firms can operate like large firms	Small firms can compete with larger firms
More integrated buildings	Less waste, eliminates redundant and wasted effort	Offers a sense of purpose and mission when first starting out
Start involvement earlier	Everyone is at the table	Creates opportunities to design, manage, and lead
More assured decisions	Focus on a single course of action; understand effects of design decisions	Entire team works toward the same goal
More sound buildings	Less investment in rework and post-construction	Improves image of the profession and industry
May raise fees if value proven	Increased value for owner if lower quantity take-offs are the result	Doing more with less improves environmental impact
Analyze and visualize project digitally before it is constructed	More cohesive integrated design	Model is utilized for entire lifecycle of a building
Design visualization; accurately visualize building appearance	More easily communicates design intent	Improves owner, user, and community satisfaction
Simulates real-world performance	Improves understanding of building characteristics	Reduces cost, schedule, and carbon footprint
Ensures well-coordinated documents	Results in higher-quality documentation and fewer claims	Reduces rework on site; increases client satisfaction

Benefit	Co-benefit	Sociocultural Impact
Streamlines delivery process	More economical use of resources	Less redundancy; more effective, purposeful staffing
Provides basis for more accurate fabrication	Fewer shop drawings; prefabrication of materials off-site; higher quality at a lower cost	Leaves less opportunity to make late game changes and therefore mistakes; shortens construction schedule
Designs are more closely tied to structural analysis and energy simulations	Produces better-performing, higher-quality buildings	Improves quality of life and experience for users and public at large
Design input occurs earlier in process	Opportunity to impact cost and functional capabilities; measurable ROI for users	Improves team relations; design intent expressed at increasingly detailed levels
Energy analysis	Determines building element location in terms of function	Determines in terms of impacts on building skin and user comfort
Model checking	Determine best routes: egress, traffic, security	Saves time and narrows down options
Information management	Manages the operations of the facility	Increases perceived value of delivery method
Improved data sharing; increased interoperability for all project team members	Reduces communication costs, errors, and omissions	Improves communication; faster client decisions
Capacity to analyze building performance	Expedites key design decisions	Reduces uncertainty, exposure, and risk
4D BIM modeling	Communicates relocation of tenants to tenants during renovation	Results in a smoother tenant experience and construction process
4D BIM	Saves time, decreases time overruns	Not always on deadline; more time to enjoy life
Compresses construction schedule	Earlier handover of risk	Attractive to owner and contractor
5D BIM	More accurate estimates; evaluate project in terms of impact on building	Results in savings in energy; reduces risk for each stakeholder
5D BIM tracks installation times	Helps trades avoid crossing paths	More logical process; less on-site disruption
Perform material quantity take-offs; fix project costs earlier	Alleviates concern about cost escalation; delivers owner a more cost-effective building	Designers reinforce role of budget stewardship; helping you attain a competitive advantage
More time in design phase (designing, not just uploading information)	Less time on construction documents, saves owners money, reduces schedule	Designers can focus on what they are good at; integrates workflow
Meets energy code requirements in just hours	Provides energy data to MEP consultant	Narrows options, frees time, meets objectives
Bidirectional associativity	A change anywhere is a change everywhere; Consequences for courses of action understood	Saves time; reduces drawing and site errors by instantly coordinating

(continued)

Table 1.1 (*Continued*)

Benefit	Co-benefit	Sociocultural Impact
DWF format mark-up capabilities	Nontechnical stakeholders are able to visualize and review end product	Input from all participants and stakeholders supports integrated design process; facilitates effective communication; and encourages collaboration
BIM model holds info accessed and utilized for project lifespan	All team players can access this information at any time	A model, tool, and process that keeps giving through project lifecycle
Ease of creating 3D views	Helps tell *the story* to communicate design intent and project goals	Helps all involved to understand design intent and goals
Earlier input in BIM model frontloads work	Creates opportunity for new billing structure	Changes can be reacted to more quickly
Less construction waste	Less overbuying; saves owner money	Less negative impact on the environment
Clash detection programs such as Navisworks or Solibri	Imports models from different trades into a single environment	Peace of mind knowing trades are coordinated and accounted for

As this book is about BIM's many unanticipated impacts and how best to navigate them, it is natural that we should pause here to elucidate what these impacts are. As Thom Mayne acknowledged about his own practice:

> Now we model not to describe a building but to manage relationships between trades, which is a totally different reason than before. What we're finding is that the more facile we are with these tools, the more we use them for whatever challenges we're tackling—it frees us up to do other things. It frees us up to deal with more complexity during early design because we now have a way to handle it. We're constantly looking for new opportunities to employ these tools that we're comfortable with. But we're also tapping into whatever is coming next. In the very near future, robots will assemble buildings. What does that allow you to do? Just the fact that it's happening, what does that allow you to do? What opportunities does that open up? And so that's what we're looking for.[15]

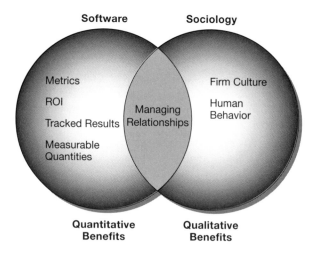

Figure 1.13   Irrespective of whether the benefits are quantitative or qualitative, we need to manage our working relationships to accomplish our BIM goals.

As the design professions and construction industry evolve from a 2D-based process to use of an intelligence-rich model, as we have shown, the benefits that once provided opportunity for the few are now shared by the entire project team. "High-performing teams are moving to BIM benefits for the whole team and a framework for pursuing peak performance from their BIM solution," says Ken Stowe of Autodesk. "Advanced builders combine excellence in BIM with *Lean Construction* principles of reduced waste and rework, better process, 'making things happen,' and a focus on value. Calculations of the return on investment will convince you that your projects can enjoy a lot of savings resulting from the transformation to model-based communications and a focus on digital cooperation."[16] (See Figure 1.13.)

Challenges and Obstacles to a Comprehensive and Effective BIM Adoption

It would seem for the practitioner new to BIM that for every benefit there is a corresponding liability—that is, one man's benefit is another's liability (see Table 1.2). Most design professionals using BIM on a regular basis don't need reminding of the challenges. There are many. In fact, there may indeed be as many technology, business, and social (mindset/attitude/firm culture) challenges as there are benefits. And yet, in terms of degree the greatest challenges to adoption aren't technological or business ones but rather sociocultural challenges.

BIM and Its Discontents

When adopted along with lean concepts, BIM helps reduce lifecycle costs. According to Ghafari Associates Inc., "the wastages in construction include:

- **Correction**—Rechecking and redoing errors occurring in design but discovered only at the construction stage
- **Overproduction**—Executing tasks ahead of schedule, thus interfering with other practical, scheduled work

- **Motion**—Time and effort lost in transit due to team moving from and to the office picking up plans, tools, or materials
- **Material movement**—Moving material from one stage to another or from one crew to another
- **Waiting**—Teams waiting for equipment, plans, instruction, materials, etc.
- **Processing**—Unnecessary reporting, expediting material orders, or excessive coordination
- **Inventory**—Material staged too far in advance on site"[17]

Ultimately, the ability to move beyond the difficulties and challenges of using BIM productively comes down to a *me* versus *we* mentality: the argument that *there is no "I" in BIM*. Successful navigation of the many hardships of BIM and integrated design—especially when firms first adopt the processes—comes down to an open-minded attitude and team-oriented mindset. In reference to an article by Stewart Carroll, BIM author Paul Teicholz writes,

Personally, I agree . . . that the primary constraint to obtaining the benefits of integrated project delivery (IPD) is the reluctance of the project team to move from a sequential to a concurrent work process. As long as each team member uses BIM mainly or solely for their own benefits and continues to work under traditional contracts, it will be very difficult to gain the more significant benefits that BIM 2.0 and 3.0 can deliver (earlier and less costly delivery of better buildings, use of model for facility management). This is true even if all team members use compatible software that minimizes the integration difficulties. I have observed at first-hand projects where various software products were used by team members in truly integrated teams. The positive results showed that technical difficulties could be overcome if there is a desire and/or a requirement to do so.[18]

One challenge, for example, can be avoided by following a simple tip: add detail as you go. There's a tendency in BIM to add too much too soon, to get carried away by the BIM model—to get bogged down in detail, especially for emerging architects. An example of this might be learning to model just enough of your project so that it communicates and displays properly, with neither too much nor too little detail. Too much information increases file size, slowing down your computer system's performance, while too little detail may undermine BIM's ability to utilize the embedded information for multiple tasks. With practice, the modeler learns to strike a balance between too much and too little information.

Building virtually prior to construction has its own challenges. There is the hope that a BIM model can predict the future, even while we were recently humbled to learn an economic model cannot always accurately predict the future. Just as economists were blindsided by overconfidence in computer models in the recent economic downturn, so too there can be overconfidence in virtual computer models to do the work for you. The model is only as good as the information that is put into it, and the knowledge, experience, and proficiency of the modeler.

First Comes the Mindset, Next the Collaboration

Some say, on one extreme, that BIM is intuitive, easy to learn and use, and "thinks the way architects think."

Barriers to BIM Adoption

Interoperability is neither the singular nor most important factor impeding BIM adoption and the general use of digital tools in design and construction. Here we posit three interrelated barriers to BIM adoption:

1. the need for well-defined transactional business process models;

2. the requirement that digital design data be computable; and, finally,

3. the need for well-developed practical strategies for the purposeful exchange of meaningful information between the many tools applied to industry processes today.

Phillip G. Bernstein with Jon H. Pittman, "Barriers to the Adoption of Building Information Modeling in the Building Industry," Autodesk White Paper, November 2004, 1.

On the other extreme are those users who admit that there are steep barriers to entry to work in a BIM environment.

> Never has a representation tool been so demanding of its user. The competent BIM operator must have an understanding of the tool, knowledge of materials and construction methods, and appreciation for professional practice. However, to move from "competence" to "excellence," I would add to this list perhaps the most important aptitude—*critical thinking*: the ability to simultaneously envision multiple aspects of a problem and their relationships before proceeding toward a solution. In contrast to the other qualifications listed above, this particular ability must be developed *before* entering practice as is best honed during an academic architectural education.[19]

Firms having to reposture and retool under times of retraction greatly diminishes the level of confidence and risk-taking.
—Michael Coston, LinkedIn group discussion, www.linkedin.com, 2009

For many who have been using the tool for some time, the BIM approach may in fact take less time and effort than a CAD approach. But to be considered truly collaborative, the team utilizing BIM must first overcome the collection of fiefdoms that limit what information can be accessed, and by what team member.

Reasons to Delay Adopting BIM

Issues such as migration from CAD to BIM, interoperability, risk, and ROI are serious—and may express concerns some have for transitioning to BIM—but do not constitute legitimate reasons for *not* adopting BIM. As Pete Zyskowski has explained, "Since Revit is not CAD, there are some migration issues to consider. Things like detail libraries can be taken to Revit, but it is a time-consuming process to make them true Revit details and may be better served on a project-by-project basis. There may be other, more immediate issues such as standard annotations, line weights, and general information sheets that can be migrated up front."[20] There are many details to work out, as there are with any significant change. But the message is clear: all of these can be overcome, have been overcome, and shouldn't discourage you from moving forward into a BIM environment. "BIM is bringing new changes to the workplace in terms of whom we hire, how we mentor, and how we share data among the parties involved."[21]

Incorporating BIM into your office raises issues as widespread and diverse as human identity—roles, how architects see and view themselves. "Human identity, the idea that defines each and every one of us, could be facing an unprecedented crisis. It is a crisis that would threaten long-held notions of who we are, what we do, and how we behave."[22] Other issues include

- The way people behave in response to new technology.
- How people manage technological change.
- How much more communication needs to occur when working in a BIM environment.

Recognizing Challenges to BIM Adoption

The most widely cited challenges to a widespread—and deep—BIM adoption are described in the following paragraphs.

Decision-Intensive Software

The modeler must consider construction methodologies when creating a model—making consequential decisions that impact the project every step of the way. No more loose (i.e., expressive yet inaccurate) sketches on trace—the expected level of detail is significant. Feeding the beast—answer-driven software, hungry for information—requires data. The model is only as good and useful as the quality of the information you put into it. For the designer, working in BIM can be constraining sometimes—information hungry, feed the beast.

Speed of Adoption

BIM has been adopted much more quickly in comparison with CAD adoption twenty years earlier. Even after the initial shock to the system, design professionals have had less time to make adjustments to practice methods, workflow, communications, and firm culture due to this virtually instantaneous upheaval brought about by the transition to BIM.

What Is BIM?

There are almost as many definitions of BIM as there are BIM users. "Over the last couple of years," says Jim Bedrick, AIA, director of systems integration for Webcor Builders, "the term 'Building Information Model,' or 'BIM,' has gained widespread popularity. It has not, however, gained a widespread consistent definition—it's like the blind men describing the elephant. But there's a lot of fuss being generated over this particular elephant."*

The six blind men in this tale go on to describe the elephant as a wall, a spear, a snake, or a tree depending on which part of the elephant—or, in our instance, 3D model—they happened to grab hold of. The message for those of us wrestling with BIM is clear: like the blind men, it is all in how you approach it. BIM is something different to everyone who uses the term.

Another analogy may serve to clarify. In Italo Calvino's resplendent fiction *Invisible Cities*, as Marco Polo describes the cities visited on his expeditions to Kublai Kahn—the city of Armilla, which "has nothing that makes it seem a city, except the water pipes that rise vertically where the houses should be and spread out horizontally where the floors should be," or the spider-web city of Octavia, and many other marvelous cities—he is actually describing details (and different takes) of his native Venice. Kahn believes he is learning about many cities when in actuality there is only one.

One city. Many descriptions. Many definitions, but only one BIM.

Some uses are grammatically challenging (*Your* BIM? *The* BIM?) The thing is that all definitions of BIM at this stage of its development are *working* definitions. One concept the best of the definitions have in common is that BIM is a process *and* a tool. Those who liken BIM to an expensive drafting tool are either skeptics or don't understand the full benefits of BIM.

---

*Jim Bedrick, "BIM and Process Improvement," www.AECbytes.com, December 13, 2005.

Time Invested in Legacy Software

For both individuals and firms, a great deal has been invested in creating and learning office standards and in mastering the use of these tools since the transition from hand drafting. Each has to grapple with the fact that years spent working in and promoting use of, say, ADT are now for the most part perceived as lost years.

Concerns about Liability

"Some project team members are concerned that increased collaboration over a shared model might make 'the chains of responsibility for work fuzzier than they are traditionally,'" explains Markku Allison, resource architect at the American Institute of Architects in Washington, DC. For instance, an architect may worry that sharing a building information model with a contractor will expose him/her to liability for means and methods. "In actuality, what we're finding is that, when it's used in practice in a collaborative fashion, claims are actually going down because we're having far fewer conflicts or problems in the field,' he says."[23] (See Figure 1.14.)

Learning Curve

In other words, equipping teams with the skills necessary to leverage the promised benefits of BIM, with limited time for out-of-office or even in-office training,

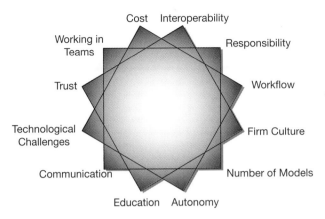

Cost   Interoperability

Working in Teams

Responsibility

Trust

Workflow

Technological Challenges

Firm Culture

Communication

Number of Models

Education   Autonomy

Figure 1.14   Twelve obstacles to successful adoption of and collaboration in BIM and integrated design.

requires a realistic understanding and acceptance of initial lost productivity.

Investment in Training

Return on initial investment may be neither immediate nor astounding. Even with training, productivity will most likely take a hit in the early stages—the first one to three months.[24] Mistakes will happen. Patience will be required of all but the most optimistic.

Implementing Change in an Existing System

Irrespective of how advanced and innovative their work products, design professionals are by nature and design conservative businesspeople. They change slowly and sometimes painfully, kicking and screaming the whole way.

Knowledge of Construction

No matter how good and capable and even award-winning a designer you may be, if you don't understand how buildings go together from smallest detail to largest system, you may not like where you find yourself working—if fortunate to be doing so—in the BIM environment. No matter where you are in your career, right-brain thinking is of little consequence for the left-brain demands made by BIM.

A Work in Progress

The software itself and the processes enabled by it are still evolving. Some firms are holding out from adopting and implementing BIM until the user interface becomes friendlier; universal collaboration tools fully mature; the software becomes more interoperable; the workflow less cumbersome; and the use as a design tool less convoluted, more intuitive, and fluid.

Whom to Trust?

Software trainers say that we need BIM training; software resellers say we need BIM software. It is hard to know whom you can believe and trust. People who say things like this, using exegesis, urgency, fear, bullying, prodding, or threatening, may have a vested interest in training others or selling outsourcing services. However, vested interest or not, they have a point that deserves to be heard out. Design professionals and AEC firms that wait to build their in-house BIM team risk playing catch-up, remaining behind the curve, cultivating a competitive disadvantage, and competing with others for the profession and industry's best talent. How long will you need to catch up: weeks, months? Meanwhile others, including contractors, have already put together their BIM teams. Don't be left out.

Managing: Information, Technology, and Staff

So far we have reviewed challenges to BIM adoption that come from outside ourselves and our organizations. Perhaps the most important challenge is managing yourself and the ever-present need to counter those who wonder why the software hasn't solved every problem, even those unrelated to design—while at the same time encouraging those who are growing weary and even leery of BIM's overpromise as a design tool. The goal remains long-term commitment by management and staff.

Managing Expectations

Another challenge to a successful adoption of BIM involves managing expectations—our own as well as others'. To address this challenge, set realistic expectations for BIM. The successful implementation of Building Information Modeling requires managing expectations and careful planning, writes Robert Green, a CAD programmer and consultant. He notes that it is important for management to support a BIM plan before putting it in place. "You can achieve management buy-in by explaining the costs, benefits, and difficulties you anticipate during implementation, so be honest and open when speaking to your managers about BIM," he writes.[25]

Using Revit, or any other BIM platform, as simply a 3D visualization or documentation production tool is like using a laptop as a hammer.
　　　　　　　　　　　—Kell Pollard, "The BIM Fad?,"
www.revolutionbim.blogspot.com, January 22, 2009

Collaboration, with its attendant file sharing, actually decreases claims.

Communication: Challenges and Opportunities

The BIM workflow requires that team members communicate with each other, perhaps more frequently than they are used to or even comfortable with. Many design professionals have been assessed on the inhibited or introverted side of the personality scale and may find the requirement to communicate verbally, face-to-face, in video conferences, and via file sharing a significant challenge. The outcome—and opportunity—driven by meeting this challenge is that your team will communicate with each other more frequently, answering questions of each other, clarifying discrepancies, and resolving problems before they occur out in the field. In time, team members will feel more comfortable speaking before others, verbalizing hunches and observations, and trying together to figure out how to accomplish tasks at hand. Some may show leadership tendencies that otherwise may have lay dormant.

"BIM doesn't work," that's very humorous and in many cases true. It doesn't work for someone whose expectations are too high, it doesn't work for someone who doesn't know how to use it, it doesn't work for someone unwilling to change the way they think, and it doesn't work for someone unwilling to change the way they work.
　　　　　　—"Senior Project Architect," LinkedIn group
discussion, "BIM Doesn't Work,"
www.linkedin.com, 2009

Table 1.2 BIM Adoption: Challenges and Outcomes

Challenge	Desired Social Outcome
Increased communication required	Teams communicate more.
Clash detection	All team members are on the same page.
Concerns about increased liability	Collaboration and sharing decrease claims.
Limited time to train	Younger staff step up and lead training sessions.
Construction wherewithal required	Interacting with team takes people out of their silos.

What's Holding You Back?

1. It seems like or actually will be punishment to do it.

2. It seems like or actually will be more beneficial to do something else.

3. The relevance of doing it is not understood.

4. There are other problems that come before or stand in the way.

Don Koberg and Jim Bagnall, inspired by
The Universal Traveler, 1976, 44.

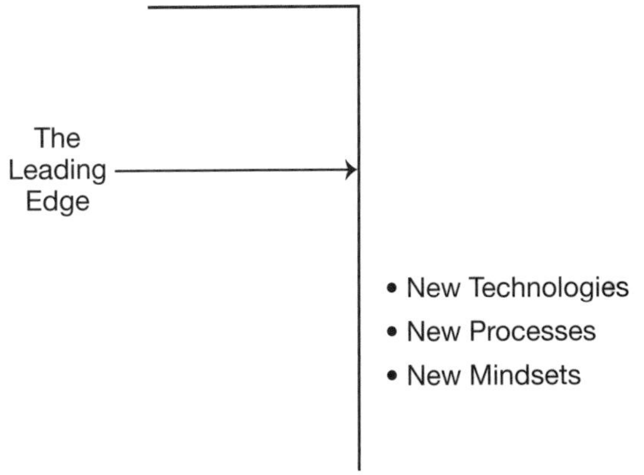

Figure 1.15   The leading edge: "There has to be a willingness to jump off and try something new."—Phil Bernstein, FAIA.

In Conclusion

Is it possible to have too much information, to gather too much advice? Possibly, raising the necessity of separating the sage advice from increasingly disparaging and discouraging comments found on websites, blogs, and online forums. For as one Australian BIM consultancy advised, "Faced with all this 'BIM chatter,' AEC stakeholders will understandably find it difficult to pinpoint what they actually need to do to reap the promised benefits of BIM. The chatter causes the change process to sound more difficult, extended, and complex than it should be. . . . This need not be the case at all."[26] (See Figure 1.15.)

Strategies for BIM Adoption

Suggestions for adopting BIM in your own office and for acquiring the mindset necessary to master the process:

Strategy 1: Think of ways in which BIM could benefit you, your team, or firm that could also be considered co-benefits for using BIM.

Strategy 2: Seek help from an expert, a trainer, or even a BIM guru that specializes in BIM adoption as

well as implementation. A recent online help wanted ad, "BIM Guru to Shepherd Office Transformation to BIM," read "Wilkinson Architects seeks a highly motivated, technology-focused Revit manager/guru with 7+ years of experience to shepherd the office's transformation to BIM . . ."[27] CAD adoption was never treated in these almost spiritual terms.

Strategy 3: If even after considering the benefits the challenges of adopting BIM still seem too daunting to overcome, consider breaking the stages of BIM adoption discussed in this chapter into smaller chunks to make them more manageable. Some firms pick a date to throw the switch from CAD to BIM and never look back. But the majority of firms approach BIM adoption more gradually and rationally on a project-by-project basis. They succeed because instead of being overwhelmed by all that is involved in the changeover to BIM, they manage to break down the psychologically and socially complex process into chunks that they and others can handle, manage, and use.

Strategy 4: Take the Kaizen approach. Similar to breaking down the vast information involved into chunks, Kaizen suggests instead taking small, incremental steps.[28] Before you know it, you'll be using—and have mastered—BIM.

Strategy 5: Adoption as problem solving. Architects are problem solvers—approach BIM adoption and implementation as an architect would. Using design thinking, tackle the task of adopting BIM as you would any design assignment. In other words, how you go about adopting BIM is the same way you would go about anything else.

Strategy 6: Steps, stages, or phases. Approach BIM adoption as a sequential series of steps. Pete Zyskowski, in "The World According to BIM: Part 1," suggests the following stripped-down, highly condensed, four-step BIM adoption process:

Step 1: Define goals. Measuring success. Other goals.

Step 2: Assess your current situation. Evaluate user skills. Identify concerns. Understand current workflow and processes. Anticipate changes to CAD standards. Assess (and upgrade) your hardware. Determine network needs. Don't forget about other software—I recommend that even the most hard-core Revit adopters keep at least one copy of AutoCAD lying around somewhere.

Step 3: Choose a pilot project. Migration.

Step 4: Make a plan. The delivery model. Training. Consultation and mentoring. Timeline and budget. Continuing education.[29]

Another example follows slightly more expansive, sequential steps—like dance steps—that can be followed one at a time:

- Agree on a common **vision** (any *defined* vision can be agreed upon; undefined visions cannot).

- Generate a simplified implementation **roadmap** for organizations to follow.

- Simplify BIM **terminology** around fewer headings.

- Identify **incremental and achievable steps** between major stages.

- Provide **benchmarks** for business improvement.

- Allow organizations to **assess** themselves and others.[30]

Strategy 7: Adoption as finding motivation to proceed. There are two types of BIM adoption: you do it freely—by choice—or you pursue BIM begrudgingly, kicking and screaming, where outside forces—the market, a client, the boss returning suddenly enlightened from a seminar or conference—pressure you to adopt and implement the new technology (BIM adoption from without).

Strategy 8: Come up with your own recipe for BIM adoption. When *Acronym* magazine editor Caron Beesley asked architect-trained technology implementer Neil Rosado, "How do you recommend organizations approach the adoption of a building information modeling (BIM) technology?" Rosado responded,

> First, I am a big fan of using a pilot project. Pilot project selection is the key to success and should take into consideration three things: One, pick a project that your team is used to working on. For example, if your team works mostly on office space projects, then selecting a project like a fire hall to implement BIM would not make a lot of sense. Two, organizations should consider a project with liberal timelines—not one with looming deadlines. Three, the project should be midsize. If the project is too small, not enough people participate, and

in a large department, word spreads from the project team and others become interested. If the project is too large or complex, the learning curve may be too steep. The idea behind pilot project selection is that you are trying to minimize the number of curveballs thrown at your team all at once.[31]

NOTES

1. Phillip G. Bernstein with Jon H. Pittman, "Barriers to the Adoption of Building Information Modeling in the Building Industry" (Autodesk, Inc., Autodesk Building Solutions White Paper, 2004), 1.
2. Rex Miller, "The BIM Mirage or BIMwashing," *Mindshift* (blog), October 11, 2009, http://the crerevolution.com/2009/10/the-bim-mirage-or-bimwashing/.
3. Jeff Yoders, "Losing Your BIM Virginity and the Giants 300," *Building Design and Construction* (blog), July 16, 2009, quoted in www.bdcnetwork.com.
4. Ibid.
5. V. H. Carr Jr., "Technology Adoption and Diffusion," The Learning Center for Interactive Technology, June 21, 1999. /www.au.af.mil/au/awc/awcgate/innovation/adoptiondiffusion.htm.
6. Kevin J. Leonard, "Improving Information Technology Adoption and Implementation through the Identification of Appropriate Benefits: Creating IMPROVE-IT," April 5, 2007. www.jmir.org.
7. Jay Moore, "Is BIM the Future?" 2009, posted at www.autodesk.com/forums.
8. Nigel Davies, "Magnum B.I.M.," January 2, 2008, *EYC* (blog). www.eatyourcad.com.
9. Lachmi Khemlani, "AIA TAP 2008 Conference," June 17, 2008. www.aecbytes.com/newsletter/2008/issue_35.html.
10. Scott Glazebrook, "Selling Short," *All Roads Lead to BIM* (blog), May 26, 2009, www.digitalvis.com
11. Nigel Davies, "(Mis)understanding BIM," *EYC* (blog), October 25, 2007, www.eatyourcad.com.
12. David Basulto, "AD Interview: Phil Bernstein," August 21, 2009, www.archdaily.com/32946/ad-interview-phil-bernstein/.
13. See, for example, www.BIMwiki.com.
14. Geoff Zeiss, "Building Information Modeling (BIM) in the Economic Downturn," April 7, 2009, quoting from Andy O'Nan, "The BIM Boom," *Concrete Construction* (April 6, 2009).
15. Robert Smith, "Thom Mayne, 2009 and Beyond: Revisiting the 2006 Report on Integrated Practice, 'Change or Perish'" (presentation at the AIA 2005 National Convention Fellows Investiture, Las Vegas, NV, 2009).
16. Ken Stowe, 2009. www.bimwiki.com.
17. Administrator, "BIM Implementation: Problems, Prospects and Strategies," August 20, 2008. www.architecturalevangelist.com.
18. Paul Teicholz, posted response to "BIM: When Will It Enter 'The Ours' Zone?" July 24, 2008, www.aecbytes.com/viewpoint/2008/issue_ 40.html.
19. Renée Cheng, "Questioning the Role of BIM in Architectural Education," July 6, 2006. www.aecbytes.com/viewpoint/2006/issue_26.html.
20. Pete Zyskowski, "The World According to BIM: Part 3," August 20, 2009. www.cadalyst.com/aec/the-world-according-bim-part-3-12881.
21. Pete Zyskowski, "The World According to BIM: Part 1," February 5, 2009. www.cadalyst.com/cad/building-design/the-world-according-bim-part-1-3780.
22. Susan Greenfield, "Modern Technology Is Changing the Way our Brains Work," adapted from Susan Greenfield, "ID: The Quest For Identity In the 21st Century," 2009. www.dailymail.co.uk/sciencetech/article-565207/Modern-technology-changing-way-brains-work-says-neuroscientist.html#ixzz1lpSA59tq.
23. Jana J. Madsen, "Build Smarter, Faster, and Cheaper with BIM," *Buildings*, July 1, 2008. http:// www.buildings.com.
24. Ibid.
25. Robert Green, "What's the BIM Deal? Part 3," September 23, 2009, www.cadalyst.com/collaboration/building-information-modeling/what039s-bim-deal-part-3-12923.

26. "Figure 6.1: BIM's Recurring Themes," January 20, 2008. changeagents.blogs.com/thinkspace/2008/01/the-bim-episode.html#tp.

27. "Revit Manager/Guru—7+ Years Experience Clive Wilkinson Architects - West Hollywood, CA," August 3, 2009. www.Archinect.com.

28. Robert Maurer, *One Small Step Can Change Your Life the Kaizen Way* (New York: Workman Publishing Company, 2008).

29. Pete Zyskowski, "The World According to BIM: Part 1."

30. Bilal Succar, "BIM ThinkSpace Episode 8," February 18, 2008. changeagents.blogs.com/thinkspace/2008/02/the-bim-episode.html#tp.

31. Caron Beesley, "Rosado on Revit," *Issue* 6 (Fall 2007), 2.

chapter 2

The Social Implications of Implementing BIM

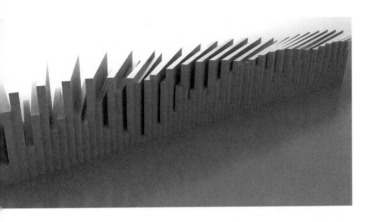

Figure 2.1   Revit- and Excel-based model generation. Use it to talk back and forth between analysis platforms for more performance-driven geometry. *Zach Kron, www.buildz.info*

You've accepted and adopted BIM—now it is time to act on it.

To implement means to give form to your plans, to take action on your decision to work in a BIM environment. Still equivocating, unsure, not convinced? Return to Chapter 1. At this stage implementation must become a focus, because BIM without implementation is just software. BIM has little value for the firm until it is implemented.

BIM is a process that brings value to organizations. You must be able to communicate that value to those with the power to implement them.

For a long time in my office, BIM was something out there that wasn't acted upon. We sat on nineteen seats of Revit for nearly two years, stored away in a closet unused—*shelfware*. Waiting for the right opportunity. Becoming obsolete. Doing no one any good. Taking up valuable storage space. Not earning its keep. And with each month unused, the software weighed on us: waiting for the right time, the right project, the right client, the right phase, the right people to put on the project, the right people to train. . . .

29

Strategic Implementation of Work Processes

There's a longstanding debate as to whether the value is in the idea or in the implementation of the idea. Along these same lines, BIM without implementation is just an idea. Implementation is a way forward. Implementation is execution. BIM without action has very little value. Or rather, BIM has value, but the value is only realized if the idea is implemented.

And yet, without BIM, there is nothing to implement. There's no need for implementation. BIM and implementation are reciprocal, intertwined, and complementary—they need and rely on each other. Just as a dollar has value, the value is only realized if it is spent or used in some way. Its value is only *potential value* as it sits in your wallet. BIM has the potential to bring value, and implementation fulfills the creation of that value. BIM's value is only real when it is implemented or used in some way.

Until BIM is put into practice, its potential and value are unrealized. The potential and value of individuals working in your firm goes unrealized as well—for it is my contention and belief that BIM makes for better architects. I have witnessed this in my own firm, and you will hear it from many others throughout this book. BIM makes of those who might have been floundering in CAD leaders, better communicators, collaborators, and more valued and valuable employees. Working in a BIM environment provides opportunities to lead that may not have been there otherwise, or that may have arisen only when the employee left your firm for another or worked for a great deal of time until eventually promoted. The *value* is found in the ability to take BIM and integrated design and make them implementable. That is what I will attempt to describe and explain in this chapter and throughout this book. (See Figure 2.2.)

Figure 2.2   Too often professionals seek a more linear process of cause and effect. Ideally, technology brings about change in practice, which, in turn, brings about change in technology.

The Human Element

BIM is implemented by people, and humans are by nature fallible. Their thinking may be flawed, their ability or willingness to communicate and collaborate may be imperfect, and their training may be inadequate.

Implementation, then, allows us to realize the value of BIM, but only if properly executed. Poorly executed, BIM will cause the value of the technology and process to be unrealized. As with ideas, true value realization is found in taking BIM and finding effective, actionable methods to implement it.

BIM in and of itself has limited potential beyond the individual who uses it. The implementation of BIM within a firm or network provides BIM with group or social value. And due to this added social value, integrated design becomes the natural next step. Only by acting on BIM is it given life.

When first considered by your firm, BIM delivers on a promise of value. Then, when implemented, BIM delivers the value to a larger group. Which is more important

BIM, while invaluable, is made tangible with implementation.

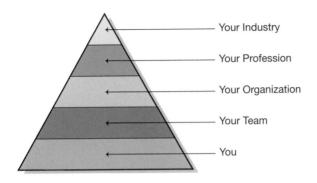

Figure 2.3   You are the foundation on which everything is determined. It all begins with you.

to an individual and which to an organization—a focus on the technology or the process?

Since good implementation seldom saves a bad idea and bad implementation seldom kills a good idea, it is safe to say that *how* you implement BIM within your organization is less critical than *that* you implement BIM. Imagine how organizations or individuals would go about achieving anything without implementing something aimed at producing or delivering the desired outcome. (See Figure 2.3.)

Agile Implementation: How Implementation Can Fail in Organizations

While it's far harder to come up with a big idea than to implement it, implementation, too, has its challenging moments.

BIM adoption and implementation is a two-step process: right-brain first (get a lot of stuff out on the table, research, gather information, brainstorm) and left-brain next (decision, selection, editing, re-design). Implementation is part of the second step. It's a test (*Can this idea succeed and produce value for us now?*) as well as the crafting of a delivery mechanism of that value.

What stands—what resides—between BIM adoption and implementation, by individual or team, is *conviction*. The selection has been made; the decision is yes—to move forward. Now what's needed is the conviction to stick with it, to work through inevitable setbacks and hardships. BIM is like marriage—you're in it for the long haul and you make sacrifices along the way for the greater good.

Put Your Pencils Down

Implementation is a call to action. Those who prefer to overthink and stew, and who have a predilection for planning and considering all options before moving forward with a decision, will find the act of implementation less thoughtful, less intellectually stimulating, less challenging. Architects who are predisposed to inaction—to question and to analyze decisions before making a move—have a tough time implementing ideas and tend to wait until the circumstances are just right, or rely on others to decide.

Implementation implies moving forward, moving ahead, with a course of action: putting your plan into action, acting on your decision to adopt the software, workflow, and work processes inherent to it.

If adopting BIM means *go or no go*, implementing BIM means *go, now what*?

The moment of truth has arrived. Implementation implies that a decision has been made. The decision can be made top-down or bottom-up. A top-down implementation is instigated from senior management, whereas a bottom-up approach is brought about by those within the office who work in BIM and want to see a change. (See Figure 2.4.)

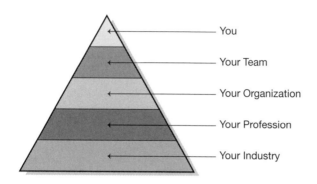

Figure 2.4 *You build on what has come before and what others have contributed.*

How One Interacts with the Model

- Insert
- Extract
- Update
- Modify*

Add a fifth interaction, *observe*. As with quantum physics and the observer effect, a person changes or modifies the model merely by observing, seeing things that others might have missed.

---

*Dana K. (Deke) Smith, "FAIA Building Information Modeling (BIM)," www.wbdg.org. Last updated: July 24, 2008.

How to Overcome Barriers to Successful BIM Implementation

BIM implementation, for many, is as straightforward as installing software and starting a pilot project using default content, standards, and templates. But as we will see in this chapter, a great deal is missed—and effectiveness lost—with this approach to implementation, including the opportunity to plan, train, customize, and adjust work processes, fitting the process to your firm's specific needs and culture.

BIM is essentially a strategy, and what is implemented is *change*.

On Implementing BIM

In this chapter we will take a look at how BIM is being implemented at firms and by individuals.

Among the questions this chapter will attempt to answer:

- Firms intend to start every new project in BIM, but do so in actuality only a fraction of the time. Why is this?

- Why does BIM take so long to implement?

The Act of Implementation

To implement is to have a predilection for action[1]—to take action on your decision to adopt BIM. Looking back to when you first worked in BIM, ask yourself: What were you waiting for?

Was it the perfect project, the perfect situation, the perfect client?

But in fact it's not BIM that you implement. What you implement is your decision, your choice, to adopt BIM.

And let this be clear: what you're implementing is not just the software. Implementation is of both technology and process. That is what you act on—what it is you have decided upon to do: Technology, because it will enable you, and your firm and project teams, to reap benefits described in the previous chapter. And process, because your existing processes will evolve with the implementation of BIM technology. (See Figure 2.5.)

No one else can tell you what that is—what is best for you or your organization to do. The answer must

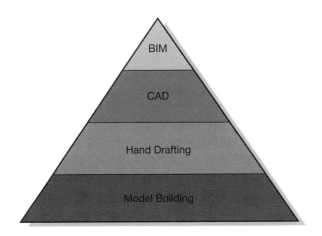

Figure 2.5   BIM has been built upon a strong foundation of earlier technologies and methods.

come internally. But once you've decided on a course of action—go or no go—it's time to launch and for the roll-out, for doing as opposed to planning, equivocating, and talking endlessly about it. Some are threatened by this stage, especially those who lean toward reason and judgment as opposed to action. Here, you are putting an entirely new way of working—and all you've worked toward—to the test.

It is now time for you to put BIM to work for you, your team, and your firm. Through best practices and lessons learned, your implementation will inform what you do moving forward. Implementing BIM will not only test your skills and resourcefulness but your resolve and patience as well. "The presenters warned, however, that the path is not easy and there is a learning curve involved. They also advised the audience to not get hung up on the technology and to avoid a long-drawn-out evaluation process to determine the 'best BIM tool'—instead, they should just go ahead and get started."[2]

And don't overlook the fact that the act of implementing will require the expenditure of resources. Just as you do in design and construction—allow for

implementation contingencies, the unexpected obstructions that turn up "below grade," unanticipated employee holdouts, and other issues that ensue that may have been unaccounted for, such as a 64-bit system and additional power and storage.

Social Implications of BIM Implementation

Anyone can load a single software license and be up and running with a program. Implementing BIM is different.

Implementation is an inherently social act. Not just the unpackaging of software licenses and seats and using the programs on individual stations, BIM implementation implies working with others in support of the project goals.

Implementation is synonymous with sharing and collaboration. BIM is implemented in a collaborative environment. In other words, integrated design doesn't automatically follow BIM adoption—but having the capacity already in place to collaborate with others predicts the successful adoption of BIM. Collaboration is not only a talent and skill but also a mindset and an attitude. Integrated design has become as familiar a concept—as prevalent and accepted—as BIM. The two concepts reinforce and serve each other in a symbiotic relationship.

Implementation as a Social Act

As the design process changes, design professionals find themselves reevaluating their current workflows and habits. One impact of this is that "the specific benefits to individuals often take priority over the wider benefits to the business and projects."[3]

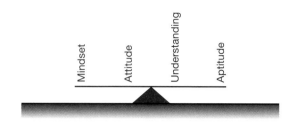

Figure 2.6   BIM balancing act.

Working in BIM introduces a number of changes to the design professional's workflow, including working earlier and for a greater length of time in the conceptual and schematic design phases, requiring a reemphasis of team members' efforts on the earliest design phases. Although architects are able to spend more time in the design phases due to the reduction in the documentation phase, this will be a hard sell for clients, such as developers, that already believe the design team spends too much time in this phase. An increase in design time would be out of the question to them. Some owners who were already suspicious that architects were spending too much time in the design phases may not be comfortable or understand why they need even more time in this phase. "Change in the workplace has a significant impact on the individual worker. . . . The introduction of new technology results in change. People are required to stop using an old, comfortable method and start using a new tool that may be totally foreign to them."[4]

BIM requires that decisions are made up front. Ideally, for BIM to provide the most benefit working on multiple levels or dimensions, the complete design and construction team is on board at the beginning of the project. This will be challenging for some project and client types—especially developers who want to wait to make decisions until the last moment. As for phases, design development (DD) is the new schematic development (SD), and construction documents (CD) are the new DD, so CD ought to be a breeze, especially if all major decisions are made up front. (See Figure 2.6.)

Implementation is not installation.

Documentation Reduction's Impact on Design Team

Most firms recognize that the greatest opportunity for making errors and omissions is in document coordination. Changes made in one part of the documents are sometimes overlooked or not addressed in others, resulting in an overreliance on general notes and requiring the contractor, when contradictory information is found in the documents, to rely on the largest-scale detail or contact the designer for clarification. Due to BIM's bidirectional associativity design, professionals can automatically (as opposed to manually) coordinate and update elevations, sections, plans, and schedules.

BIM affects architects' well-being because a lot of the drudgery of coordination is taken care of by the program. Although this does not replace checking one's work, the likelihood for human error lessens, allowing architects to focus on what they are best at.

How you staff your team—more up front, and fewer later—may be the opposite of what you previously prepared for. The makeup of your staff, from one that is mostly technical with a smaller design presence, may become more balanced—pairing design with technical from the beginning of a project. Architects who formerly specialized in CDs or detailing may now find themselves paired up at an early stage with designers and BIM operators, and may need to retool to do so effectively.

The makeup of a traditional architectural project team is governed by the huge effort required to produce a construction document set, with roles corresponding to drawing types: plans, elevations, sections, details, and so forth . . . Revit significantly reduces the documentation effort, thus rendering this traditional project structure obsolete. Instead, a Revit building information modeling team should be organized around functions such as project management, content creation, building design, and documentation.[5]

Project team makeup and size is also affected by the new technology, process, and impact on workflow.

Firms will also find that they can budget for much smaller project teams as they reduce the overhead of traditional documentation and CAD tools. In some cases, as few as half as many people are required to complete a BIM project compared with traditional ways of working. The smaller team—three to five people is the most common size we find—encourages agility during the implementation period and sets the right expectations for the rest of the firm that BIM doesn't require resources beyond conventional methods to succeed. . . .[6] (See Figure 2.7.)

We've Implemented—Now What?

What should you do now that you've implemented BIM in your workplace?

- Create a feedback loop

- Meet on a regular basis to "rest," observe and comment on how your implementation is going, provide feedback, and make necessary adjustments

- Have a goal for your BIM use and keep your ideal outcome in mind. Envisioning it makes it more likely to happen

Factors potentially impacting the success of your firm's BIM implementation include the following:

- The economy

- Training

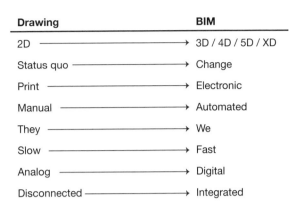

Drawing	BIM
2D	→ 3D / 4D / 5D / XD
Status quo	→ Change
Print	→ Electronic
Manual	→ Automated
They	→ We
Slow	→ Fast
Analog	→ Digital
Disconnected	→ Integrated

Figure 2.7   BIM biases. *After Michael LeFevre, AIA, Holder Construction Co.*

- Burnout

- Resizing of firm; staff adjustments in manpower or in paid hours available

- Skilled in CAD versus BIM

- Attitudes—willingness and interest versus feeling coerced

- Available resources

- Senior management oversight, leadership, interest

- Role models, mentors, coaches

- Project availability

- Client on board versus passive or indifferent

Architect and consultant Aaron Greven went about implementing BIM at his previous architecture firms in a variety of ways, depending on the focus and size of the firm. He explained that one moderate-size established architecture firm started a pilot project with a very small-scale commercial project with a team of three. "We were all self-taught at that point using Revit 5.0. The project type was the kind that we could do in our sleep, therefore no learning curve for project type and the billing was handled as part project time, and part overhead as 'IT training.'"[7] A second firm, he explained, was focused on large-scale design-build projects and trained small groups of staff in a more orderly, structured way using an outside consultant.

When our initial pilot project went on hold, we then integrated Revit into a large-scale multiphase project by looking for opportunities to gain value, and demonstrate to a broader group within the firm that we could pull it off. We had the advantage of working with a structural design build group that was already in 3D. And hiring an HVAC sub that produced shop drawings in ABS. Leveraging that info to improve the construction and design coordination process was actually easy—when compared to using ADT 3.3, and layered up drawings on a light table.

We also did some scope and bid analysis, rendering views, sunshade analysis, LEED quantity take-offs, etc. . . . Ultimately the problem was the economy, as the projects and opportunities dried up. The firm's more measured and elaborate approach, was this due to firm culture being measured and elaborate or because they were architects? We started with a larger stable of experienced users. Focused on building content libraries, templates, and documentation that matched the existing graphics of the firm so that the transition was as seamless as possible. In-house mentoring was critical to successfully "spreading the knowledge," using tips and tricks meetings often across project teams.[8]

Moving to BIM: Five Common Concerns

As firms consider their move to BIM, these five typical concerns commonly arise.

1. Productivity suffers during the transition to BIM.

   Yes, productivity can be expected to decrease by an average of 30 percent during the learning period and first project or two. However, these initial productivity declines are generally made up with subsequent productivity gains.

2. BIM tools are difficult to learn.

   There is always the matter of understanding the hows and whys of the way any tool works. When this is mixed with the anxiety that any change brings, learning these new tools can appear much more daunting than it usually is.

3. BIM disrupts established workflow.

   The two dimensions to the concept of workflow are the *progress* of an activity as it moves through a company,

and the *rate* at which this progress takes place. Does BIM affect workflows? Absolutely, BIM affects workflows—the progress as well as the rate. But the reality is that the workflows it disrupts are inefficient ones.

4. The benefits of BIM are not shared equally among the designers, contractors, and owners.

   By reducing the duplicative efforts of conventional drafting and coordination methods, BIM allows the design and engineering team to focus more on high-value design, understand more about the design earlier through analysis and visualization, and deliver as much value to the owner as possible.

5. BIM increases risk and exposure.

   BIM provides a way to reduce the risk of errors occurring in the design process.

Jarod Schultz, adapted from "Moving to BIM—5 Common Concerns," February 7, 2011, www.jarodschultz.com/?p=138.

Working toward BIM Implementation

There are a number of checklists available for implementing BIM. Most recommend these basic steps:

- Seek assistance

- Map out new workflow

- Identify key players and map out your BIM dream team

- Select a pilot project

- Create a feedback loop

- Consider lessons learned and establish best practices

The important question is how BIM is best learned. While learning BIM will be covered in greater detail in Chapter 7, during the implementation stage it is important to ask: Is BIM best experienced—and learned—in linear steps or in stages? What's the difference?

Steps are a linear sequence of activities, like a recipe: first you do this, next this, and so on, until you're up to speed. The problem is, it can be a recipe for disaster. People move at different speeds. Not every step is necessary for every individual for every project at every firm.

That's why implementing in stages makes some sense, as discussed in the following section.

BIM in Stages

Because there are so many individual steps in the path to implementation, and because each firm will take its own steps and exclude others, it is more helpful for many firms to approach implementation in stages.

Ten Steps to BIM Implementation

Here are the key steps in the process of transitioning an entire office, no matter how big or small. If you follow this process as outlined, you *will* be successful and there will be no turning back. BIM is here to stay! Here is the condensed version of the transitioning process.

1. Establish full commitment from principals; this is essential.
2. Choose a change champion.
3. Develop an implementation plan.
4. Select a pilot project and initial team.
5. Hire a BIM consultant (an embedded expert).
6. Setup initial formal training.
7. Change vocabulary, change perception.
8. Evaluate the implementation plan.
9. Create a BIM manual.
10. Repeat above process on remaining project teams. Start all new projects using the BIM process.

John Stebbins, "Successful BIM Implementation," June 12, 2009. www.digitalvis.com/successful-bim-implementation-learn-it-love-it-live-it.

Most firms begin their exploration of BIM doing comfortable 3D visualization and move systematically through more complex uses; the most advanced users integrate their project approach using BIM throughout the supply chain. `Almost by definition, more advanced usage—such as analysis and production—requires collaboration throughout more of the project team.

—John Stebbins, "Successful BIM Implementation," June 12, 2009. www.digitalvis.com/successful-bim-implementation-learn-it-love-it-live-it.

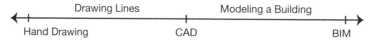

Figure 2.8   *The drawing/modeling continuum.*

Some propose making implementation a phased, iterative, and incremental approach so that the initial steps are cheaper and thus fewer resources may be wasted. Others favor deciding and moving forward full throttle, no holding back—giving 100 percent of attention and resources to the execution of the plan. "Unlike adopting a new technology in isolation, BIM implementation has to be undertaken in stages."[9] (See Figure 2.8.)

Implementation Recommendations and Opportunities

Implementation of BIM and integrated design requires an understanding of how you and your employees best assimilate process change. As every organization is unique and there is no one way to effectively implement BIM, you must understand existing processes within your organization before applying technological solutions.

While there's no one best way to implement BIM and integrated design in an organization—there are just too many variables to take into consideration, each requiring subtle changes or not-so-subtle adjustments—there are a number of tips and tricks you might consider, if you feel they will be a good fit for your team. Within each stage, place the individual steps that will best serve your firm—here presented in no particular order.

Office Standards

Early on in the implementation, come to an agreement on office standards, including title blocks and wall tag callout box sizes and styles. That said, don't let the decision on fonts, title blocks, and object styles hold you back from moving forward with your progress in BIM. If necessary, consider utilizing the standards out of the box while farming out the decisions for how to make the program approximate the look and feel of your existing office standards to your in-house quality, BIM, or CAD committee; technical head; or IT personnel. Memorialize these early decisions as early wins in the form of a BIM manual to be distributed—and signed—by all participating employees on the receiving end.

Level of Detail

Monitoring and if necessary controlling the amount of detail you put into the model becomes a challenge—not only for yourself when working in the model, but also from a management standpoint. The temptation to micromanage here is keen. BIM may be overkill at the start—you may want to opt to work in conceptual design programs such as SketchUp or Rhino prior to farming your design into BIM.

Avoid over-detailing—it is easy to go too far at any stage of the design. At the same time, BIM requires a great deal of information upfront—the payoff for a great deal of effort filling in dialog boxes and plugging in information is minimal at this stage. The key is to identify and prioritize the kind and amount of information and detail required to (1) meet the goals and expectations for the phase you are in and (2) make progress toward addressing later phases and team requirements. Just as important is to identify the details that do not need to be drawn, either because they are not critical to the construction of the project, do not represent criteria of the 80/20 rule (where 20 percent of details adequately address 80 percent of the conditions), or can be best addressed by others.

Leave the Past Behind

It is important to recognize that you are implementing both software and processes into an established situation and practice—not into a vacuum. "Oftentimes, one of the greatest barriers to the adoption of new technology is dovetailing it with existing process and workflows."[10]

Architects are certainly familiar with the concept of introducing new buildings or interventions into existing conditions—being sensitive to what came before. With the implementation of BIM, it is much the same. The firm—with its culture, habits, practices, workflow, and processes—can be thought of as a series of pre-existing conditions that you will need to be sensitive to when introducing something new.

One note to consider: once working in a BIM environment, you'll be tempted to leave CAD by the wayside, and for good reason. But you don't want to entirely abandon CAD just yet. As one firm recommended, keep a copy on hand so that, in a crunch, you can read a file sent to you in that format. And avoid the temptation to detail in CAD. Put less emphasis on 2D CAD, but don't abandon it altogether.

Conduct a Self-Assessment

Conduct a self-assessment for yourself and for your firm (see sidebar). Ask yourself: what type of firm are you—design? Delivery? Before fully implementing new technologies and processes is a good time to revisit your firm's mission, if it has one.

You will hear this suggestion from BIM trainers and consultants hawking training services. One size does not fit all. Do what works best for you and your firm. It has to work for you. This is a question of fit—good fit.

BIM Self-Assessment

Here are a few questions you would be wise to ask yourself prior to implementation:

1. How computer literate are the people who will be using the program?
2. What is the time frame for the ROI? Will it be six months after the training before users are using Revit?
3. How much time do you have to commit to helping individuals?
4. How many people can attend the class? I would imagine there are restrictions. Can a selected group learn the fundamentals and teach others on an as-needed basis?
5. How much work is planned for the Revit platform? It doesn't make sense to have everyone trained when you are still in your pilot projects phase.
6. Can these fundamentals be learned elsewhere, maybe from a book or in a tutorial you could lead with small groups? Or are there webcasts or videos available? Providing the instruction is both a service and a skill!
7. Can this money be better spent on specialized courses—Autodesk U, etc.?
8. Can you begin with "simple" (they always start out that way) pilot projects with defined expectations? Defined expectations may include your role in the project (template and project setup is a *huge* factor), what will be modeled, how will details be handled (AutoCAD versus Revit), deadlines (I suggest having more aggressive deadlines in earlier project phases to accommodate for more time in CDs), etc.

emgeeo, from comment posted on RevitCity forum, July 2, 2008. http://www.revitcity.com/forums.php?action=viewthread&thread_id=10171

Have a Plan

Assure senior management's support while engaging the design team—in other words, instigate both a top-down and a bottom-up approach. Engaging those who will be involved in the BIM work to assist in the design of the new workflow required by the technology assures that they will be onboard when it comes time for rollout; assures buy-in from constituents, users, and stakeholders allowed to participate in the decisions that led to the implementation; and at the very least, decisions are communicated and explained even if the process is not entirely transparent and democratic.

Adjust your implementation plan as necessary. With the concept of fit, what you are aiming for is an approach to BIM that's integrated into and dovetails with the way your firm works. Given how important context is to most architects in design, it is surprising that the concept of fit—good fit—is often ignored or overlooked when implementing BIM. Meet on a frequent basis, get feedback, adjust.

Assess Your Team's Progress

Assessing your team's progress is relatively easy to accomplish. Meet on a regular basis, establish protocols where everyone's encouraged—if not required—to chime in, and solicit feedback. In turn, supply any data that may have been gathered concerning ROI, percentage through project, hours spent, etc. (See Figure 2.9.)

Train Your Staff

Acquiring a comfort level with BIM tools, an understanding of how to use the programs, and familiarity with the work process and the potential impacts it can have on the members of your team as well as

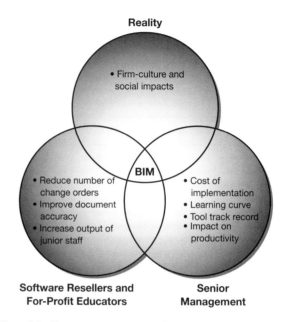

Figure 2.9   The greatest progress with BIM occurs at the confluence of multiple forces and inputs.

those working outside of BIM are all critical in making strides toward a successful implementation.

While learning is an important component of BIM implementation, there will also be some unlearning involved. Learning BIM, for example, will be hardest for those who are already familiar with CAD. There's a tendency for CAD users to try to get BIM to do things their way or to be more like CAD. Some advice is in order here: Don't try to get BIM to be more like CAD—you'll only get frustrated. Instead, learn how the BIM program thinks—even if the marketing materials say that the program already thinks like an architect. For those in the know, irrespective of marketing claims otherwise, BIM thinks like a good contractor. A contractor thinks about how to build a building—how the components come together. When working in BIM, it is important that you attain the mindset where you ask yourself, "How am I going to build this building?" (For more on training, see Chapter 7.)

When I was first trained in BIM, our junior team members learned so much more about construction by modeling. You may have come to the conclusion that your staff is strong in computer skills but otherwise weak in familiarity with building construction—The BIM Conundrum: Computer Skills vs. Construction Knowledge. One of the issues that cannot be stressed enough is having a strong understanding of how a building is put together. Unfortunately, many of the young graduates we see entering the profession do not possess the fundamental understanding of constructing what is designed. In the new BIM environment and the current move toward integrated practice, this core competency is one that is significant. Many of the young constituents of the profession have strong computer skills, including proficiency with a BIM platform, but the level of construction technology is seriously lacking. Our experience is that a team member with sound construction technology expertise will be required to mentor the young intern and work side-by-side with BIM integration. This cannot be overemphasized."[11]

Training Tutorials versus Pilot Projects

When design professionals contemplate how best to implement BIM into their firms, they often consider utilizing the technology on a practice project—not necessarily a real one—or on a real project that is temporarily on hold. They're concerned about client expectations and already-set parameters such as schedule and budget. They wonder whether choosing a smaller project versus a larger one makes sense, and are concerned as well about the importance of the project having repetitive elements or systems.

Many believe that utilizing BIM on a real project is the best option because it makes you think about what you are doing—not just going through the motions and steps of even the most detailed tutorial or on- or off-site training: "The firm went through Revit basic training as a team, attending on-site training. . . . The training familiarized staffers with basic Revit functionality and introduced them to the free online libraries of architectural components available for use in Revit models. However, when employees returned to their production environment, specific details of real-world projects took a toll on staff productivity."[12] Additionally, depending on the project scope, there's the opportunity for your team to work in worksets—where two or more people work on the model at one time. "While we knew how to use most of the functions in the software, it was harder to translate what we learned in the classroom to our own projects than I had originally thought," said firm principal Jon Covington. "You do not realize how much you don't understand about the software until you try to make things work for real."[13]

Don't wait for the right project—jump right in and test the water. "Among the uninitiated, there are no doubt many firms that would like to move to BIM but are waiting for just the right project—one that is sufficiently complex to take advantage of the technology's potential benefits, but still straightforward enough to allow team members to become comfortable with unfamiliar tools."[14] Once an initial group of employees is up to speed with the technology, one key social opportunity is to let those who want to teach—or have a gift for mentoring, coaching, and teaching—train the next tier of employees in the use of the tools. This is a vastly overlooked incentive—to provide on-the-job training by fellow employees. As an intrinsic reward, it might even offset the need for an annual pay increase for employees providing the training—if necessary—the following year.

After Training, Practice

Here, follow the 10,000-hour rule. Initial training is one thing, but your ultimate goal is mastery of the software and process. The sooner you become proficient at it, the sooner you will start addressing new information, taking it to the next level. (To look for ways to knock the training time down, see the next item.)

Coaching

You can certainly familiarize yourself with, train to use, and learn BIM without a coach. But what a difference a coach makes! A BIM coach will keep you focused on immediate and long-term goals and provide you with shortcuts, tips, and tricks geared specifically for you at your stage of development and the situation you find yourself in. Perhaps most important, a coach will show you how to master BIM in less time—perhaps cutting the ten thousand hours to mastery in half.

BIM Training Resources

While not officially a stage or step in BIM implementation, a good resource or two for speedy and exacting responses to BIM questions and conundrums will save you time and a great deal of frustration. Why reinvent the wheel when others who have gone down the same path are available to show you the ropes—and, unlike coaches, often for free.

Since sources are constantly changing, being added, and updated, I will provide but one example here of how an online resource has helped our project team. Brad Beck posted screen shots of a double (compound) curved wall problem on AUGI's online forum, and within two hours he had received two solutions. The answers were expert and almost immediate, and the consultancy free. That said, at all-volunteer sites such as AUGI you are requested and even expected to contribute knowledge of your own. As you yourself become more expert, you will find this to be a rewarding component of working in BIM.

Select the Right People

As Jim Collins suggested in *Good to Great*, "Get the right people on the bus."[15] The best people to venture into your initial BIM efforts aren't necessarily those who are most proficient at CAD. The opposite is more often the case. As we'll see, those who have worked in CAD may have many habits to unlearn before being able to pick up the specifics of working in a BIM program and environment. Instead, identify and select for your initial BIM efforts those who are quick, willing, and able learners and who are self-motivated. In other words, choose those who are flexible and open to training and learning new skills, rather than self-described experts.

Challenges and Opportunities while Implementing BIM

As with the benefits of working in BIM, the challenges, covered briefly in Chapter 1, are well known and legion. Suffice it to say that any change to the way you work will introduce obstacles, some easier than others to overcome. It is the known challenges that you can anticipate and therefore address as you initially implement BIM into your workforce. "Many BIM processes are undefined today, partly because the approach is new and partly because the effort depends on all stakeholders working together. When a client asks if an architect can 'do BIM,' but doesn't fully understand what BIM entails, the architect must become a trusted advisor to consult on what BIM is and how it benefits the process and stakeholders."[16] It is for this reason that it is important to do your homework ahead of time, before a full rollout of the program. "New software is but one aspect of building information modeling—be sure you understand all the challenges of this new approach to the building cycle."[17] (See Figure 2.10.)

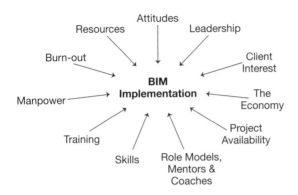

Figure 2.10   Multiple forces potentially impact the successful outcome of a BIM implementation.

Increased Hardware Requirements

When you first start out in BIM, especially if only one or two people are working on the project, file sizes will be manageable and you'll most likely be able to rely on your existing hardware to support this effort. Once people are added to the team—internally or by way of consultants and engineers who may also be working in the BIM model—depending on the size of your file(s), you may find that you need to add memory to your system.

Expectation Management

You will discover almost immediately that it is important to manage the expectations of those who are working in BIM as well as those who are not. Since the learning curve is sometimes steep, the perception of progress may not be apparent to those who expect results to be immediate—or at least in a time frame comparable to previous efforts using CAD. This includes owner's expectations, but also those within your firm in senior management who may have agreed to the implementation begrudgingly. It is important that everybody understands that this will take time—and where additional time is not available, a greater effort—at least for the short term, until everyone is up and running with the program and the process.

Just as when a tower goes up ASAP, then just seems to sit there for weeks while electricians are laying conduit and wire, the same process occurs with BIM, as the team fills in dialog boxes behind the scenes and inputs information into the model. As at least one architect has discovered, you can trim interior walls to exterior walls all week without anything to show for it. To be sure, progress is being made; it just may not be apparent to everyone. Your job is to monitor as well as play up the progress. Set expectations based on when that data is available and you are able and prepared to update the model.

Consider the appropriate team makeup (those who performed well in CAD make not be the best candidates for a strong BIM showing), project and team size (larger projects may overtax the firm's number of available BIM-trained talent), and appropriate use of the model at each stage (don't overpromise if the level of detail—or data—isn't there yet).

More People to Manage, Sooner

With more people at the table, sooner, more decisions will need to be made. This is one of the key differences, challenges, and opportunities once BIM is implemented. Architects need to remind themselves that this is what they always asked for: increased early presence at the table. And yet architects don't always see it this way. Instead, they ask themselves: "We could have more input and say if invited to the table early—but who invited everybody else? Who are all these other people?" (See Figure 2.11.)

The Question of Identity

One of the things you'll soon notice while working in BIM, but especially in integrated design, is the apparent lack of reference to the "architect" on the team. Where's mention of or reference to the architect? The

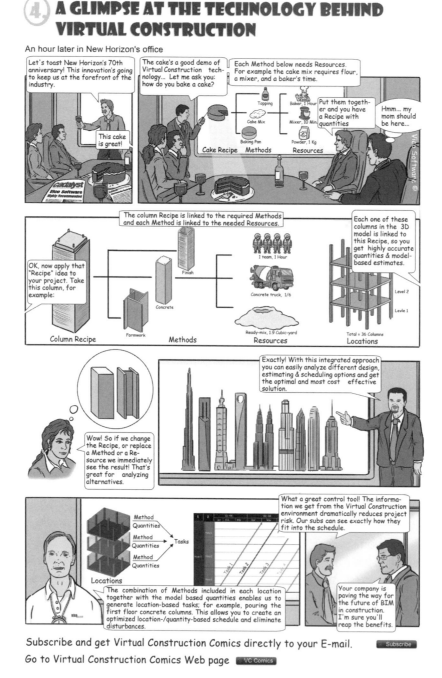

Figure 2.11   Comics seek to humanize the often hard edges of virtual construction technology . . . or sell more seats? *VicoComic No. 4, Vico Software Virtual Construction Comics.*

architect asks: "All I see is 'design' or 'designer.' Is that *me*?" Architects want to know that they are still relevant, not marginalized—or at least given equal status with anyone else who might offer an opinion and pass it off as expertise. Architects, like any other human being—no more nor less—want to be loved, enamored, given their soapbox, heard, understood, acknowledged, and valued.

Impact on Others

Needless to say, when you are working in BIM, ask yourself, what larger implications are there for this? Who else is impacted by this decision? What are the consequences for this course of action? These are questions that always should have been asked, even before working BIM—but it is all the more critical to ask them once BIM is implemented in your firm.

Impact on Schedule

If all goes as planned, before long you will notice a huge productivity gain from your implementation of BIM. ROI is one thing—from a business perspective. The perception of productivity by others within the firm, as we've seen, is as important.

To realize these productivity gains, you will have to assure that those working in BIM have an understanding of how buildings get built. More mentoring will be required, but in time you'll witness this knowledge-based ROI. But there's also the monetary ROI that will be realized once you are well into the (former) construction document phase, which depending on project size can last 4 to 5 weeks versus the 16 to 18 weeks you might have formerly experienced. This will have social implications as well as financial ones, especially for those whose careers until now have been focused on the later stages of project delivery.

In addition, you will have more time to design if you keep the same timeline as you currently have working in CAD. For the sake of this example, we'll say 32 weeks in CAD:

8 weeks in Schematic Design (SD)

8 weeks in Design Development (DD)

16 weeks in Construction Documents (CD)

Now, compare this with the 24 weeks working in BIM:

12 weeks in Schematic Design (SD)

8 weeks in Design Development (DD)

4 weeks in Construction Documents (CD)

The implication ought to be that in exchange for taking a reduced amount of time overall, you can spend more time in the initial design phase. One immediate question about the sudden reduction in project time, however, is this: *Our clients are used to 8 weeks in SD, 8 weeks in DD, and 16 weeks in CD. Why would they give you 12 weeks in SD when they are used to giving you 8?* And, they might add, *The clients already thought 8 weeks was too long.*

The answer is clear: there is the very large chance that a client or owner will still expect you to produce the same work in 20 weeks that formerly took you 32 by maintaining your original phase length of 8 weeks in SD. This is where your ability to describe, explain, and justify the importance of gathering more information and making decisions earlier—in other words, your skill in persuasion—becomes critical.

Reduced Productivity Due to Technology Training

The question is how much time—and with it, productivity—is lost in the implementation of BIM in the workplace? One study had this to report: "A recent online survey of Revit customers reported that although there was an average productivity loss of 25 to 50 percent during the initial training period, it took most new users only three to four months to achieve the same level of productivity using Revit as they had with their previous design tool. Building on that statistic, the estimated long-term increase in productivity as a result of migrating to Revit ranged from 10 percent to more than 100 percent, with more than half the respondents experiencing overall productivity gains of more than 50 percent and close to 20 percent experiencing productivity gains of more than 100 percent."[18] While results differ for each user, the idea that productivity may be reduced working in BIM is short-term thinking.

Opportunities for Increased Communication

Seldom do design professionals consider the positive social outcomes of their initial forays into BIM. And yet BIM model visualizations facilitate communication within the team and with the owner. Be sure that you are communicating what you intend—see the cutaway view, rendering, or fly-through from the viewer's perspective, and ask yourself what it is that they are looking for.

BIM implementation provides project teams with opportunities for increased communication with not just the owner but with all parties. With increased communication comes increased coordination across all trades. Assuring that information traded and shared is readable and interoperable will increase communication and speed up the design process.

Case Study Interview: Paul Durand, AIA, and Allison Scott, Winter Street Architects

Paul Durand, founding principal of Winter Street Architects, and an adventurer by nature, was an early adopter of BIM and IPD. Allison Scott, director of business development at Winter Street Architects, is a strategic marketing and communications professional with a strong background in technology and design.

You mentioned that your transition to BIM was "hard and expensive" and "a year of havoc and frustration." Please talk a little bit more about the transition your firm went through in adopting BIM. What were the biggest challenges and obstacles for WSA? Were they more technical (hardware/software) in nature, or firm cultural?

Paul Durand: All of that, all of the time. The transition was more than we could have predicted. We were committed to it. In 2003 we bought our first license. At that time we decided it was the thing. We have someone in our office that is smart, good at it, and thinks going home at night and playing with the software is fun. She's always our test driver. We started a project—so we could understand how we do it, understand how we'll roll it out, understand how we'll educate everyone in the office. Unfortunately, her understanding of things didn't always translate down to everybody else. We did that to some success. The software—out of the box—wasn't there yet. We knew that. But we knew even then that this was going to be the thing of the future and it was going to give us a leg up. We just jumped in. We changed all the licenses over. Everybody had to learn it and get it done.

Allison Scott: We don't not do BIM. That's our motto. (See Figure 2.12.)

PD: Everybody was trying to get Revit to do what AutoCAD did. Everybody's trying to print and meet deadlines and all of a sudden the printer wouldn't work and the hardware froze up. We changed all of the hardware, bought $40,000 worth of new printers. We had some naysayers—those ten- or twelve-year AutoCAD users—who didn't want to go over (and this is still a problem). Despite this, we made it happen. It was painful, expensive, it caused great tensions in the office, stressed the culture. We just had to be a little evangelical about it, saying, "This is the way. Trust me, this is the way!" And it all worked out. We were twenty-five to twenty-seven people. That's not so hard. If you're a big firm or small firm, it must be harder. We found our biggest problems were a result of lack of proficiency. I believe that was the whole thing with CAD, too. We went into CAD early as well, and people then would say it's faster to draw it by hand than to put it in the computer. But once people were proficient at it, nobody would go to hand drafting again. BIM was the same way. Once the proficiency was there, nobody wanted to go back because everything else was easier and better. It was painful and it rocked our world. My partner and I could sit there on our pulpits and preach, but the masses were angry and stressed because they were the guys who had to make the deadlines. But we did it. It took time—probably a year. But we got better and better.

It has been said that people who have never used AutoCAD have an easier time learning and using Revit—because you are not predisposed to think in terms of two-dimensional drafting.

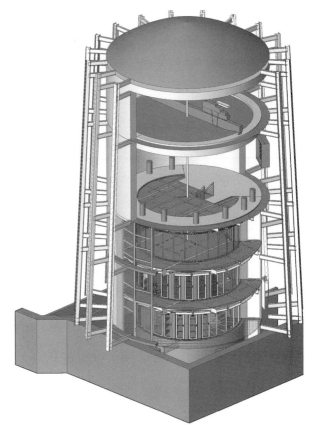

Figure 2.12   BIM model isometric cutoff of interior configuration of adaptive reuse, *CLUMEQ* Data Center. © *Winter Street Architects*

PD: AutoCAD is like drafting with computers. And Revit is like building models. They're two different things, two different skill-sets, and you go about them in different ways. The problem with the die-hard AutoCAD users is that they keep trying to do what they do in AutoCAD in Revit, so they end up dumbing down Revit to a drafting tool. When what they really need to do is understand that it is a model-building tool, a virtual building tool. Our goal is to virtually build.

AS: We've found that a lot of expert AutoCAD users know how to fake a lot of things. And in Revit, you can't fake things. (See Figure 2.13.)

PD: It's a proficiency thing; it's a habit and getting the idea right—that you're model-building. It's hard because they know what they need to do and they're under pressure to produce CDs or a design. And it's frustrating because they can't get where they want to go easily. Now, several years later, several people are good at Revit. Some of our principals that don't draft are still not

(Continued)

It just made so much sense to us. Because philo-sophically we've always been collaborators: we know what contractors and others are good at and we know what we're good at. And they're not good at what we're good at and we tend to not be so good at what they're good at.

— Paul Durand

good at it. We supplemented—we have a mentoring program with a local college. We have this pilot–copilot thing where it's great for the intern, where they get to deal with real, important projects, and the old dogs—not working as much in Revit—can orchestrate what they want. I have the vision— I don't know how to get there. They have to figure out how to get there in BIM. My partner and I—we continue to press the troops to bring it to another level.

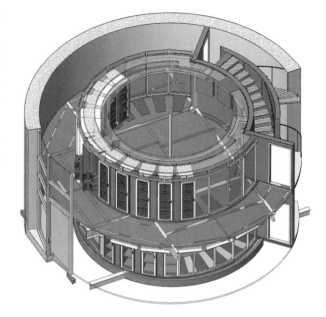

Figure 2.13   BIM model of two level interior configuration of adaptive reuse *CLUMEQ* Data Center. © *Winter Street Architects*

What came first for you—use of BIM on projects or inte-grated design? Does your office perform BIM projects without integrated design and vice versa, or do you see the two as integral and codependent?

PD: BIM came first. We got into it early—in 2003. It was presented to me by a few of the people here who thought it's the latest, greatest thing. I'm not typically gripped by software or even technology, but when I read a little about this I instantly saw this chang-ing our industry. This gives us the tools to do our job better, the way we always should have been doing things. In reading about it I came across IPD and a year later we implemented IPD. It just made so much sense to us. Because philosophically we've always been collaborators: we know what contractors and others are good at and we know what we're good at. And they're not good at what we're good at and we tend to not be so good at what they're good at. The collaborative process has always been informative to us. The earlier we've collaborated in the process, the better the projects have been for us. Because what we've found is where you don't do that you have to change your position. We end up compromising the design down the line, which was always painful. We get married to our ideas—we hate to give them up. We feel that we've lost something, we've compromised. I'd much rather deal with reality up front so that we get it right and don't have to suffer the compromise. (See Figures 2.14 and 2.15.)

You are now able to create a section—or even a detailed perspective view—for the client instantaneously. Do you have any concerns that you wouldn't be able to invoice for your time working in BIM—especially because of how open and transparent your process appears to be? You mentioned that your investment has resulted in time and cost savings to our clients. How about for yourselves as a firm?

PD: I don't have concerns about not being able to invoice for everything we do in BIM, for every section we're able to cut, because it's not more work. We sell service and ideas. And BIM is a tool that helps us to communicate those ideas, which improves our

Figure 2.14   CLUMEQ Data Center existing exterior conditions. © *Winter Street Architects*

Figure 2.15   CLUMEQ Data Center site visit during construction. © *Winter Street Architects*

service. So we look at that to consider what it takes for us to do a job, and state, "That's our fee." We used to have additional services for additional renderings and views. I find this particular tool allows us to provide more for our clients—for no additional money—within our fee. (See Figures 2.16 and 2.17.)

Have you found that clients come to expect more when you utilize BIM?

PD: This is still fairly new to clients, and there aren't a lot of people who have mastered BIM. We have a variety of work and a variety of clients. Clients are still pretty surprised at how easily and quickly we can provide these things and not at an additional cost. Eventually they will learn this and know that these things are available. But at the present it has really given us the heads-up against our competition. When clients ask for presentations, we go and demonstrate just how easy it is to use these tools to create views, renderings, and print models built in plastic. For example, at a town meeting, someone from the neighborhood asks, what can you see from my back yard? And you can show him. It's impressive and has taken a lot of the objections away.

(Continued)

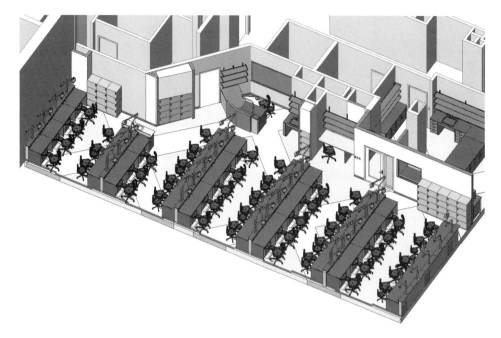

Figure 2.16   Maloney Lab Expansion, 3D axonometric view of classroom and lab. © *Winter Street Architects*

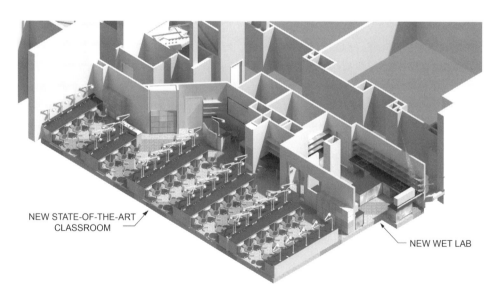

Figure 2.17   Maloney Lab Expansion, rendered 3D axonometric view. © *Winter Street Architects*

Figure 2.18   Maloney Lab Expansion, perspective view. © *Winter Street Architects*

Figure 2.19   Maloney Lab Expansion, rendered perspective view with lighting effects. © *Winter Street Architects*

You are given approvals quickly. When we've tried to get departmental approvals for an office design and one person is really the hard person to please and asks, what do you see from my desk—we can show her in seconds. (See Figures 2.18 and 2.19.)

We struggle to make our work relevant to clients. How can we make their business better through design? We look to the latest technologies and trends that could benefit our clients. We're not the kind of architect that waits for clients to bring us work—we think of solutions that we can bring to clients.

— Paul Durand

Your firm is a success story in these economically challenging times. What factors can you share that distinguish your firm and the way you do things from others that might be struggling? How important are certain firm-culture factors—such as open and frequent communication, a collaborative spirit, and trusting natures—that contribute to this success?

PD: What separates us is that we're entrepreneurial. Contractors have told us that they like working with us because

(Continued)

we treat architecture like a business. And we used to be insulted by that. I understand more clearly now what they mean by that. We're entrepreneurial; we bring creativity, vision, and daring to our business practice, likely due to our design work. But we struggle to make our work relevant to clients. How can we make their business better through design? We look to the latest technologies and trends that could benefit our clients. We're not the kind of architect that waits for clients to bring us work—we think of solutions that we can bring to clients. It's almost like a technology firm. When things are hot, money's flowing, and there are projects—we have found that's a good time to be investing in research and development, by asking what we're good at and what will be needed by our clients, for when things do slow down. When we come out of this economy, what are people going to want to do? Last year we hired a person who's a workspace planning expert and had this idea of the future of the workspace and what's it going to look like. So we spent twelve months investigating what we call the transformative workplace that takes advantage of virtualized workers. We developed a reference design for a leaner, meaner, greener workplace. We're asking: how does the workspace change when you virtualize employees? People are asking: We've got to grow—how can we do this without increasing our real estate? We've kept our workers employed and even grown the firm at a time when they have a dozen friends that are unemployed. (See Figures 2.20 and 2.21.)

Figure 2.20   Maloney Lab Expansion, wireframe perspective. © *Winter Street Architects*

You make great use of Web 2.0—social media. Have you seen a benefit?

AS: In response to the economic downturn, we knew that we weren't going to have the same amount of funds to apply to a traditional marketing plan. This worked out for us because we didn't want to go the traditional route. We wanted to keep

Figure 2.21   Maloney Lab Expansion, rendered perspective. © *Winter Street Architects*

pushing things and changing the way we do things because so many of our clients were moving progressively forward in their technology. We were becoming more and more exposed to the technologies that they were using. And so we started to adopt them. In the last year we've integrated a fairly deep social media marketing campaign. It has grown exponentially. We're seeing some great traction. Being with you on the phone with you today is a result of our blog. Paul, Mark (Paul's business partner), and I all have a strong passion for the role technology can play. I saw that in Paul and Mark, and I saw that in Winter Street with their early adoption of BIM and the way they were developing new processes around it to support their client model. Coming from a place like Kurzweil Technologies, involving Mark and Paul in a discussion with Ray Kurzweil on how the convergence of design and technology had become imminent and we can't ignore it. The fact that we are embracing it and utilizing it so deeply while other people might be running away from it or afraid of it [gives us] a distinct advantage.

We want to be partners with our clients. I had a professor in my MBA program that told me, "Good designers aren't taxi drivers. They don't just take you from one place to the other. They are actually tour guides that help you to understand the landscape." Taking into effect not only how we are going to build a better building, but how it is going to impact our business. How is it going to make our business better? Paul says we want to walk in our client's shoes. BIM, and the integrated design process, certainly helps us to do that. (See Figures 2.22 thru 2.38. Note: Figures accompanying the following interview are for illustrative purposes and are the work of WSA.)

Case Study Interview with Aaron Greven, BIM Consultant

Aaron Greven, a consultant advancing the use of BIM to contractors, design firms, and owners, has led large-scale projects as a project architect for several firms and served as project director for a design-build development firm.

What was your first exposure to BIM software and what was your initial reaction to it?

Aaron Greven: Over six years ago I was looking for new tools to simplify the documentation process. I was looking for a small-scale pilot project to explore the potential of Revit (then 4.0) after doing my own research. My initial reaction was one of frustration, but excitement, about the potential. I'd always been focused on add-on tools to help automate and speed up the "drafting drudgery" of the architectural documentation process—and Revit seemed to promise a release. [It was] frustrating initially because of the vacuum of best practices, help books and resources, and proven project success examples.

Working my way up as an architect with CAD responsibilities—my personality is more of a troubleshooter never satisfied with "this doesn't work"—I'm always looking things up and finding new ways to solve problems. Always looking for new tools. Revit [is] a tool focused on how architects think. The way it's being marketed now is too much *Revit's going to solve all of your problems; push a button—instant building*: an oversimplification of the tool's capabilities.

In the last three years user-to-user communication has revolutionized how people learn. You don't have to wait for a magazine to arrive. The amount of information that's online is unbelievable. Certainly there's a lot of garbage, and you have to know how to pick and choose. There's I wouldn't say inaccurate but incomplete information out there. You need a reliable source. One of my favorite sites is designreform.net—their tutorials, reviews, and all sorts of software. Some of this can be daunting for new users. Develop the ability to filter through the information to find what's valuable. David Ivey's BIM and IPD Group is a diverse group of people—not just Revit nerds.

At what point, if ever, did you decide that BIM is the future for the design profession and AECO industry?

AG: After the pilot project, I went to work with Optima in a design-build capacity and saw the true value and potential of the model information to the entire project team and not just a better drafting process. With a very small team of architects, we

(Continued)

were able to produce DD level documents quickly and accurately, sharing quantities with early bidders, and really understand so much more about early project-design decisions and how they influence cost and scope. This made it clear to me the value that intelligent drawings and smart models can

> *Most firms I'm working with now see [BIM] as an investment in getting new work.*
>
> —Aaron Greven

provide to the entire project team. If architects don't see the ROI to their internal processes, owners and contractors eventually will, and will demand the information be shared.

BIM software is costly. How did you justify the expense?

AG: My professional experience has largely been with mid- to large-size firms that have specific technology budgets prepared to absorb the cost of BIM technologies. Most firms I'm working with now see it as an investment in getting new work. Also in this current climate, RFPs that went out to five firms one or two years ago now go out to at least ten to fifteen. It's a more competitive environment, where firms realize they need to differentiate themselves more and expand their services to win new work.

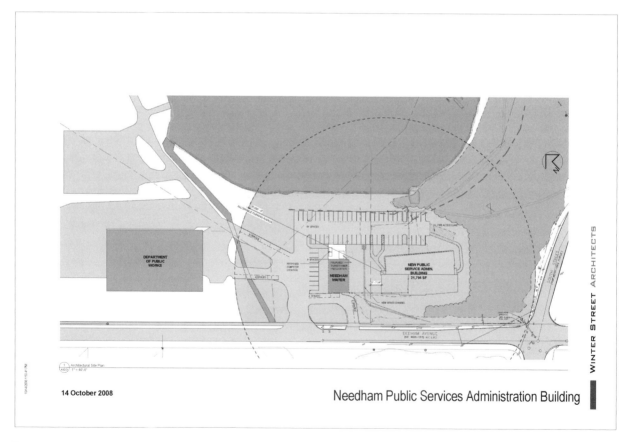

Figure 2.22   Needham Public Services Administration Building (PSAB) site plan. This 21,000-sq.-ft. office building is nestled into a grove of pine trees alongside the Needham reservoir, a response to ecological constraints, setbacks, and its relationship to the adjacent Water Building. © *Winter Street Architects*

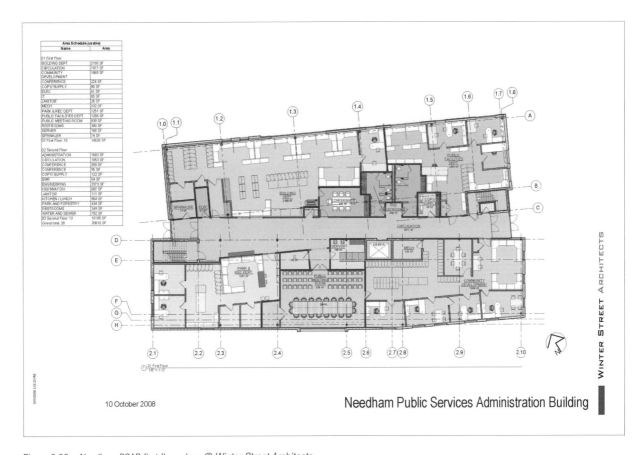

Figure 2.23   Needham PSAB first floor plan. © *Winter Street Architects*

How has the workflow between you and those you work with been affected by utilizing BIM, as compared with working in CAD?

AG: Definitely do more with less, including smaller project teams. Working in one model file requires more communication. There's more of a focus on using 3D views and renderings as part of a design process. In the traditional approach, 3D and renderings were used as static presentation tools that were more about validating a preconceived design intent as opposed to creatively solving a problem.

Did you hit any snags in terms of communication, technology, or the collaborative work process?

AG: Yes! [We had] IT concerns throughout in terms of CPU power and network capability, but this went with the territory. Communication with leadership was very difficult, as they didn't understand the underlying processes that went into design and documentation in the first place, let alone the changes BIM entailed. A few top leaders did understand the issues, challenges,

(Continued)

Figure 2.24   Needham PSAB perspective—early concept. © *Winter Street Architects*

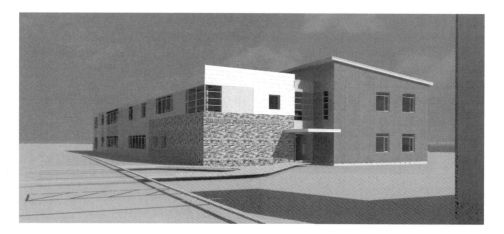

Figure 2.25   Needham PSAB perspective—added detail. © *Winter Street Architects*

and opportunities—yet failed to manage expectations among other firm leaders. Using new tools with new users represents a risk and is fraught with challenges.

There's a preconceived idea floating around that BIM is best for larger, repetitive, new construction projects. Would you recommend certain project size/scale/scope/new versus existing conditions for BIM? How about an ideal firm size for BIM use?

AG: It depends *entirely* on the experience level of the people involved in the project. If my team were four or five architects with at least four or five years experience using Revit, then I'd say any size project is appropriate. It depends also on what you're starting with and the competency of the entire design team. Again, experience is critical, both with the tools and with the project types.

At a basic work level, the tool enables you to do more with less. I have found personally, on the projects I've worked on over the past four or five years, project teams can be smaller.

—Aaron Greven

Once teams are up to speed—on, say, a firm's second or third project—can teams be smaller and get the same results?

AG: And seen as a threat! Yes, at a basic work level, the tool enables you to do more with less. I have found personally, on the projects I've worked on over the past four or five years, project teams can be smaller. Looking down the road, project teams will be smaller because deliverables will be different.

The role of CDs and where they fit in the grand scheme of things is changing. Whether the model is the contract—I don't know where that is in the future. The state of 100 percent CD documents is going to change. The value of that as a document, and deliverable, is lessening.

If you take documents away from architects, and contractors are more comfortable with design as their territory, they're chipping away at the architect's domain. I see trouble.

AG: I agree. CDs are a short phase in integrated design and in BIM. Once you articulate the model to an extent, getting to CD documentation is easier. That said—it's easier; but it's not push-button easier.

In your previous firm, did everyone use BIM? Were there positions or roles that you feel did not need to learn the software?

AG: Those who did not learn were managers and designers who saw it as an extension of a 3D rendering tool to produce imagery instead of solving design problems—not digitally savvy in the first place.

Figure 2.26   Needham PSAB entry perspective—rendering (*top*) and during construction (*bottom*). © *Winter Street Architects*

Figure 2.27   Needham PSAB completed project. © *Winter Street Architects*

(Continued)

Some say that BIM will be utilized primarily by younger, emerging professionals.

AG: I agree to some degree—depends on people's desire and comfort level with "the new." Using digital tools requires self-starters interested in figuring out how best to use a new tool that isn't well documented.

Do you design in BIM, or utilize BIM to develop the design and documents once the building has been designed in other media?

AG: BIM can be a tremendous design tool in experienced hands. New users run into the frustration of being more efficient and faster with other tools. BIM allows for design with more intelligence.

BIM: Just a tool, evolution (from CAD), or revolution? Which one, and why?

AG: A "revolutionary tool"—"tool" because it represents other software that when combined with non-3D-based software adds to how an architect delivers an idea. "Revolutionary" because it represents such a dynamic shift in thinking about how to document a project.

BIM can be a tremendous design tool in experienced hands. New users run into the frustration of being more efficient and faster with other tools. BIM allows for design with more intelligence.

— Aaron Greven

Figure 2.28   Portsmouth Fire Department Station 2, completed project. © *Winter Street Architects* © *Damianos Photography*

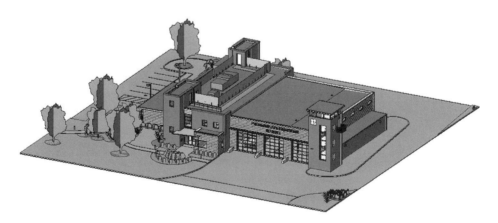

Figure 2.29   Portsmouth Fire Department Station 2, site model. © *Winter Street Architects*

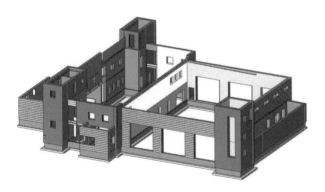

Figure 2.30 Portsmouth Fire Department Station 2, building envelope model. © *Winter Street Architects*

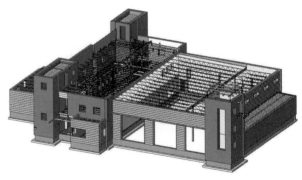

Figure 2.32 Portsmouth Fire Department Station 2, structural model. © *Winter Street Architects*

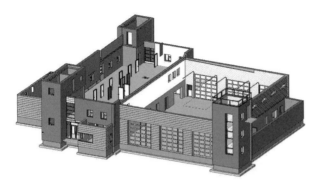

Figure 2.31 Portsmouth Fire Department Station 2, building envelope model with doors and windows. © *Winter Street Architects*

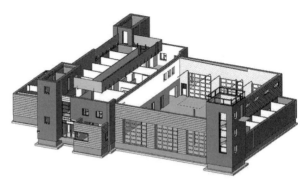

Figure 2.33 Portsmouth Fire Department Station 2, model with interior walls. © *Winter Street Architects*

If BIM technologies have in fact been around for decades why do you feel, in the vast majority of firms, BIM hasn't been fully adopted? What obstacles, if any, do you feel are keeping firms and companies from adopting the technology and work processes enabled by it?

AG: It's hard to beat the efficiencies of AutoCAD—there aren't enough skilled users in the marketplace to support the demand. I think, to a large degree, firms are very conservative and risk-averse, especially throughout the last five to seven years. There hasn't been a market demand to innovate above and beyond "efficient CAD"—but I think this is coming. Competition for work will demand firms look to expand and evolve their services to keep up.

Successful BIM implementation involves changing the attitudes and mindsets of the people who will use the technologies, which unlike the latest software and hardware required to support the new technologies, design professionals have within their control. Agree or disagree?

AG: I agree that it involves an attitude and mindset that is focused on facing challenges and "finding a better way." Revit how-tos and BIM project processes aren't as well documented as traditional approaches—so team members have to be willing to

(Continued)

learn on the fly, research, and find an answer to a problem. I often say in an anecdotal way that a new Revit user will have a question every twenty to thirty seconds, and if someone isn't sitting next to them answering these "micro-questions," then they won't become a power user and won't be able to do things as proficiently as they could the old AutoCAD way.

Having now worked on multiple sides, having crossed over from architecture to design-build to construction to running your own consultancy, which side do you prefer working in BIM on? Does one get it and one not get it?

AG: It's a really good question. It's something that's going to change over time. It's a question of who gets the most value out of the information in the model. Architecture design firms are using their models in such a limited capacity—to generate more efficiently the same old documentation they have always been producing. I feel that's such a limited-value proposition. Architectural design firms—at least the ones in my experience—I don't think they fully get it because it involves ultimately changing what you deliver. Changing how you ultimately deliver a project to an owner—it's not just a set of drawings anymore. It has to be so much more analysis-based, so much more focused on using the information that comes out of the model to help inform and improve the project as a whole for the owner. Looking at sustainability issues, not just hiring a consultant to give you the answers. Really using the design at an early stage to look at alternative concepts and schemes that are evaluated beyond just their design and aesthetic approach.

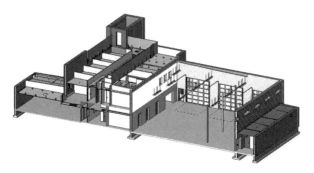

Figure 2.34 Portsmouth Fire Department Station 2, model with ceiling and lights. © *Winter Street Architects*

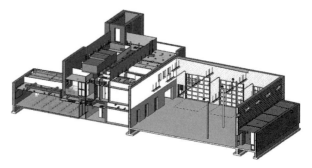

Figure 2.36 Portsmouth Fire Department Station 2, mechanical model. © *Winter Street Architects*

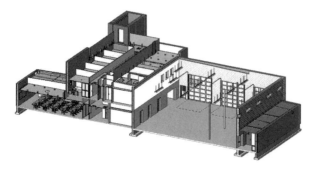

Figure 2.35 Portsmouth Fire Department Station 2, furniture model. © *Winter Street Architects*

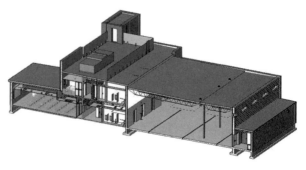

Figure 2.37 Portsmouth Fire Department Station 2, plumbing model. © *Winter Street Architects*

Contractors get it the most because their business is tied more closely to the kind of information that we can get out of a model in terms of constructability, sequencing, scheduling, cost and quantity. A lot of that right now is quite frankly low hanging fruit—the easy stuff. The hard stuff is prototyping, form analysis, energy analysis, and lifecycle costing. Working with existing models, pulling data, and using that data to help inform cost and schedule, constructability I believe is much more attainable.

Any other thoughts or experiences on BIM or integrated design you might like to share?

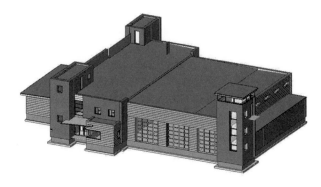

Figure 2.38   Portsmouth Fire Department Station 2 building model with envelope and roof. © *Winter Street Architects*

AG: I've accentuated the need for experience to ensure success. A good example of this comes from a recent project MEP coordination meeting I attended. The meeting involved eight or nine subcontractors working on a large hospital project, all using BIM tools to coordinate their work. An engineer from the GC was leading the group with the project file in Navisworks on a projector. The technology was impressive, clearly showing conflicts and issues that wouldn't have arisen otherwise. But there was a problem—no one was taking notes, no one was assigning responsibility, there was no agenda. In essence, no one was leading the meeting. This young engineer from the GC was leading because he knew Navisworks and was proficient in the technology—but he had no idea how to run a coordination meeting. At a basic level, this young GC engineer still needed to be able to lead a meeting, establish action items, track responsibility—do all the things his predecessor would have done while using the traditional light-table coordination approach. Technology alone can only takes things so far. In my mind, we're replacing project experience, the real knowledge of how to put a building together in a collaborative way, with "technology users"—a recipe for failure.

NOTES

1. Don Koberg and Jim Bagnall, *The Universal Traveler* (William Kaufmann, 1976), 80–93.
2. Lachmi Khemlani, "BIM Symposium at the University of Minnesota," February 15, 2006, www.aecbytes.com/buildingthefuture/2006/BIM_Symposium.html
3. "Why BIM Implementation Goes Wrong," August 1, 2009. /www.bimjournal.com/category/issue-07/.
4. Craig C. Kuriger, "Workplace Change and Worker Fears," July-August, 2006. www.bnet.com.
5. Rick Rundell, "Implementing BIM, Part 2: Planning for Process and Staffing Changes," *Cadalyst* (2004).
6. Ibid.
7. Aaron Greven, interview with author, August 25, 2009.
8. Ibid.
9. "Optimising your BIM Implementation," August 1, 2009. www.bimjournal.com/2009/08/optimising-your-bim-implementation/.
10. Tim Rice and Art Haug, "Managing Submittals," December 21, 2007, www.aecbytes.com/feature/2007/ManagingSubmittals.html.
11. James A. Walbridge, "BIM in the Architect-Led Design-Build Studio," October 2, 2007. www.aia.org/akr/Resources/Documents/AIAP037644.

12. *Cadalyst* staff, "With BIM, Practice Makes Perfect," July 24, 2008. www.cadalyst.com/aec/with-bim-practice-makes-perfect-3748.

13. Ibid.

14. Joann Gonchar, "Diving Into BIM," *Architectural Record* (December 2009).

15. Jim Collins, *Good to Great* (New York: HarperBusiness, 2001), 47.

16. Brandt R. Karstens, "Do You Do BIM? Part 2," *Cadalyst* (June 6, 2006). www.cadalyst.com/management/quotdo-you-do-bim-part-2-5617.

17. Ibid.

18. Rick Rundell, "Implementing BIM, Part 3: Staff Training," *Cadalyst* (January 15, 2005). www.cadalyst.com/aec/implementing-bim-part-3-staff-training-2920.

chapter 3 Who Works in BIM and Who Doesn't

Nearly every day, there are new announcements for BIM Modelers, BIM Managers, BIM Coordinators, and BIM Operators. Does this proliferation of BIM-related titles merely reflect the current state of transition of the industry from CAD to BIM, or are there real distinctions between BIM- and CAD-related roles?

BIM Roles and Responsibilities

In the profession and industry, who works in BIM? First, it is important to recognize that BIM—whether tool, technology, or process—is something different for each entity that uses it.

Who Works in the BIM Program and Who Doesn't?

The role of interns and emerging professionals in the past was sometimes described as a succession of menial 2D-related tasks. While those just out of school are still sometimes given the equally menial BIM-related tasks associated with tedious creating objects and families, the majority are given opportunities—by working in BIM—that they may not have seen in an earlier generation until later in their career.

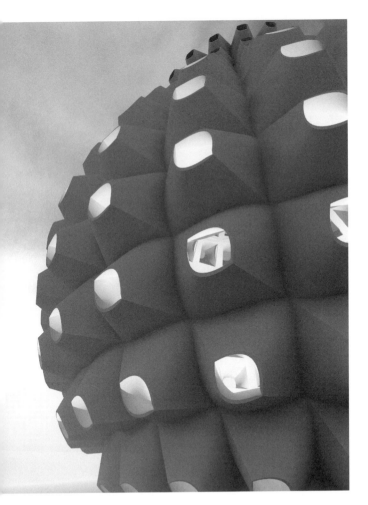

Figure 3.1   Curtain panel–based form inspired by looking at sea barnacles.
Zach Kron, www.buildz.info

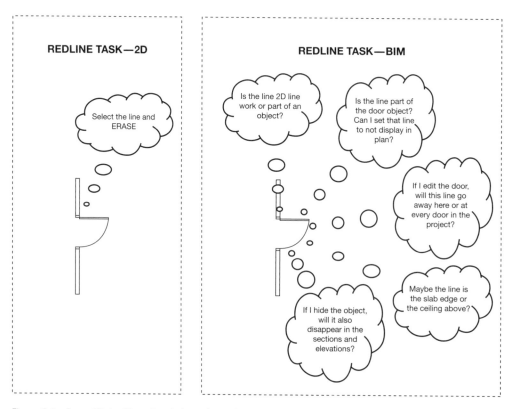

Figure 3.2 From 2D to 3D redline task: perhaps the clearest statement about the difference between working in CAD and in BIM. © 2009 Morris Architects

According to Lauren Stassi, of Morris Architects,

BIM gives an intern access to see the coordination of a project far sooner than they would in a 2D world. By working in plan, section, and elevation simultaneously, an intern, and the entire project team, is able to understand how to put together a building. Since the intern is generally the team member who will become the most skilled in 3D modeling, they are also the most likely to discover unresolved issues as they build the model. . . . BIM allows an intern the opportunity to see these issues and learn how to resolve them much earlier in their career than 2D drafting did. The greater the

intern's knowledge of building systems the better equipped the intern will be for this new responsibility.[1] (See Figure 3.2.)

Stassi adds,

In BIM, an intern has a much longer learning curve before they can complete tasks on their own because redlines are not a simple task of moving or trimming a line anymore. An intern needs to understand the software to determine if they need to adjust an object's location or type in order to "delete a line." They need to ask themselves and their team members— what are the impacts of editing an object—did

Acoustician Architect Attorney Audiovisual Consultant BIM Manager Building Inspector Building Maintenance Workers Building Researcher Business Developer Cabinetmakers Carpenters City Planner Client Owner Client's Representative Client Relations Code Expeditor Consultant Code Reviewer Community Representative User Conservator Construction Contractor Construction Manager Contractor Copy Editor Cost Estimator Developer Drafter Editor, Author, Critic Electrician Energy Conservation Consultant Engineer Acoustical Engineer Civil Engineer Electrical Engineer Environmental Engineer Mechanical Engineer MEP Engineer Plumbing Engineer Product Engineer Process Engineer Structural Engineer Transportation Environmental Consultant Estimators Exhibit Designer Expediter Facilities Manager Facility Planning Consultant FF&E Contractor Financial Services Foreman Furniture Designer Dealer Geotechnical Consultant Graphic Designer Historic Preservationist Housing Designer Illustrator Industrial Designer Insurance Bond Agent Inspector Building Interior Decorator Interior Designer IT Consultant Journalist Kitchen and Bath Designer Land Surveyor Landscape Architect Landscape Architect Interior Lawyer Lender Lighting Designer Manager Manufacturer Marketing Client Relations Material Scientist Material Testing Consultant Metalworker Model Builder Model Manager News Reporter Owner Client Owner's Rep Parking Consultant Photographer Plan Examiner Product Designer Product Supplier Professor Programmer Building Project Manager Public Relations Publicist Realtor Rehab Consultant Representative of a Community Representative of Owner-Client Representative of Building Products Salesperson Security Consultant Signage Space Planner Stage Designer Stonemasons Student Surveyor Teacher Transportation Planner Urban Planner Users of the Project Vendor

Figure 3.3   Complexity: the vast array of players typically involved in construction projects today. *Ryan Schultz*

every object of that type in the entire project just change? If the object is adjusted, will there be a gap in the model? Is it necessary for that object to be modeled in that location, but the display in plan needs to be adjusted? Because so much of the documentation is tied to what is built in the model, an intern needs to develop not only their software and building technical design skills at a much quicker rate in order to complete what were once simple "redline" tasks.[2]

Job Titles and Descriptions in the Age of BIM

It used to be that there were clear-cut roles, easily distinguished based on areas of focus. These areas were paths architects often went down after they passed the registration or licensing exam. Most often architects in larger firms would specialize, selecting from a limited palette of options—whereas those in smaller firms were required to perform multiple roles, and thus if they had a title it was often ceremonial. (See Figure 3.3.)

Larger firm positions were based on the acronym MAD, for Project **M**anagers, Project **A**rchitects, and Project **D**esigners.

With BIM and integrated design, just as the familiar project phases SD, DD, and so on are being replaced, so too are the former job titles, as well as the responsibilities.

The BIM process is also blurring distinctions between managers, technical staff, and designers. "There is a breakdown of traditional hierarchical roles to a much more granular level where all team members are important," says Allan Partridge, principal of HIP Architects, an Alberta-based firm, at the time in its fourth year of full BIM deployment. "Technologists are being involved much earlier in the work flow," he adds.[3]

Concerning BIM and the identity of the architect, somewhere along the way architects began to be referred to as "designers" or coupled with other designers—interior designers, product designers, structural engineers (where engineers weren't explicitly called out)—and they were often offended and scared for their professional well-being, as though they had fallen asleep and woken up to discover that they weren't special but clumped in—usually in PowerPoint presentation diagrams and the like—along with others. This has become a major concern to architects as it threatens them, causing them to defend who they are and what value they provide. For the purpose and urgency of implementing BIM, this can be seen as much-needed prodding of the architect by others.

IT Manager versus CAD Manager versus BIM Manager

A shift in the industry has taken place. Formerly, the architect was responsible for managing the client, process, schedule, budget, and team. Today, we need to emphasize the importance of this shift toward the architect's role of managing analytic data. For example, a request to perform "BIM drafting" communicates a lack of understanding about the basic tenets of BIM. (See Figure 3.4.)

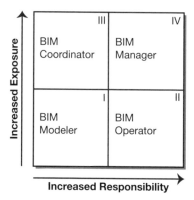

Figure 3.4   The unspoken hierarchy of BIM-related roles and titles.

Am I a CAD Manager or a BIM Manager?

You could argue that it is semantics. Am I a CAD manager or a BIM manager? If you support AutoCAD, then the first; if Revit/ArchiCAD, etc., then BIM. The jobs aren't that different in the trenches, but some of the smarter cookies have found themselves much closer to upper management because their firms have recognized the revenue potential that exists. If not revenue, then perhaps at least a newfound respect for the impact such a role can have on the bottom line. CAD has been reduced to a "factory floor" sort of mindset. With BIM, the way it affects how and why a firm does things, it makes it possible for the truly innovative CAD manager to step into a bit brighter limelight.

The titles I see now vary because firms are struggling to define who or what we are according to BIM. We call it modeling now; in the past we called it drafting or drawing. The tasks getting assigned to a BIM leader or manager are not all that different from their prior roles; they are just getting recognition now for the tasks (conflict resolution, design verification) that should have been part of a firm's regimen. They are actually getting priority with BIM.

Some firms had a project CAD leader because they recognized the importance of oversight from that perspective. These firms have BIM leaders now, project-focused, too, because they already understood their importance. Firms that don't recognize or that dismiss it are being confronted by its importance now that they are tackling BIM. The newness of the software and methodology is actually causing firms to confront things they've ignored to their detriment.

It's both the transition *and* that firms are realizing that there are things that ought to be done. There are new opportunities to mine if attention is applied to the fact that these old wishes/ideas are finally practical on the personal computing level.

——————————

Steve Stafford, AEC Advantage, email to the author, August 20, 2010

BIM Modeler (Model Manager) Roles and Responsibilities

One role that is widely advertised for is the BIM model manager. BIM model managers, unlike BIM managers,

- Perform hands-on production work.

- Address infrastructure requirements.

- Create a collaboration plan.

- Identify the level of detail.

- Coordinate disciplines and trade models.

- Facilitate the coordination meetings.

- Coordinate clash resolutions.

- Facilitate analysis done on those models.

Job Description of the BIM Model Manager

The job description of the BIM model manager depends on which team entity she works for. The architect's BIM model manager coordinates and manages the AE team's consultant models. Including those of the architect, structural engineer, MEP consultant, interiors, civil and site design, landscaping, and specialties such as labs, etc., each team entity's model

Figure 3.5   Collocating as part of the integrated design process. *Image courtesy of Tocci Building Companies and KlingStubbins*

manager—including that of the CM and owner—will have their own requirements. (See Figure 3.5.)

The BIM Manager

The BIM manager

- Assists in the coordination between disciplines.

- Develops a BIM Execution Plan.

- Creates a staffing plan for the execution of the plan.

- Coordinates BIM software and hardware requirements.

In addition to some of the same requirements of the BIM model manager

- Is responsible for office BIM standards: templates, libraries, and best practices in BIM workflows.
- Is tasked with setting up a BIM department and with creating BIM standards and manual.

The BIM manager is often tasked with organizing an internal BIM committee—similar to the firm's CAD committee or quality task force. There's a need for a BIM manual, and this is one of the committee's first tasks. The office manual allows for another employee to continue modeling in the previous operator's wake in the event the assignment needs to be handed off for whatever reason. Everyone on the team follows the same set of model-making rules with the confidence that they can continue their task without having to backtrack. (See Figure 3.6.)

The role of BIM Manager did not exist at all in the industry five years ago. This position demands excellent communication skills. Often the integrated construction manager has to work with all project team members, from construction executives to labor foremen, which requires a variety of communication skills. One aspect of the BIM Manager position is technology evangelist. The ability to objectively discuss the risk/reward aspects of the use of the new technology is a very important and difficult skill for BIM Managers to acquire. This is especially difficult because they are so close to the technology and have difficulty understanding the skepticism of seasoned construction professionals.

—Peter Rumpf, Mortenson Construction

Figure 3.6   Sometimes collocating entire integrated teams benefits the project. *Image courtesy of Tocci Building Companies and KlingStubbins*

The BIM manager is best situated to assure that the integrated design team delivers their contracted responsibilities and deliverables. Ideally, for the sake of neutrality, this ought be a consultant that is independent of the larger integrated design firm.

BIM Manager: Roles and Responsibilities

The BIM manager is primarily responsible for implementing and leading BIM efforts across multiple disciplines and office locations on a variety projects.

Other Roles: BIM Champion

GSA, the United States General Service Administration BIM Team, famously named their key BIM proponents of the technology "BIM champions." As Charles Matta discussed GSA's BIM success with Kristine K. Fallon, FAIA, "GSA avoided the major pitfalls in BIM implementation," which Matta describes as "trying to do too much and believing that BIM technology is ready out of the box." A step GSA took, which Matta believes to be indispensable, was the development of BIM knowledge and leadership in all of its eleven regions. These 'BIM champions' ensure that, when a BIM deliverable is requested, the agency is getting what it asked for."[4]

One of the most important steps a firm can take is to identify a BIM champion within the firm to serve as an example, help get those working in BIM to the next level, and push the technology—and process—further.

Case Study Interview with Jack Hungerford, PhD

Jack Hungerford, PhD, is a clinical and organizational psychologist and professional training and coaching consultant. With a background in engineering, Jack works with design professionals and others in the construction industry.

To date, many in the AEC industry will work collaboratively only when forced to do so by the owner or contractually in integrated design. Can one expect architects to work collaboratively and cooperatively out of their free choice and not by force or coercion?

Jack Hungerford: Unless there's a major benefit to them, I don't see architects doing it at all. They've killed themselves to get their architectural license, and remain at risk with others who are not licensed architects, even after they retire. I think that's a lot to ask. If you can demonstrate to them that there's tremendous benefit—makes their job easier, shares some risk with others—then definitely it can work. It's more about benefit than motivation.

What would you suggest to an architect when offered an opportunity to work on a project utilizing an integrated design platform—with shared risk and shared reward—and their reaction is along the lines of "No way! Why would I risk my profit on someone else not making mistakes? Why sign on to a project whose payoff relies on the other guy not screwing up?"

(Continued)

JH: If I were advising them, I would tell them as part of the advisory board to conduct an incredibly technical and detailed background check of every person who's going to be on this team. A complete due diligence: all the way back to what they were doing in college. Find out from other projects they've done, other owners they've worked with, other developers and architects they've worked with, how many suits they've had, what their story is. If there's a red herring or a red flag, I'd want to be all over that initially. Would they be able to work together? If everyone sees it as a benefit to everyone involved, if it's a requirement for my getting the job, then I'll have to weigh it against other projects I may have going at the time and the market outlook. It seems like less of a headache if I can make it easier on myself and sign a contract that says this is what I'm responsible for, the heck with the rest of you. On paper, it looks fantastic. Get everybody to sit at the same table, hammer out all the details, so we can avoid some of the hassles that normally arrive later. I see tremendous advantages for being able to do it, if everybody trusts everybody

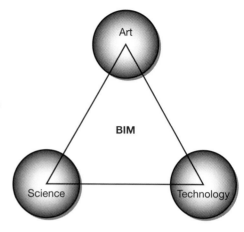

Figure 3.7   BIM, like architecture and construction, is a product of competing cultures.

at the table; you can save yourself a lot of trouble. If I'm a developer, I'm thinking, hey—I can save a lot of money. These guys are going to save me a lot of money and get the project done on time, done in the way I want them to. (See Figure 3.7.)

Studies have shown that architects would sooner work with others that have worked with BIM before than with consultants and engineers that they have long-standing relations with but that have not worked in BIM.

JH: If my best friend doesn't know anything about cars, I'm going to go to the mechanic rather than my best friend. It makes sense to go to someone who knows what they've been through before. And hopefully keep me from stepping in the holes that might be there. (See Figure 3.8.)

Some see integrated design requiring one to "gamble on the other guy not screwing up." What might be another—more helpful or productive—way you might suggest that they look at the situation or opportunity?

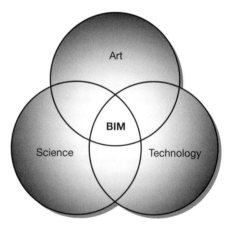

Figure 3.8   Ideally, BIM occurs at the sweet spot of its overlapping cultures.

JH: As we're going to be collaboratively solving the problems of this project, as a contractor I would hope the architect would ask me what kind of issues I've had with this kind of building before. How did I solve it? What did I do? As an architect, even though I may have had all kinds of years of experience, the contractor may have had a great deal more experience in this particular kind of project. I want to hear what kind of problems they have to solve, which ones didn't get solved, and which were ones where he didn't feel like he wanted to be part of a project like that.

Integrated design has to be a win-win. Anyone who walks away from the table and feels that it's not going to fly…will potentially ruin the whole project.

—Jack Hungerford, PhD

While IPD is at essence a contractual relationship, integrated design is an attitude, mindset, or ethos—about sharing information, sharing in risk and reward, being entirely transparent, trusting one another, and working collaboratively toward a common outcome. Do words such as attitude, mindset, or ethos hold water/count for anything in your estimation? If so—what?

Figure 3.9 Mastering both the technology and the process ought to be every project participant's goal.

JH: Not a whole lot. What you just described, I'm picturing everyone holding hands singing "Kumbaya" before we sit to nail things down. Now, I have to admit, a couple of times in California where I was helping to negotiate the sale of a business between partners, I had them do some breathing exercises together before we got started just to get them on the same plane and get them relaxed. And had the lawyers leave the room while we did that. It lowers the stress, lowers the tension, allows everyone to be as creative as possible and really go for the win-win. And integrated design has to be a win-win. Anyone who walks away from the table and feels that it's not going to fly—or that they got screwed—they will potentially ruin the whole project. (See Figure 3.9.)

Would you describe those that work in the AEC industry as primarily conservative and risk-averse when it comes to money, their business, and learning new technologies?

JH: Architects are risk-averse as well as those working in the architectural realm. They have to protect themselves dramatically; they're on the hook like doctors in terms of being sued. By virtue of that alone they have to be conservative, or even defensive. Because at every turn they can see their careers go away.

Building information modeling (BIM) digital technology requires that design professionals design and otherwise work in 3D—a completely different way of working and thinking from CAD and freehand drawing. What is your impression of those in mid-to-late career learning a new technology such as BIM and learning to work in a completely different way than they have been used to?

JH: A lot is determined by the size of the architectural firm that the professional works in. If they're in large firms, they get training along the way, incentives to attend seminars and stay abreast of things. Others see it as learn or get out, and still others as— "I just want to move into management. I don't have to know all this technology! All I need is some young neophytes who do. I'll manage them. I'll be the project manager. I'll be the rainmaker and will let the young guns do the grunt work." They see learning the technology as a big hassle to learn all that software. When in fact many of these architects in their fifties and sixties, when they were in their forties dealt with CAD. My first CAD manual was 1,200 pages. It was so daunting and intimidating—to draw two lines that crossed took forty-two different keystrokes—these professionals told themselves that they'd never learn CAD. Then as CAD became more user-friendly, many were so turned off by the experience that they said the hell with it and continued with paper and pencil. It's not a factor of age. I've worked with architects in their sixties who are very sharp when it comes to technology. What will be interesting will be to see how many professors stay on top of the technology—as compared with students. For example, at New Trier High School in Winnetka, Illinois, they have architectural software and machinery that few architectural firms have. (See Figure 3.10.)

(Continued)

Architects and contractors have historically had an adversarial relationship. BIM and integrated design require that they not only work together,
but that they do so with the entire team in place from day one. What will it
take for them to get along?

JH: No matter what my position is at the table, what it really comes down to is,
"What's the benefit for me?" If it's a requirement, a deal-breaker, the only way
I'm going to get this project, and I'm really hurting to get some business, then I'm
going to have to learn how to do this. For some, it would be a tremendous opportunity: this is the wave of the future—I'm starting at the ground floor and can really
learn something and this will serve as a marketing piece for me later on after this
project's done. Yes, there's some real benefit there. As for architects who have
been turning down opportunities to work on integrated design teams because
there's too much risk—due to the shared risk, I remember when I first started as a
builder architects took 7 percent of the GSF for their fee, which included construction management services. That's where architects really earned and learned their
expertise.

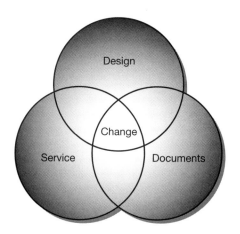

Figure 3.10   The one thing all design professionals
produce is change. Today, they do so in the midst of
unprecedented and enormous industry transformation.

Concerning architects and contractors—is it a class thing, an education thing, a cultural thing, or more pragmatic than
that—they each want different things?

JH: It's an experience thing. When I was a contractor, there were three architects
that I regularly worked with that I knew would take care of me. If they screwed
up on their design, I knew we could hammer it out. And they knew I wouldn't
mess with them so they would refer business to me. It was a situation of mutual
admiration and mutual trust. We both win. On huge projects, where the general
contractor brings in not only subs but other contractors as well, it gets very complicated. I don't know this guy—why should I trust him? That's human nature as
well as the architect knowing that her butt's on the line—and so the due diligence
up front. What recourse does she have when, three months into it, she realizes
that she signed up with a bunch of idiots? What's her out? (See Figure 3.11.)

In most cases it seems like it is the architect that is upset, throwing chairs.
What would you say to an architect who is unwilling to cooperate or collaborate with a contractor on an integrated team?

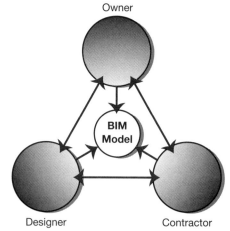

Figure 3.11   A question of identity: Where is the
architect?

JH: You're not in this—you need to be an independent practitioner working off to the side, doing your thing, cut out of all the
major projects because integrated design is the wave of the future. Either learn it or leave. If someone came to me with this
problem, I would have them break it down into as many doable parts as possible, addressing their risk and concerns, and create a long checklist of all the things that are needed for this to happen, for them to move forward with the integrated design
team. To others at the table you may look like an obsessive compulsive, but in fact, this is the way we're going to do it. This will
guarantee we're all safe.

In the film *Sketches of Frank Gehry*, the architect is seen discussing professional issues with his personal therapist, Milton Wexler, described in the movie as serving other architects over many years. As someone who has worked professionally with design professionals, what are some issues or themes that pop up again and again with architects and other design professionals that might help them succeed in adopting and accepting the new work process of BIM and integrated design?

> *The most problematic architects I have worked with don't see themselves as architects. They see themselves as artists.*
>
> —Jack Hungerford, PhD

JH: The most problematic architects I have worked with don't see themselves as architects. They see themselves as artists. Architects who see what they do as a learned skill with some creativity involved, they're far more workable, can make amends and work out details in the integrated design agreement. But the artist sees himself as an artist, this is my vision and I'm not bending on it. How do you help someone like that? You ask, what are the ups and downs of that? You ask them, how can you take care of yourself in this new context? How can you be an advocate for yourself without giving up all of your vision? And be able to work it all out so that you're comfortable with it. When I was working in a prison, the warden was a brilliant administrator and person. I was his assistant. Two department heads came in wanting to do completely different things on the same project. He listened to each, asking why do you think each will fail, made a decision, and said to one: OK, you're going to do it, you're going to have to support him. When they left I asked the warden, why didn't you work out a compromise? The warden said: Because it would have been completely screwed up. Neither one would have invested in it. This way, this guy's responsible and that one's got to help him. And it worked! It's absolutely a mindset.

What's the goal? To prove that you're a great artist? A great architect? To get the project done so you can move on to the next one? It's extremely important when I talk to someone I'm coaching that they can say what's the outcome they're looking for? What's the big payday for you? What would failure look like? The really smart people will tell you there's no failure—just a result. And the result may not be what you were looking for, but we'll make it happen. I would recommend that all design professionals go online and take a free Myers-Briggs assessment to know what type they are, Google their four-letter response, and find out where they're at. I haven't had any false results. When I worked with McKinsey consulting, the two issues we addressed to those who were going to be hired were: a sense of urgency and dealing with ambiguity. That's all there is. (See Figure 3.12.)

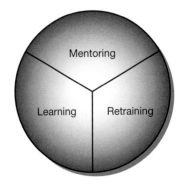

Figure 3.12 The role of senior management in the BIM environment. How best to use one's middle and latter years beyond project work? It is best for midcareer professionals to see themselves as constantly reemerging.

Working on an integrated team poses many challenges for all involved. The professional literature—including contracts—simply states that those on the team need to share, trust, respect, etc.—without any hint as to how that will come about or happen. How would you suggest a design professional—such as an architect—approach each of the challenges of "trust," sharing information (transparency), and sharing risk/reward?

JH: And nowhere does it explain how to do that, right? You have to check your ego at the door. You cannot be part of this team at the table with an ego. There's the old adage, architects have a major in architecture and a minor in arrogance. Knowing

(Continued)

what architects have to go through—they've earned a certain amount of arrogance. Architects are one of the three major professions—along with lawyers and doctors—that I've helped change careers from more than any others. They became architects and I helped them become something else. Perhaps it is less true today because there's more reality pounded into kids in school, especially with BIM in the curriculum, but these kids

If they didn't have anxiety, I'd be concerned, because architects are way too trustworthy. Anxiety is a healthy reaction, it's absolutely required.

—Jack Hungerford, PhD

thought they were going to be able to put up these magnificent buildings and in many cases ended up doing room additions in the suburbs. So check your ego at the door and focus on the goal. The goal here is to complete the project as best you can. Not for me to be the right guy, not for you to be the right guy. It's about the project.

The architect's role, moving forward with BIM and integrated design, is still largely undefined and unclear. Would you expect a situation such as this to create anxiety in the architect? Would it be natural to feel anxiety?

JH: Hell yes. If they didn't have anxiety, I'd be concerned, because architects are way too trustworthy. Anxiety is a healthy reaction, it's absolutely required. Andy Grove: *Only the paranoid survive.*

In conferences, seminars, and publications, the title "architect" is now largely replaced with "designer." Architects in the audience get upset when they see this, wondering if they are left out of the picture, if they are even needed in the process. Based on their emotional reaction, this seems to impact them—hit them—on a very visceral level. How important would you say a professional's identity/title/role is to them? And how flexible can design professionals be expected to be in this situation?

JH: The architect's title and role are extremely important to them. It's a major part of their identity. They don't do architecture, they are architects. They own it. In fact, you can't be good at it unless you own it. Now, does it define you completely? Unfortunately for some of them it does. And so consequently when someone with fewer credentials treads on their territory, it hurts—because they've earned their stripes. Some interloper will come in with little or no experience, degrees, or credentials and call himself a designer. Given that, I'd excuse an architect for asserting their title and identity. If it borders on arrogance—they've got to check that at the door. How are they going to engage people in a healthy way? The number one phrase I've used to help the architect dealing with the client or the contractor is "Help me understand." People respond to help. But "you're wrong!" "That'll never work!" Now we're off in a battle. "Help me to understand how you arrived at that decision." "Help me understand how that's going to work." A lot of teams will need a facilitator—but unfortunately it's more like a striped shirt and a whistle! (See Figure 3.13.)

Figure 3.13   Firm transformation brought about by BIM.

Comfort with ambiguity and flexibility are seen as two competencies of the architect. BIM software is seen by many to be highly inflexible, coupled with the demands of the integrated design process, which are decision-driven, evidence-based, fast-paced, and linear. Does this call for the redesign of the architect?

JH: Yes. They're going to have to initially compromise in their effort to find something to work for these guys. But hopefully, as the architect, I'm going to change what needs to be changed. Their evidence has to be overwhelming. It can't be just "intuitively

I think this is the way it is." Show me the data. And if we have to experiment, let's try it. Coming into this field as an engineer, people come in to this room, sit in this chair and tell me exactly what's wrong, what they need to change, and say, "I don't know how." And like an idiot I would jump in with both feet and say, "Let me show you how!" Pert charts, critical path charts, we have these kinds of diagrams—try this one! Didn't work? Try that one. It's not "How?" "How?" is about 10 percent of it. Ninety percent of it is "Why?" With an architect, if the reasons are big enough, they'll change. Unless they feel hurt, depressed, angry, upset, disappointed, without that there's no leverage to change. People change when they can no longer stand the way they're living, and architects are no different. Architects are going to have to change when they can no longer stand to practice the way they're doing it and realize that they have to change. They'll be forced into it. When the reasons are big enough, they'll change.

Architects—generally introverted by nature—must communicate and collaborate at all times on all projects working in BIM and integrated design. What challenges do you think this will create for the architect and what recommendations would you make?

JH: My experience is that the ones that are introverted aren't on their own. They're working for someone else. The extroverts are the rainmakers. The rainmakers are the ones who have the big firms, the most successful firms. The other guys are waiting for someone to walk through the door. The architects I've worked with are extroverts. (See Figure 3.14.)

With BIM—and the collaborative work process enabled by it—there's a lot for the architect to learn. For architects to truly collaborate, bad habits—developed over a lifetime—have to be unlearned. What are your thoughts concerning an architect's ability to unlearn certain behaviors that might be considered as detrimental to both their ability to work productively with others and the successful completion of their work?

JH: Unless the feared pain of changing is less than the feared pain of not changing, I'm not changing. It's not, "This is good for you." I'll fight you to the death on that one. This was very hard for me to learn early on in my career as a psychologist. People

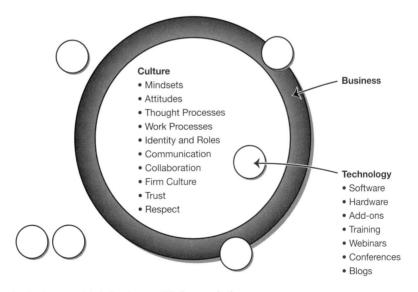

Figure 3.14   Business and technology as catalysts for change within the organization.

(Continued)

don't change because it's good for them. They don't change for people. I've come to appreciate the quote "negative" feelings. I need those. That's the leverage. Now we're going to change. It's all part of cognitive behavioral therapy. It's all quantifiable and you can show results.

Concerning the above questions and situations, does any analogy with tennis come to mind?

JH: If I want the best out of my doubles partner, I've got to keep building him up and just laugh at his mistakes with him. Give him feedback along the lines of "hey, that's cool," and "we'll get the next one, let's go." I'm considered a very good doubles partner not because I play better but I can get in the head of the person I'm playing with and make sure they're having a good time. If they're having a good time, they're going to be playing great tennis. Same thing with an architect and his team. If we're having a good time, and I really enjoy getting together with you as an architect, it's going to help me tremendously. It's not uncommon for some social connections to happen. Going out with the spouses may be helpful—even part of the due diligence. Anyone we hire at the executive level—no way do we do so without there being dinner with their spouse. Because if the support isn't there—this isn't going to work.

Case Study interview with Kristine K. Fallon, FAIA, Kristine Fallon Associates

Kristine K. Fallon, FAIA, Kristine Fallon Associates, has been a pioneer in applying information technology to architecture, engineering, and facility management and in helping AEC firms and government and corporate facilities groups evaluate and implement technology systems.

In the *AEC Survival Guide*, you wrote that there are three classes of barriers that inhibit the adoption of new technology: technological barriers, organizational barriers, and lack of understanding. Would you say that these are the same barriers to the widespread adoption of BIM and the collaborative work process enabled by it?

Kristine Fallon: These are definitely the same barriers. They're almost exactly the same as the research I did for the National Institute for Standards and Technology (NIST) in 2007 on the subject of information exchange in the AEC industry. Those were (1) commercial issues (the business and organizational barriers), (2) expectations and change management (the sociological elements), and (3) emerging technology and inadequate technology infrastructure (the technological elements).

Have you found that there's a hierarchy to these elements?

KF: There's quite a bit of sociology there, but I really think it's the lack of understanding. With a computable description of a building we're dealing with things in very different terms. This is a schema—a framework—that's totally unfamiliar and people are not taking to it or are not mastering or understanding it. This is what I am seeing even with people who are doing a lot of work on this. I see huge gaps in comprehension of how this actually works under the hood and what's necessary to make it work well. To make this work you have to get two domains to work hand in glove: people who know how to build a computable description of a building, how to code that up and map it, and the folks who understand how the construction industry

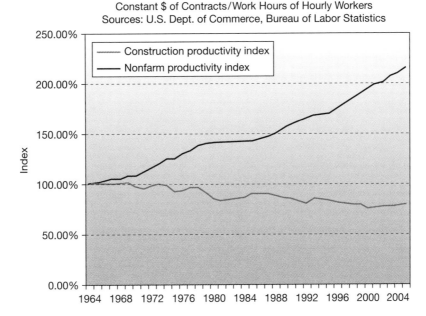

Constant $ of Contracts/Work Hours of Hourly Workers
Sources: U.S. Dept. of Commerce, Bureau of Labor Statistics

Figure 3.15   Construction Productivity Index. *Graph courtesy of Paul Teicholz, founding director, Center for Integrated Facility Engineering, Stanford University*

operates. The people who get the technology don't necessarily get the subtleties of those relationships and the fact that you can't just redefine them on the fly. The folks who are clear on the (construction) responsibilities don't have a clue and don't want to know what needs to be done to successfully define the technical aspects. (See Figure 3.15. Note: The figures accompanying this interview are for illustrative purposes and do not represent work of the interviewee.)

There's almost no interest among design professionals today to really master this stuff and get down under the hood, figure out how it works and tweak it to work the way we want it to work. That's been left to the software guys, who don't really get what needs to be done.

— Kristine K. Fallon, FAIA

When we were young kids at SOM, there really weren't computers in architecture. People like Fazlur Kahn and Bruce Graham supported our use of the technology vehemently because they thought it was part of being a great designer and engineer. That's really gone away. There's almost no interest among design professionals today to really master this stuff and get down under the hood, figure out how it works and tweak it to work the way we want it to work. That's been left to the software guys, who don't really get what needs to be done.

You concluded the book with these words: "The seeds were planted thirty years ago. The industry is in the cultivation period. With sustained vision and commitment we'll achieve a bountiful harvest. The information revolution

(Continued)

is underway. There is no turning back. Change is affecting every economic sector. There will be big winners and big losers, but no business will remain untouched. The AEC's ability to prosper in the twenty-first century will depend on its ability to use this information technology to augment industry-wide effectiveness and innovation." That summation could have probably been written yesterday. You reference Midwestern imagery. Has there been any advantage or disadvantage for you by working in the Midwest as opposed to one of the coasts?

KF: When I started my career, SOM Chicago was an absolute leader in applying technology to architecture and engineering. That experience—the first six or seven years of my career—has been incredibly valuable to me. Beyond that, no. If you talk about design analysis—if you think of Intelligent Building Modeling—the Midwest is not particularly a laggard. We have, for example, Joe Burns of Thornton Tomasetti. (See Figure 3.16.)

Architects often ask whether BIM will pay off. You don't seem to have that problem. A recent press release read: "In a highly competitive, qualifications-based procurement, the U.S. General Services Administration (GSA) awarded Kristine Fallon Associates Inc. team a $30 million GSA nationwide indefinite quantity IDIQ contract." What was that like?

KF: We had done work for GSA before the RFP came out. It wasn't like they were a big, scary federal agency. I really understood their goals and had done good work for them before. They had set aside a small number of awards for small businesses. I built on my understanding of their needs and approach. GSA is a pretty complicated organization, but I did understand the motivation behind their BIM program. I assembled the right resources in terms of focusing on expertise that they need and

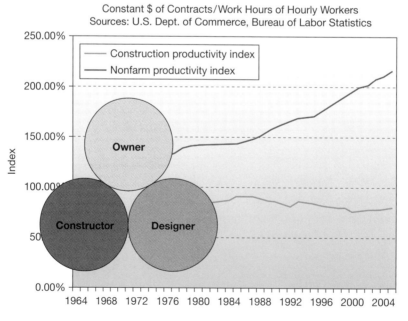

Figure 3.16   Owner/Constructor/Designer Productivity Index. *Sam Spata, Architect, AIA, LEED® AP BD+C*

presented a team that already has some credibility. What amazed me was the number of competitors, which I didn't know until after the award.

Does GSA understand BIM primarily as a technical tool—or also as a process? How well does the GSA get integrated design?

KF: GSA is a mammoth organization. For any project over $3 million they have to do a preliminary design, get a cost estimate, and go for individual congressional appropriation. This makes it difficult to get everybody together. They are highly constrained in what we would call process or integrated design. The central office—which originated the BIM program—has very little control over what the regions do. Each region is organized entirely differently. GSA's Charles Matta, FAIA, Director of Federal Buildings and Modernizations, has been focusing on the business challenges. They're looking for ways to do work with fewer people, greater quality, and repeatability. They're looking at automating things. (See Figure 3.17.)

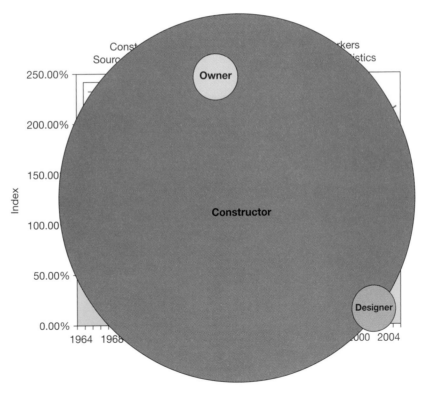

Figure 3.17   Owner/Constructor/Designer Productivity Index. *Sam Spata, Architect, AIA, LEED® AP BD+C*

(Continued)

How do you describe the work you do to those who have no understanding of it?

KF: We provide information technology consulting and services related to design and construction.

KFA has followed the evolution of BIM technology since the early '90s. Given your intimate involvement with the early stages of BIM, are you surprised that it has taken this long to catch on?

> *I am always surprised that things take so long to catch on. I've always been right about what's going to happen—just way off as to what decade it's going to happen in!*
>
> — Kristine K. Fallon, FAIA

KF: I am always surprised that things take so long to catch on. I've always been right about what's going to happen—just way off as to what decade it's going to happen in! The big mistake we all make is to think that what we do isn't very complicated.

I don't think there is any other industry that is as organizationally complicated as the design and construction industry. In terms of their roles, the requirement to follow the design intent, the architect can't get into means and methods—these are very complicated interactions. An RFI is the most complicated thing in the world. Someone looking in from the outside says it's just a question and answer. No. It's a claim, a change order, a cost overrun, a schedule delay! People have so internalized this complication they don't even realize it's there. They're operating with all these checks and balances in their heads. Professional regulation is on a state-by-state basis—consider changing that for a moment! And there are a lot of small players playing by these rules. Some people want to see consolidation in the AEC industry so we can get things done efficiently. I don't believe the answer is to consolidate everybody into big project delivery behemoths. It's much more complicated than the automotive industry. Even with rollouts of repetitive building types you have local codes and unique site conditions to contend with.

How do you adjust to the different audience/client types that you find yourself working with?

KF: For a long time I've said technology is not about technology. It's about getting business results. I always try to start with what problem are you trying to solve or what kind of competitive advantage or benefit are you trying to gain? You always have to work with other people in this industry. If you come up with a technology strategy that does something for you but creates a big problem or additional work or liability for someone else, it's not going to be very acceptable. We help people to develop a viable, implementable, win-win strategy on these things. It's something we're pretty facile at. If you can do that pretty predictably and consistently, we've found that this is rare among consultants. That's why we mostly hire people with a background in design and construction—to think like our clients, see the big picture, and not get so caught up in the immersive experience of technology. (See Figure 3.18.)

What do you make of contractors having so quickly and effectively adopted and implemented BIM over design professionals and others?

KF: There are a couple takes on this. One is: some of it is marketing hype. The other is: it's kind of a no-brainer for them. For coordination—it will always be cheaper to develop a computer model than to build the [expletive] thing and discover it doesn't work! Depending on the building type, what is the probability that the drawings are 100 percent perfect? Yes, it costs something

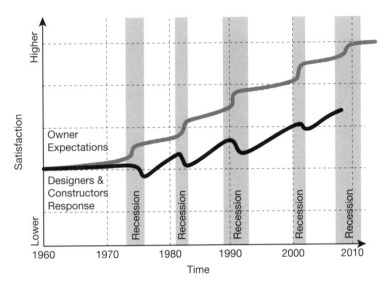

Figure 3.18   Owners' expectations; designers' and constructors' response. *Sam Spata, Architect, AIA, LEED® AP BD+C*

up front—but it is so much cheaper. What did Walsh say concerning Sherman Hospital? Twelve people in the trailer leveraged 550 people in the field. One deviation discovery on the project—in the first week of coordination—more than paid for a year and a half of our doing modeling and coordination.

There's a good chance that the architecture firm will go away.

— Kristine K. Fallon, FAIA

What would you say is the number one concern for you and your business right now?

KF: To be on the leading edge of the technology curve. We work very hard to be ahead of the rest of the industry. There's no real roadmap for doing that. I worry about whether we're identifying good technology directions and quickly galloping up the learning curve and getting good at these technologies before they're in big demand. I actually have an incredibly vast, international network of contacts. A lot of the leading edge stuff isn't particularly published—it's in people's heads or buried somewhere. Not stuff you can Google. So you have to go to the people. That's why I am so active in so many organizations. That and staying in touch with people—it's something I got used to doing very early in my career. (See Figure 3.19.)

What would you say is the number one concern for the architecture profession?

KF: There's a good chance that the architecture firm will go away. At this point, in England, I hear that the architects mostly work for the contractors. At that point—why have a firm? What is the role of the architecture firm? There are certain training, skills, capabilities, and qualities that architects do bring that engineers and contractors don't bring. There's a role for those skills and capabilities. As for being able to rely on the architect's model for construction documents—if architects drag their feet for

(Continued)

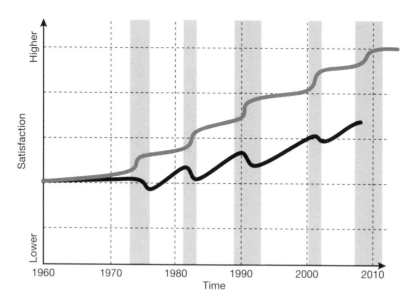

Figure 3.19   Time/satisfaction chart: owners' expectations; designers' and constructors' response. *Sam Spata, Architect, AIA, LEED® AP BD+C*

much longer about that, people will find a way to do without architecture firms. Because it's just such a stupid waste of time. People will perceive firms as adding absolutely no value. You want an architect on your team somewhere to come up with creative ideas and solve problems. But why would you need an architecture firm?

What would you say is the number one concern for the construction industry as whole?

KF: I see the potential for the agglomeration—for the contractors getting absorbed into a couple big firms. That said—for all my championing of change—I enjoy the industry as it is. I love the fact that you work with different people, personalities, and teams. I find that really invigorating.

KFA has developed training curricula and conducted training in multiple BIM products. What would you say is the best method for someone unfamiliar with the technology to learn BIM?

KF: BIM is easy to use. It's much easier than CAD. It's pretty complicated under the hood, but architects and engineers no longer feel like they need to understand what's under the hood. I feel that's a mistake—they do. The firms that are doing well with the technology—it's because they understand what's under the hood and they tweak it. To understand and use BIM is really very simple. We do a four-to-six-hour Revit quick-start, and in that amount of time we take a bastardized Palladian building and we do plan, section, elevation, rendering—we talk about the construction techniques, the integrity of the 3D model. If you come from 2D CAD—a lot of people bloody their foreheads trying to make Revit behave like AutoCAD. It's a different analogy, and so you have to approach it differently. From there, there are some great online tutorials. (See Figure 3.20.)

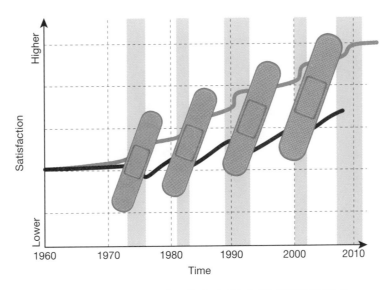

Figure 3.20   A series of Band-Aids with each successive recession. *Sam Spata, Architect, AIA, LEED® AP BD+C*

With a business immersed in technology, does it make any sense for design professionals and others to concern themselves with the collaborative work processes and delivery methods enabled by BIM and related technologies? Or are these just beside the point?

KF: They're quite central, actually. If the designer does a great BIM but then at the last minute makes some AutoCAD changes to the drawing, the BIM is useless downstream. It introduces more waste and the possibility of error where it doesn't need to be. So knowing the process is very important to the effectiveness of BIM.

Women in general have not been well represented, at least numbers-wise, in the architecture profession and less so in the construction industry. The numbers in technology for these fields cannot be much better. Have there been any obstacles or deterrents that you've experienced in the work you have done based on your gender?

KF: If you're asking have I encountered obstacles to realizing my potential—I would say yes, I have. There continues to be a discounting of women in design and construction. I do believe were I a man, with the same experience and intellectual capacity, I would be more highly respected than I am. I say something in a meeting and everybody ignores it; then a man says exactly the same thing and everybody thinks it's a great idea. (See Figure 3.21.)

KFA has developed its own training curricula for the Revit product family. How did you make the decision to work with one software program over another, such as ArchiCAD?

KF: We're consultants. We do care about where the demand is. I did a lot of work for Autodesk in the '90s, and then when started doing work for Revit, before Autodesk owned Revit, we had a little divorce. I liked Revit. In 1999 there was this little

(Continued)

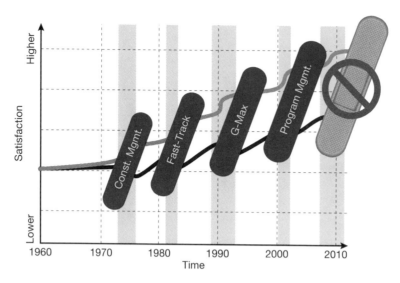

Figure 3.21   An end to Band-Aid solutions for the construction industry? *Sam Spata, Architect, AIA, LEED® AP BD+C*

company with ten people called Charles River Software where somebody recommended me as a consultant. I went in with a colleague—another woman—we spent a day with these guys, and I was just blown away with this product that was in pre-alpha. I was very impressed with it and the people who founded the company. I worked with them before the initial product release, and I was there when they released the product. We had a real wake-up call since we were the first people who ever saw it. We encouraged people to use it—we were paid to do so back in 2000 or so. Revit was acquired by Autodesk and the divorce got healed. Now we probably do more work with Navisworks than with Revit.

With your work helping design firms with the transition to BIM, what have you seen as the biggest obstacles to the successful adoption and implementation of BIM by firms you have worked with? What advice would you give to a firm still considering the move to BIM?

KF: The biggest obstacle is the conception, by the architect, of what the architect is and what he does. They look at BIM and say this isn't architecture; these aren't the metrics I use.

If you can't work yourself into this new commercial environment, you're not going to survive. I do think there are people out there who cannot get their minds around it. Assuming you can get around that—that this is what an architect does—then you have the issues of reworking all of your work processes, all of your metrics, which isn't easy. If you're a small firm, you can calibrate very easily. But if you're an HOK or SOM going into a two- or three-year design project and you know everything is going to be different—it's all pretty scary.

To what extent does the successful transition to BIM rely on a firm's culture?

KF: I would call it attitude. The firms that would go to BIM are the firms you would consider entrepreneurial, aggressive, asking is there a better way to do something. If there is, I want to be the one to do it the better way. The firms that are particularly

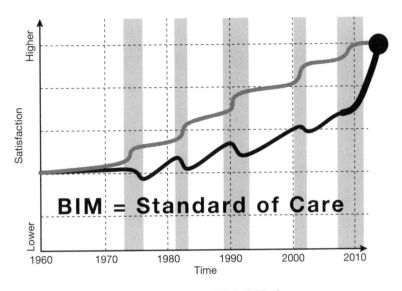

Figure 3.22   BIM bridges the ever-widening gap. *Sam Spata, Architect, AIA, LEED® AP BD+C*

successful in BIM are the firms where the principals develop a relatively deep understanding of—not necessarily twenty-eight ways to intersect walls in Revit, but how BIM works, why it's different, what it means, what are the potential uses. It's not the BIM manager doing the presentation—it's the principal of the firm, because it sets an example and because they're the decision makers. (See Figure 3.22.)

> *You need a conceptual understanding of BIM, and some people who have tremendous operational skills don't have very good conceptual understanding of the technology.*
>
> —Kristine K. Fallon, FAIA

You have written that as with any technology initiative, you must have the right product, the right people, and the right perspective to succeed. Who are the right people to work on BIM? Are they necessarily those that have excelled at CAD or other programs? Is it even a requirement that they are technologically inclined? Or is it more about their attitude and mindset—and if so, how would you describe the ideal mindset to excel working in a BIM environment?

KF: You need a mix of skills. We're moving beyond the architect as a solo performer. What I find is that there's great value within an organization to have someone who can make the software sing and can help other people through modeling or content issues. Some firms need a person who can tweak the applications, get into the API to get it to do special things. There's the strategy of the application, of the technology. That is different. You need a conceptual understanding of BIM, and some people who have tremendous operational skills don't have very good conceptual understanding of the technology. When interviewing, I can't tell whether a candidate has this conceptual awareness. I know that my weakest point is the ability to judge, through an interview process, whether somebody is going to be able to work well in my organization.

(Continued)

You have written that "BIM . . . is no longer an IT issue. It has become a business practice issue. Principals must take time to think about how BIM will fit into their future business strategy, as it is a matter of business survival." From your perspective working in IT, how would you describe the relationship between technology, business, and people when it comes to working effectively in BIM?

KF: My first client when I started my firm was Sears. I worked for their store planning and construction group. They would turn to me when they had a technology question. Whenever Sears had a business challenge, they looked to technology to be a big component of the answer. It was just their mindset. They wouldn't consider approaching a business problem without considering what technology could contribute. I don't see that enough in design firms. How do we pursue a business goal? We define it. Then what do we do? Try to figure out how to get there. What do we use to get there? We've got marketing. We've got production. And we've got technology. So we want the marketing guys to go out and sell this idea. And we want the production guys to ramp up to be able to deliver. Is there something we can do with technology that could give us a competitive advantage? That would make the ramp-up easier? Or we're moving into a new service and need the technology to provide it. I don't see enough of that. Technology is an afterthought with most firms. BIM is no exception. It's like "Oh [expletive], we ought to do BIM!" It's hardly a strategic approach. To a great extent, design firms are late adopters of technology. (See Figure 3.23.)

BIM has been called elsewhere a young person's game. Do you agree or disagree?

KF: No. To use BIM effectively you have to be extremely knowledgeable. Especially in knowing how to put buildings together.

When you hire—what do you look for?

KF: What is important is finding people who are experimental. Who are willing to push the technology. Who are curious about other products, other approaches. What's happening under the hood? How can I make it do what I want? I look for people like that. I find that people who are smug about their skills are probably not the right people for us.

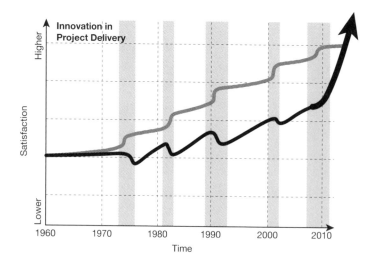

Figure 3.23   Together, BIM and integrated design can lead to increased productivity for design and construction. *Sam Spata, Architect, AIA, LEED ® AP BD+C*

A recent McGraw-Hill report stated that firms would sooner team with other firms that had experience in the technology over firms that they have a long-standing working relationship and a history of working with—has this been your experience? Is this something new? Has technology caused this marketing disruption?

KF: That knocked my socks off when I first heard that. It used to take a long time to break into the industry because people liked to work with whom they worked with before. Now, you get a reputation for being really good at BIM and they want you. My most recent GSA project team was put together based on what they could do in BIM.

Stewart Brand has been quoted as saying, "Once a new technology rolls over you, if you're not part of the steamroller, you're part of the road." Do you agree?

KF: I guess so. It's a little extreme. Does technology roll over you quite that way? I don't know.

Do you agree that much of the inadequate interoperability rests on the shoulders of the architectural community? If so, why architects and not software providers or contractors?

KF: People assume that software companies will just do the right thing. That's not really true. Software companies need to know what people really want in their products. And particularly when you get to interoperability, they have some real disincentives. If you've got 10 percent of the market, you want interoperability because then the people who use your software are equal to anybody else because they can exchange models and get data back and forth. If you're a company with big market share, all you can do is lose market share by making your software interoperable. You don't see how you can gain market share. The only way to convince them to do it is to demand it. To say, I really need to you to support these interchanges, because it's important to my business and I'll go to another vendor if you don't do it. Architects haven't done that up until now. My students say the technology will take care of interoperability, and I have to tell them *no, it won't!* Not if you don't know what you want and demand it.

How big a problem would you say interoperability is today, and when—if ever—do you anticipate that it will be adequately addressed—that is, no longer a stumbling block to collaboration in the industry?

KF: There are two parts to the problem right now. One part is that because BIM is new, the interoperability requirements are not well defined. There's a need for industry participants to get active in doing geeky stuff to define those requirements. This is a huge problem because of the near-total abnegation of interest on the part of design professionals in these issues. I can count the number of people in the United States on two hands who can fruitfully participate in such a discussion. We're working on it. We're going to build that expertise because it's important.

The promise of BIM is that you can move this information into multiple uses. The one thing that's working really well right now is interference checking. But that's because of Navisworks. But we don't have interoperability. We can't just say here's a really comprehensive building description packaged up in this BIM, let me hand it to someone with eQUEST and have them analyze the energy performance. You need to create a whole new model. It doesn't happen with cost estimating. You have to do a lot of manual checking to make sure you modeled it right. And interoperability doesn't exist for facility management. You have owners demanding Revit as-built BIMs that include all building systems and detailed information on every piece of equipment for facility management. I don't know what the hell they think they're going to do with them. These are big, big questions.

NOTES

1. Lauren Stassi, "Extreme Collaboration: Interns in a BIM World," Texas Society of Architects, September 11, 2009, texasarchitect.blogspot.com/2009/09/guest-blog-extreme-collaboration.html.
2. Ibid.
3. Joann Gonchar, "Transformative Tools Start to Take Hold," *Architectural Record,* April, 2007, construction.com/CE/articles/0704edit-1.asp.
4. Kristine Fallon, "Charles Matta Discusses GSA's BIM Success," Summer 2008, info.aia.org/nwsltr_tap.cfm?pagename=tap_nwsltr_200807.

part **II** Leading Integrated Design

In Part II, the focus is on working alone and with others in BIM; obstacles to successful BIM collaboration and how to overcome them; and why collaboration is the way forward for our profession and industry.

Read these chapters to familiarize yourself with challenges to BIM collaboration including interoperability, workflow, firm culture, education, technological challenges, working in teams, communication, trust, BIM etiquette, one model versus multiple models, cost, and issues concerning responsibility, insurance, and liability. Learn about the one critical skill set design professionals need to master if they are to survive the current professional, economic, social, and technological challenges, as well as strategies for making collaboration work.

Read these chapters to better understand why owners and design and construction professionals have been slow to adopt integrated design and how we can rectify this situation. A brief but incisive overview of integrated design is offered to help you promote the process to owners and your team, and learn how BIM and integrated design together help design professionals achieve their ultimate goals: well-designed, high-performing buildings that deliver value to owners while benefitting all involved, including future generations.

In this part, learn how a major architecture firm's chief information officer is contending with near-constant change brought about by BIM; learn from a major constructor regarding their experiences working on more than one hundred integrated BIM projects; and hear from the author of the industry's first integrated project delivery (IPD) case studies on where IPD is headed.

chapter 4 Working With Others In BIM

Figure 4.1   An architectural designer turns snippets of unintelligible code into a button to push and watch wonderful things happen. *Zach Kron, www .buildz.info*

It's not as easy as saying *OK, work collaboratively*— or by working collaboratively you'll save the owner millions. Some collaborations fail—and many don't pan out to be a more effective method. Collaboration that works right for everyone involved is the key—not "Kumbaya." For many, working alone is more comfortable, effective and predictable. And yet, for our profession and industry, collaboration is the way forward. So how to find a way to work collaboratively that is beneficial to the owner and fulfilling creatively and professionally?

The ability to collaborate and work productively in teams—historically subjects felt better left to psychologists and operations—will be the most critical skill set design professionals will need to master if they are to survive the current professional, economic, social, and technological challenges. Especially with the growing use of BIM and integrated design–led projects, the need for collaborative skills will be felt by every design professional. If they are able to acquire the mindsets, attitudes, and skills necessary to truly collaborate with others—and learn how to design buildings that are optimized to give owners, contractors, and other team members what they need— then architects will be trusted, newly esteemed, and return to their rightful role of Virtual Master Builder.

As Ernest Boyer has said, "The future belongs to the integrators."

Working Alone in BIM

At the 2008 AGC BIM Forum, contractor John Tocci compared and contrasted the then-new terms *lonely BIM* and *social BIM*. As explained in one review of the BIM Forum, "These concepts would gradually weave throughout almost all the subsequent panels and presentations and seemed to be a clarification of the terminology set forth in the book *BIG BIM, little bim*, by Finith Jernigan. The 'lonely' variety depicts BIM when utilized primarily for production gains within a single company. In contrast, being 'social' implies the sharing of building information models with others either downstream or upstream in the building lifecycle."[1]

While many will continue to use BIM more as a tool than as a process—by working alone—this is not the ultimate BIM solution. The goal is to work collaboratively with others to garner the best solution for all involved. One of the greatest benefits of BIM is the collaboration it enables—something missed out on when working alone.

Working alone is at best suboptimal and defeats the purpose BIM was developed for. The "I" in BIM, ironically, is meant to be shared and truly only exists in a meaningful way when it contains *Input* from other parties.

Using Revit, or any other BIM platform, as simply a 3D visualization or documentation production tool is like using a laptop as a hammer.
—Kell Pollard, "The BIM Fad?" www.revolutionbim.blogspot.com, January 22, 2009

Some don't have a choice in the matter. But architecture has always been a team sport. No one individual can do it all. If you find yourself working alone, think of it as a temporary situation. Many design professionals work alone in BIM when first starting out. During that time there is a great deal you can do in terms of training and self-development—on your own—to improve your chance of success later, when working with others in the BIM environment. For collaboration—as difficult as it can be—when it works has superior results (see Figure 4.2).

Working with Others in BIM

It makes designing fun again. We're not drawing lines, we're building a building.
—Peter Downs, "BIMming with Enthusiasm," www.stlouiscnr.com, January 1, 2009

You work in BIM to get things done—more efficiently and effectively—not because you want to see change

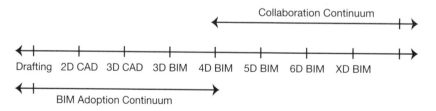

Figure 4.2   The BIM collaboration continuum picks up after BIM adoption leaves off.

in your business. And yet one unmistakable outcome of working collaboratively in BIM is *change*. For better or worse, BIM is a transformative tool—ignore this at your peril.

BIM is a business process supported by technology. To optimise use of the technology it is necessary to deploy the process. It is absolutely critical to understand this, as in the construction industry traditional methods use technology in isolation, but the BIM process uses technology in collaboration. This scenario is not unique and lessons can be learned from the past. During the 1980s, manufacturing, automotive, and aerospace faced a similar situation to construction today. Driven by the need for dramatic improvement in efficiency due to international competition, rather than a volatile property market, it was clear that disparate and isolated work groups, each shrouded in their own environments, were not the platform for success. The solution was to adopt new technologies that encouraged collaboration.[2]

Collaboration

The best buildings result from active, consistent, organized collaboration among all players.
—WBDG Aesthetics Subcommittee, "Engage the Integrated Design Process," October 30, 2010, www.wbdg.org.

Collaboration is too often considered just a buzzword—but the future of the profession and industry is about collaboration, and that future begins *now*.

Collaboration has impacted all fields, not just the design and construction industries. And because of this many are scrambling to learn how most effectively to work together in a way that all benefit. In the best of worlds, a successful collaboration ought not be a sacrifice—in terms of risk or reward—on the part of the design professional so that others might gain.

Some argue that we're wired for cooperation, but that it comes at a price.

The highly linear process of traditional design is starting to go away. In the new integrated, collaborative scenario, multiple designers have to think simultaneously about a design, and they need to figure out not only how to define their own self-interest but also to defer their decisions to the cause of the larger good. BIM does provide an environment where all the players can work together for the common good, which is why it is one of the key trends abetting collaboration. While BIM is not a radically new concept, the new advances in hardware and software have put it well within the reach of the average AEC firm, enabling them also to work in a collaborative mode a lot more easily, both within the firm and with other players.[3]

Collaboration is mentioned earlier as a co-benefit of utilizing BIM, where a benefit for one entity positively impacts others, serving to dissolve silos while ostensibly paving the way toward collaboration and integrated design. Phil Bernstein was asked if he could think of other benefits in his experience that are also co-benefits for using BIM:

BIM is probably the mechanism that will allow the advantages of social networking or collective conscious or crowdsourcing—whatever you want to call the phenomenon of a great number of minds—that will improve the likelihood

Figure 4.3   Collaboration, as a reliable skill set and tool, results from the development of multiple personal attributes.

of a good result. That's one co-benefit because the degree of transparency of the collaboration is so obvious that you get that co-benefit. So you've got this first idea about collective consciousness.[4] (See Figure 4.3.)

The power shift due to BIM and the collaborative work processes is most often described as one between architects and contractors, but the same can be seen between architects and engineers.

During the '90s, the structural engineering profession felt that it had become commoditized to some extent, via the widespread implementation of CAD and simple off-the-shelf analytical software on the one hand, and with the architect often being seen as 'the sole author' of buildings on the other. However, Carfrae now perceives a swing back towards the structural engineer, through the potential in advancing and extending building information modeling (BIM) and allied techniques, as part of the collaborative design process.[5]

But what if engineers become too powerful for their own good in the process? "Carfrae sees that the most straightforward way around this potential problem is always to be found through multidisciplinary collaboration—'to keep talking', as he puts it—allied to a shift in the outlook of the engineer."[6]

Obstacles to Successful Collaboration

If the utility of a building model results from its collaborative potential, then obstacles to that collaboration need to be identified and either successfully worked around or, where possible, removed altogether. The thirteen most commonly encountered obstacles include:

• Interoperability

• Workflow

• Firm culture

• Autonomy

• Education

• Technological challenges

• Working in teams

• Communication

• Trust

• Etiquette

• One model versus many models

• Cost

• Responsibility, insurance, and liability

Interoperability

Interoperability of software and applications is a significant barrier to collaboration between involved parties.

Of course, there are still some additional technological challenges to collaboration such as large file sizes, secure access to the model,

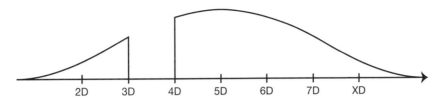

Figure 4.4   Practice and conviction will help you make the leap from visualization to coordination, and later to sustainability, fabrication, and operations. Having a plan in place will help to bridge the gap.

an effective way for multiple team members to work on the same model, better interoperability between different tools, better integration of the modeling process with other workflows such as project management, and so on. But all of these are far from insurmountable and should eventually be resolved. What we really need to work on is better education on collaboration, which is missing in most schools teaching architecture, engineering, and construction. Integrated design and construction courses are rarely taught, and this is a huge challenge. If collaborative practice is the envisioned future of the AEC industry, that future is not going to be realized unless collaborative and integrated design become an integral part of AEC education.[7] (See Figure 4.4.)

Interoperable software and systems come up again and again at conferences and seminars and in online forums and user group discussions as the number one issue for the foreseeable future inhibiting collaboration between all parties.

When I asked Aaron Greven if his firm shared their models with others, he said, "Yes, in my past, I've shared with structural firms, MEP firms, HVAC subcontractors, curtain wall contractors, other architects. With WE O'Neil, we've received design models to help provide preconstruction services with more accurate pricing and scheduling analysis early on."[8]

Interoperability continues to be a work in progress for the professions and industry. According to Kristine Fallon,

> Today, project teams are engaging in information handovers on a daily basis. Many are even exchanging BIM data. However, this process is neither automated nor seamless. It works if a motivated team devotes several man-weeks to defining the information to be exchanged and the protocols for doing so. Often, the BIM is incomplete for its intended downstream use and must be augmented by verbal or text explanations and information. There are still technical issues to be overcome, particularly if a two-way exchange of intelligent model data is the goal.[9]

Workflow

While integrated design changes when data is shared, BIM changes *how* data is shared. And this can be seen most vividly in BIM's impact on workflow.

A workflow is a "depiction of a sequence of operations, declared as work of a person, a group of persons, an organization of staff, or one or more simple or complex mechanisms. Workflow may be seen as any abstraction of real work, segregated in workshare, work split, or other types of ordering."[10] Most have come to believe that the introduction of BIM disturbs a firm's existing workflow despite the fact that others have called this a fallacy.[11] But if the continued use of existing inefficient technology perpetuates the cycle or traditional handoff with the inevitable changes and subsequent opportunity for errors occurring at every change, then perhaps a disruption to a firm's traditional workflow would be welcome.[12]

I asked project architect Brad Beck how the workflow between him and those with whom he works has been impacted by utilizing BIM, especially as compared with working in CAD:

> Collaboration is the biggest difference from the old process when a sketch from a senior was handed to a junior team member to draft, then handed back to the senior to redline, then back to the junior to revise. With BIM, the process involves a senior who will give the modeler a sketch—and sit down with a modeler and go through that sketch after it has been built to find things that need to change, working together to make it all work. It's a much more collaborative process, and you learn more. It's a more empowering process, where team members have more of a say in how things get modeled, than if you were just highlighting redlines. It forces those who are a bit shyer and a little less willing to put their opinion out there. Personally, I've always been the guy who'll walk in and say, "Are you sure you want to do that?" But for those who don't have that in their personality, working side by side in BIM can make it easier for communication.[13]

In fact, software architects practice a style of working called *pair programming*, in which a "driver" and "navigator" sit side by side, as opposed to getting over-the-shoulder input from a colleague. This method has

---

BIM without a broad team effort is likely to fail. BIM is a team sport and ought to be played like one.

---

much in common with the way team members work together in BIM. "It might sound as if the person writing the programming code would find it distracting to work this way, but it's not. It's a collaborative effort . . ." where senior and junior developers are paired. "It's also a way to bring junior programmers up to speed quickly, because they benefit from the more senior employee's knowledge."[14]

Social interaction remains a barrier to a proper workflow. "One barrier to adoption of BIM is not the technology itself, but the implications for changes in the relationship of all the members of a project team. Because BIM allows architects, their consultants, owners, and contractors to share information and expertise more easily and earlier in the life of a project, many proponents see it as a catalyst for the use of more integrated delivery methods than design-bid-build."[15]

When Beck looked back at his first professional position prior to working in BIM, he had this to say about what really changes and what stays the same:

> What changes is the workflow. The way you used to sketch, hand off, and redline is completely different now. The mindset of what you're doing with your drawings and 3D model, the process of creating that model, and the communication between team members— all of that changes. The final result is the same— you're still creating a set of documents that describes the building, whether a 3D model that's a file or a set of drawings. A firm's hierarchy is something that needs to remain in place,

for without the hierarchy you just won't have successful projects. The concept of what you put out there is the same. You're able to create a better product—a better set of documents— because of BIM. But the concept of what you're creating—a building that's coordinated, everything is well thought out—that concept remains the same because that's the role of the architect and what was expected of us. The liability we've all assumed as architects is because that output was not what we needed it to be. That output had holes in it. The drawings were missing details. The responsibility of the architect to lead the team and understand construction costs, budgets, and timelines, stays the same.[16] (See Figure 4.5.)

Beck went on to describe his current project's workflow, how he worked internally and externally with others, and what challenges this introduced.

CHMR is an interesting case because the way we started with it is that we were given a set of 2D documents and contracted to build a 3D building [model] from those documents. At first we didn't have much more of a role than being the virtual builders. We took the drawings and built what we could. What it has evolved into has become much more complex and rewarding because what BIM has allowed our firm to do is garner some trust from Smith-Carter, the architect of record, and that trust has led to an expanded scope of work for us. It increased our responsibility on what we are contracted to do. The expanded scope can be a double-edged sword in that when you're out on a limb further than expected or contracted. But it makes sense for you to take on this added scope in BIM—for in order for you to have the quick process and building, everyone has to

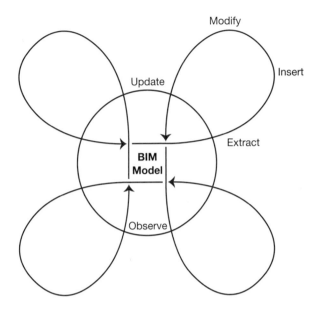

Figure 4.5   The collaboration cycle revolves around the BIM model and how we interact with it.* *After Dana K. (Deke) Smith, "FAIA Building Information Modeling (BIM)," Last updated: July 24, 2008, www.wbdg.org.

be on board. It's better overall for the project to have those working in BIM take on this added scope. Once you put together the base building you start to see the conflicts and clashes, and because we're in the model every day it's easier for us to point these things out and even to coordinate. So now we are coordinating between the architect and structural engineer, the architect and mechanical engineer. There have even been some instances where we've been asked by the architect of record to coordinate between mechanical and structural, coordinating the consultants rather than coordinating them with the architecture. As confusing as that can be, they trust us enough to ask us to do that. Whoever is doing the model needs to be part of that process because it is so inherent to what you are doing every day. As for the workflow, it has changed—but I think it has moved in a positive direction.

Beck continued:

> Antoine Predock's office, lead design architects
> for CHMR, are the "keepers of the geometry,"
> to use Yanni Loukassis's phrase. What we've
> done—and done a good job of—is making
> sure that that geometry stays true to what
> Antoine Predock's office's design intent was.
> That said, being the keepers of the geometry
> is something that will drive the whole BIM pro-
> cess moving forward and forcing architects to
> lead more than they have been up to now.[17]

Concerning workflows in firms as they are currently
set up to operate, in *Reinventing Collaboration across
Internal and External Project Teams*, Patrick Aragon,
senior product marketing manager with Adobe
Systems Inc., came to this conclusion: "The project team needs to evolve from a linear, sequential to
a concurrent work process. What is evident is that
workflows dependent on paper or native application
files often hinder collaboration."[18]

Firm Culture

If BIM is 90 percent sociology and only 10 percent
technology, then firm culture has to be taken into
account as a major factor in both encouraging and
discouraging collaboration. Discussing collaboration shifts in the construction industry, the editors of
DesignIntelligence had this to say:

> A culture of collaboration is more likely to hap-
> pen in a workplace environment that is more
> informal and where there are shared social
> activities, communities of practice, or social
> enterprise structures. Professional practices
> are becoming more complex and new col-
> laborative forms and cooperative cultures are
> emerging to build value delivered to clients.

It is one of the most pressing issues for leaders
in professional practice and one of the most
exciting areas of best practice development.[19]

You not only adopt BIM but along with it collaboration, and an emphasis on performance and ROI.
"Integrated modeling changed how the firm works,"
according to Paul Seletsky, senior manager of digital
design in the New York office of SOM, "but adopting BIM requires adopting 'BIM culture'—a new way
of thinking about building design based on performance, not just form."[20]

Culture is a word with multiple meanings, so it is important to define it clearly here. "The culture of a group
can now be defined as: A pattern of shared basic
assumptions that the group learned as it solved its
problems of external adaptation and internal integration, that has worked well enough to be considered
valid and therefore, to be taught to new members as
the correct way to perceive, think, and feel in relation
to those problems."[21] More simply put, firm culture
is *how things are done around here*. "Managing
cultural change in the construction industry poses
a greater challenge than any technological transformation as Building Information Modeling (BIM) gains
traction. . . . Building industry partners will no longer
be able to be adversarial, but will have to work as
true collaborators," according to Derek Smith. "Silos
will not work."[22]

It should be clear by now that technology is only part
of the equation, that the larger part involves having
an attitude of either hesitancy and reluctance or
commitment and acceptance. "In many cases, contractors and architects have a misconception that
they can become BIM-compliant by rushing out and
purchasing software systems that boast support for
3D, 4D, and 5D. It's only after purchasing these software applications that reality sets in; they don't have

an internal culture that supports the practical use of these tools."[23] Culture change comes about due to collaboration. "Before you ask yourself whether or not your company has money in the budget to purchase and implement a suite of BIM (Building Information Modeling) software applications, you should first ask yourself whether or not your company has a culture that supports collaboration."[24]

BIM has been called a disruptive technology—and this can have physical implications beyond culture. While CAD may have been disruptive in its time, BIM disrupts a firm's physical surroundings in a way that CAD, relegated to the back room, never did—by penetrating the front conference rooms, taking over the kitchen when team meetings grow too large, rearranging seating, opening up cubicle-like workstations, and requiring more and larger hardware and monitors.

> Companies are finally realizing what their employees have known for ages: cubicle cultures just don't work. With concerns about knowledge sharing among older and younger generations of employees skyrocketing, organizations are concluding that impersonal 'cube farms' discourage collaboration, stifle employee engagement and, as a result, strangle innovation at the exact time when it's desperately needed.[25] (See Figure 4.6.)

Individuality and the Mistaken Promise of Autonomy

The design professions as a rule attract introverts, lone workers, and those who are hell-bent on believing collaboration equates with compromise. Even when told that lone genius types are not valued, many architects secretly hope that they will be considered the sole exception.

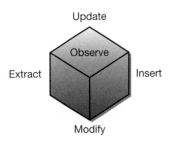

Figure 4.6   Five ways to interact with and transform the BIM model.

The publication title "Keepers of the Geometry[26]" sounds autonomous. I asked its author, Yanni Loukassis, if he had a concern that autonomy is the enemy of collaboration: "Professionals," he explained,

> are always trying to do two things: on the one hand develop a sense of autonomy and individuality and on the other trying to build bridges to other people. They're trying to do both at once. They want to collaborate and work with others. In order to do that they have to develop a common language, common set of references, representations; and technology is very useful for that. But they also need to distinguish themselves and articulate why they are valuable. Dana Cuff wrote that every person in an architecture firm is trying to define the way in which they are creative. In which they are a designer, regardless of their role. I think it is necessary for people to do both. You cannot submit completely to the collaboration; otherwise everyone is fighting to preserve their own identity at the same time.[27]

Education

When asked what, if anything, he feels is missing from students' education these days, Loukassis responded, "How important is it to prepare students for the profession when 50 percent go on to work outside traditional practice?" What does he think can be given greater emphasis, and what does he feel is overemphasized?

Collaboration, for one, is underemphasized in education. Engineering students are often forced to collaborate on some projects in school—they can learn a lot from that. Architects have privileged architectural representation way too much. In school, architects need more often to think and work quantitatively and through writing—because those are the predominant languages people outside the profession use. If architects want to collaborate and cooperate, they need mastery over those languages. Quantitative thinking and mathematics will give them access to everything from science to economics and a whole range of issues architects traditionally separate themselves from.[28]

What we really need to work on is better education on collaboration, which is missing in most schools teaching architecture, engineering, and construction. Integrated design and construction courses are rarely taught, and this is a huge challenge. If collaborative practice is the envisioned future of the AEC industry, that future is not going to be realized unless collaborative and Integrated Design becomes an integral part of AEC education.[29]

Technological Challenges

Technology is what we use to get things done, and new technologies that purport to improve our productivity have been a fact of life for some time for the profession. Yet it is counterproductive to force design professionals to learn new technologies. Meanwhile, BIM, as a technology, is disruptive because it does not build incrementally on previous software, instead requiring entirely new competencies. While technology changes constantly, one early reader commented, the way people behave in response to new technology, in contrast, does not change. (See Figure 4.7.)

Many today still believe that one of the most significant obstacles standing in the way of integrated design is presented by the new technologies available to the industry. What it really comes down to is motivation: if the desire or need is strong enough, you can overcome anything. As Paul Teicholz wrote, "I have observed at first hand projects where various software products were used by team members in truly integrated teams. The positive results showed

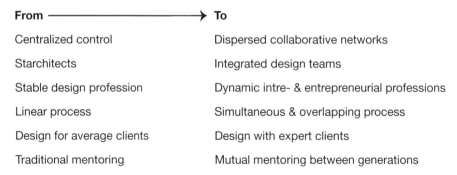

From ⟶	To
Centralized control	Dispersed collaborative networks
Starchitects	Integrated design teams
Stable design profession	Dynamic intre- & entrepreneurial professions
Linear process	Simultaneous & overlapping process
Design for average clients	Design with expert clients
Traditional mentoring	Mutual mentoring between generations

Figure 4.7   Shifts required for a move toward more collaborative integrated design teams. After "From the Editors," September 15, 2007, www.di.net/news/archive/from_editors/.

that technical difficulties could be overcome if there is a desire and/or a requirement to do so."[30]

Collaboration is too often discussed in terms of technology, not people—especially where the lack of collaborative tools within the construction industry is given as the reason for inhibiting productivity gains within firms.[31] It is meaningless unless people are addressed—and are the focus of collaboration. The intent is for technology to support, rather than hinder, collaboration. That unfortunately is not always the case, for where there are new technologies there are challenges to overcome. "Of course, there are still some additional technological challenges to collaboration, such as large file sizes, secure access to the model, an effective way for multiple team members to work on the same model, better interoperability between different tools, better integration of the modeling process with other workflows such as project management, and so on. But all of these are far from insurmountable and should eventually be resolved."[32]

Architect Brad Beck's current project involves collaborators in different countries. When asked if he found that videoconferencing or any other media or tools help foster collaboration while working in BIM, and what would need to improve for collaboration to run more smoothly, he replied:

> We use WebEx conferencing, but there are a host of them. Teleconferencing is absolutely essential, especially when you're working on a project, like CHMR, where you have consultants in different places and it's too cost-prohibitive to get everybody together all the time. It does more than foster collaboration—it makes asking questions easy. Sometimes asking those questions is a little too easy. A negative might be that it's hard to focus on what you're supposed to be focused on. Once you build parts of the model, there are a lot of placeholder elements. You'll be in a teleconference specifically talking about structural steel but the people with you in the teleconference can also see that the walls are misplaced, or that the finish on the floor is not what it's supposed to be. You're focusing on where the structural steel's supposed to go, and they're saying "What's going on with that floor?!" So while it may be a little too easy to ask questions—you understand that there's no negative connotation intended. In these situations someone with the meeting agenda needs to be running the teleconference. So when someone goes off-topic, they can say we'll cover that at another time, but right now we're focusing on this. One lesson learned is that when you do a WebEx, have a set agenda. Otherwise it'll be a free-for-all, pointing out where everything's wrong about the model. It's a good thing in that it opens up a line of communication where you might otherwise be afraid to ask and not say anything. The dynamic is critical: in a WebEx you're sitting apart and don't see the other people, so it's easier to ask, "What's happening here?" Whereas when you're all gathered at a table, if you see something's wrong, you're less likely to bring it up because everyone's in the room. It keeps everybody honest, saying what they're thinking. Even with a facilitator, it's very difficult to keep the conversation focused on a similar level of detail. The process should be like an onion where you're building an onion backwards. You're putting on the overall scope and slowly putting in each layer inside until you get all the way down. It's very difficult to do that in BIM because the first time you put in a wall it asks you how thick is your drywall? Not impossible but difficult in BIM.[33]

Larger firms are outfitting their major offices with prototype videoconferencing rooms to display images, video, documents, and even live views of computer desktops. Using a series of projectors and flat-screen TVs in each room, multiple ideas and documents can be displayed at one time, and all meeting notes can be saved, printed, and emailed instantly to participants. Your team has managed to make progress with less. Is this larger-firm fit-up now—or will it become—a necessity as BIM becomes the standard? Beck continued,

> I don't think it's a necessity. It certainly makes communication easier, and will become more commonplace—but not because of BIM. It'll become ubiquitous because it is technology and it's the next step. BIM will help it along a little faster. It's something that has been slowly evolving outside of the BIM world and would become prevalent even if BIM were not involved. Architects might use it more because of BIM to the extent that it helps them coordinate. Meeting notes that are saved, printed, and emailed in WebEx is a great feature—if you take advantage of it. The danger is sometimes communications are forgotten in WebEx and left unanswered.[34] (See Figure 4.8.)

BIM's biggest frustrations and challenges so far: Technical? Communication? Human nature? According to Beck,

> Technically, the software's not there except for very simple buildings. What BIM has really been sold as is not on the market yet. The biggest communication gap occurs because many senior members at firms who aren't familiar with BIM think that what it is selling is what it is. And it's not there yet. It has not fully realized its potential—especially for complex buildings. We're seriously pushing Revit on the CHMR

Technically, the software's not there except for very simple buildings. What BIM has really been sold as is not on the market yet.

—Brad Beck

> project, and everyday there are hours lost due to technical issues. That's probably the biggest frustration. Human nature is a challenge on any project whether you're using BIM or not. One thing that's exasperating is that the engineers that developed the software drive the output and possibilities. That's my biggest pet peeve—that I can't change an elevation to the way it is supposed to look for our office. Things that software engineers don't think about or care enough about to make a priority—are a big deal to the profession. There are wish lists on AUGI, but any BIM software is only as good as the engineers who make it. Engineers not being in tune with what is needed creates a whole host of issues for their users. If I was in charge of Autodesk I would definitely [have] a consulting group of architects who can look at the software and tell me what's lacking and then fix it before I send out a release. To force it to work for the profession and not the profession working for BIM.[35]

Working in Teams

> Now the grail hero is one who acts out of his own spontaneous nature. . . . The meaning of the grail, and of most myths, is finding the dynamic source in your life so that its trajectory is out of your own centre and not something put upon you by society. Then of course there is the problem of coordinating your well-being and

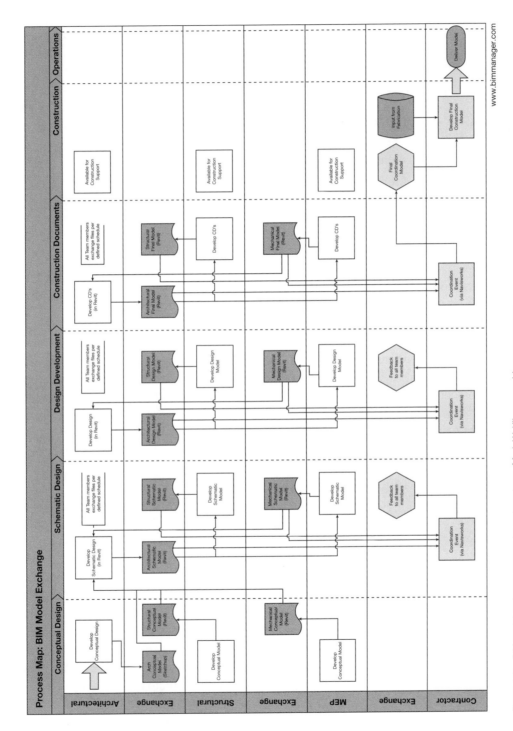

Figure 4.8   BIM model exchange process by project phase. *Mark W. Kiker, www.bimmanager.com*

your virtue with the goods and needs of society. But first you must find your own trajectory and then comes the social coordination.

—Joseph Campbell, from *Hero with a Thousand Faces*

Working in teams can be fraught with difficulty.

Collaboration occurs when you combine the experience, knowledge, and talents of a variety of professionals with the intent to cooperatively contribute to the design, documentation, and construction of a project in a way that is potentially more productive than had each team member performed their tasks separately. Collaboration is, by this definition, the basis for integrated design—requiring team members to work cooperatively, transparently, trusting and respecting one another, communicating openly, and accepting the ideas of others as equal to one's own. How that is accomplished is never explained very well and left to each team member to figure out individually. As Mike Whaley, director of preconstruction for J. H. Findorff and Son Inc., put it, "To maximize the full potential of IPD, we also need to focus on team building as an organized step in the process."[36]

Concerned about how little team building as a discipline has been addressed, that is exactly what Whaley has done—by asking the right questions: "There are four aspects of team building that need

---

Sharing information is not only beneficial to expanding the professional body of knowledge, but . . . it is our ethical duty to do so. This is a challenge that will certainly test our ethical stamina!

—Carol Jones, "Collaboration: The New Professional Paradigm," December 21, 2005, http://www.di.net/articles/archive/2450/.

---

to be considered: First, how do you build a team? Second, is the relocation of the team to one central location worth the investment? Third, how does BIM figure into the team equation? And finally, after the team planning, is everyone performing as a team?"[37] It might be beneficial to think of BIM as an additional—*and* instrumental—team member. As overheard at Autodesk University, "Tools are not simply means to an end. The tools are now part of the team, the culture, the entire business enterprise."[38] This working arrangement is especially critical for less experienced staff. "It is important for the success of a project that an intern has direct communication with team members with technical design and construction experience to guide them to model pragmatically in order to complete accurate usable documentation."[39]

Working collaboratively creates a social context for the BIM model. Since it is generally understood that information acquires meaning only through social context, the wider the social context the BIM model works within, the more meaningful the model. (See Figure 4.9.)

Just how important is emotional intelligence when working with others in BIM? Architect Brad Beck believes

> it's just as important as it is working in teams that are not using BIM. What you get from working in BIM is the cooperation that was lacking in traditional architectural practice. The apprentice was learning from the professional but not vice versa, and what you got was a top-down experience. What you get with BIM—and the communication and emotional intelligence that is needed to work in BIM—is the down/up and up/down teaching. Because BIM is still relatively new, it is a bit more prevalent now. As BIM permeates the industry and is used by everybody, it may go back to the top-down approach.[40]

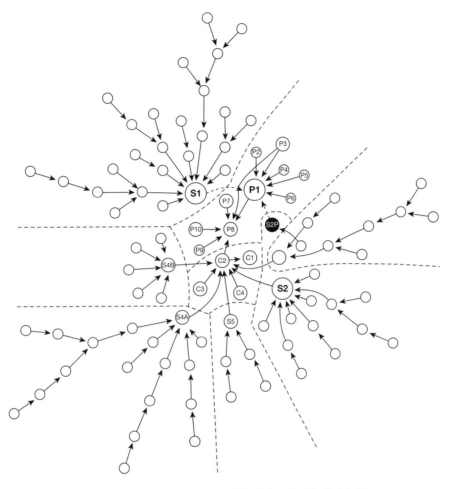

Key Client Body Stakeholders:

S1 = Deputy Head of Client Section 1
S2 = Deputy Head of Client Section 2
S2P = Client Section 2 Programme Manager (assigned Project Sponsor role)
S3 = Deputy Head of Client Section 3
S4A = Deputy Head of Client Section 4A
S4B = Deputy Head of Client Section 4B
S5 = Deputy Head of Client Section 5
C1 = Head of Procuring Client
C2 = Deputy Head of Procuring Client
C3 = Procuring Client's Programme Manager
C4 = Procuring Client's Senior PA

Key Project Provider Stakeholders:

P1 = Architect/Project Manager
P2 = Office Furniture Supplier
P3 = Cost and Procurement Manager
P4 = Interior Designer
P5 = Planning Supervisor
P6 = Main Contractor
P7 = Facilities Manager
P8 = Client's in-house Estates Services
P9 = IT Contractor
P10 = Operations Manager

Figure 4.9   Illustration of social complexity. Organogram illustrates the ambiguity of the boundary between the client and the construction team that had been allowed to emerge in a project. Diagram produced by observing patterns of documented communication (email) between the construction team and client representatives. *Image courtesy of Dr. Derek Thomson, Heriot-Watt University, Edinburgh, Scotland, d.s.thourson@hrv.ac.uk.*

It has become increasingly apparent that the ability to collaborate and work productively in teams—historically subjects felt better left to psychologists and operations personnel—will be the most critical skill sets that design professionals will need to master if they are to survive the current professional, economic, social, and technological challenges.

Especially with the growing use of BIM and integrated design–led projects, collaboration—and utilizing collaborative skills—will be required of every design professional.

Until architects agree that all of us is better than some of us, that teamwork always results in better solutions, that architecture, including the design of buildings, is always improved by involving others, including contractors and clients who may have competing or otherwise completely different goals than your own—until that time, BIM and integrated design will not catch on and architects will become gradually irrelevant.

I asked Aaron Greven what his experience has been like so far using BIM with others on the design team and whether everyone is on board. "Experience and skill level are all over the map, and difficult to gauge." Difficult?

> MEP design firms are the last involved in the industry, frankly because their services are more geared to a sketch and draft workflow that is systems-based. Their output and involvement throughout a project process has been marginalized well ahead of the impact BIM has had—so they have less fee and less scope to work with. Many are only contracted through a specific bid phase to provide very cursory, performance-based scope information that doesn't lend itself to investing the time to produce articulated Revit models.[41]

Integrated design needs integrated behavior, not just a collection of specialists.
—David Mar, S. E., Principal,
Tipping Mar + Associates

Communication

BIM puts special demands on teams, especially when it comes to communicating. There are now seminars dedicated to communicating effectively in a BIM environment. One session was advertised as such:

> The enormous potential of BIM focuses on design and construction, but there is another vital area that demands attention: the dynamics of interpersonal communications. The art of information exchange is changing with the new technology. Person-to-person information exchange in the new BIM workplace requires "BIM cooperative communication"—starting at the earliest project meeting. Team members, owners, attorneys, and subconsultants must strive to present ideas effectively. Without clear understandings in place, miscommunication can dilute project delivery. This session explores ways to structure and deliver information, both formally in meetings and informally in discussions and conversations, so that all parties involved "get it" and proceed with the same understandings.[42]

With all of the collaborative tools and platforms available today, distance is perhaps less an impediment to communication than at any other time. In fact, collaborating at a distance has become almost ubiquitous among design professionals and others on the project team. "Although most collaboration occurs among project team members at the same office, nearly three-fourths of those who collaborate also do so with people outside of their offices. In fact, compared to the other AEC professionals in the study, architects and engineers are significantly more likely to collaborate with outside consultants and service providers."[43]

While many innovative design firms see prefabrication as the answer to lean construction and integrated design, one Philadelphia firm, Erdy McHenry, is "trying to streamline construction by resetting the relationship between the architect and the builder. They may have a better chance of achieving their goals than their more utopian counterparts." According to the firm founders,

> They argue that the lack of communication between the professions is the real reason for the high cost of construction. Erdy McHenry believes it can save money and speed up the process simply by engaging in a collegial back-and-forth with the craft trades—steelworkers, carpenters, electricians—before construction. . . . Rather than wait until a design is finished, [Erdy McHenry starts] sharing computer models with contractors as they're developed. The builders, they argue, can spot mistakes early and suggest a more efficient way of accomplishing the same task.[44] (See Figure 4.10.)

Trust

Trust can be a difficult subject for those in the AEC industry to discuss, especially when there's the implication that one party—or their work effort or product—cannot be trusted. One thing is certain—trust speaks to the need for meaningful social relationships among people who work together. So who will take the first step?

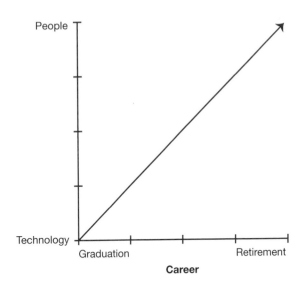

Figure 4.10   As your career progresses, technology becomes less important, while people issues become more important.

Some believe the owner has to set the stage for a trusting working environment and process:

> The first step in the development of a collaborative relationship is taken by the owner. The owner or owner project representative must be open to working in a new environment, one where all communication is valued. The owner must understand that knowledge does not just exist in one location but is located throughout the construction industry. The trick is to get the knowledge as well as the best and the brightest people working on your side of the table. For this to occur, trust must be developed.[45]

However you define it, trust is one key to working collaboratively—without trust, there's just coercion in one of its many forms. Collaborative organizations and teams rely openly on trust, on the belief that members of one's team are fundamentally good and capable of drawing the best from people and providing them with the means to succeed. Ask if management trusts project team members enough to let them get their work done.

Others attest that trust in integrated design is a result but not a prerequisite. "It's not about trust—it's about process," says Scott Simpson. "If the process is set up properly, trust will follow."[46]

Etiquette

Not only that team members find a way to work cooperatively, but also *how* team members work together is important. Playing nice is not just common sense practice; it is a privilege and our duty as design professionals. This point is spelled out by Jarrod Baumann in "How to Play Nice":[47]

- **Make it predictable.** Having a predictable linking point is essential.

- **Deleting objects versus changing types.** When making changes to the architectural model, one common thing to do is delete an object and redraw it. This is entirely reasonable for the architect but can create more work for your consultants. If you delete and redraw the wall, however, these elements will be orphaned and will need to be rehosted to the new wall. The same goes for changing a wall or ceiling type. Select it and change the type instead of deleting and re-creating it.

- **Reduce the need for duplicate elements** within the compiled building models. This should be one of our goals as cooperative BIM modelers. In this effort it would be desirable for the lighting designer to model and place lighting fixtures in lieu of having them reside in the architect's model.

- **Green analysis.** Energy-efficient construction is an important goal for everyone in our industry to pursue. BIM has the potential to make this pursuit easier.

In order to fulfill its potential, designers from all disciplines will need to cooperate in the creation of high-quality models for use in model-based analysis. Much of that responsibility rests with the mechanical and lighting engineers. However, a well-constructed architectural model will make the task of detailed analysis much less difficult.[48]

One Model/Many Models

An object seen in isolation from the whole is not the real thing.

—Masanobu Fukuoka, *The One-Straw Revolution: An Introduction to Natural Farming* (Rodale, 1978), 26.

An inevitable obstacle to architects and contractors working together collaboratively comes about when the question is raised as to whether there ought to be one or more BIM models. Architects are on the fence—while insisting that their models are complete enough for contractors to use for construction, for reasons of liability they are grateful not to have to. With all team-related issues, it helps to communicate early about intentions for the model. As blogger and BIM expert Brad Hardin explains, "If you're building a BIM to provide a construction tool that helps better coordinate the project, [then] build the model to a level of constructible detail that a GC can use and build from. Start the dialogue with the contractor to find out what they need as well."[49]

Owners, as well as some architects, need to understand why one model isn't adequate for the entire effort—why there may be a need for a separate schematic model, design model, construction model, and facilities and operations model. A great deal depends on the use of the model—for design, for construction,

I recently was asked how to use architects' models if they're "trash." While it seems like a good question and easy to ask if you aren't an architect, I have been asked the same from engineers and fabricators by contractors and heard from the architects, what kind of model is the contractor looking for? Basically everybody is asking why they can't use each other's models.

—Brad Hardin,
"Composite Model Strategy," March 21, 2009,[1]
www.bimcompletethought.blogspot.com.

for analysis. "From the owner's perspective, if the architect is BIM-savvy and produces a 3D model as part of his work product, why can't the general contractor and subs use that model to plan construction and fabrication? Or more to the point . . . why should the owner pay the GC or the subs to make another model(s)?"[50]

As enticing as a one-model approach sounds, the norm is to use multiple BIM models. In fact, there were relatively few projects where only one BIM model was created and used by all of the disciplines. One project can have as many as eight models that

The GSA has had over 100 BIM models on a single project, according to ENR—and the count may reach 220! I have been in more than 100 meetings over the past 4 years where people at the conference room table just wanted there to be 1 model that did everything and wanted me to say so. But true to my beliefs, there is a need for more than 1 model.

—Don Henrich, "I rest my case! 200 Models?"
April 30, 2009, www.vicosoftware.com.

are used for different purposes.[51] Here's what other industry experts have to say on the question of one model versus multiple models:

> BIM is not a single database or "single building model." This is one of the main confusions with regard to adopting BIM. A lot of people believe BIM has to be a single database from which every party extracts their information in the format they require. . . . It is better to think of BIM as a series of models.[52]

Another report relates: "Although BIM users constantly refer to 'the model,' in actual practice, a multidisciplinary project team is rarely, if ever, served by a single, seamless database. Instead, teams rely on a series of models usually organized by discipline, and are often dependent on different software platforms. The models are generally updated and coordinated at regular intervals, often via a project extranet."[53] It is clear from a construction standpoint that the need for multiple models is the way to proceed for the time being.

Cost

Since information is costly to produce but inexpensive to reproduce, to work efficiently and effectively the design professional should spend the least possible amount of time modeling. Creating firm-centric families in your BIM program for the first time will be more costly than producing later instances.

Working collaboratively with others has a price tag. "One of the costs many companies explore cutting in difficult economic times is technology. So you can bet that professional service firms around the world are taking a close look at the overall value of the technology they employ."[54] BIM adoption should be considered holistically and not on a piecemeal basis, as something that benefits the firm for all the reasons spelled out earlier—not the least of which is as a vehicle for working collaboratively—and not just as a business tool.

Responsibility, Insurance, and Liability

To be sure, this is an important topic that is not yet resolved and could fill a volume of its own. Here, I would like to limit the discussion by touching on one or two points that serve as potential obstacles to effectively working together, and on how working collaboratively can actually lessen the legal and liability ramifications of working in integrated design. "Although there are concerns about liability and authorship, a collaborative environment has [been] shown in large-scale projects in the United States to reduce the perceived need for defensive documentation."[55]

At the 2010 BIMForum, Gregg Bundschuh of Ames & Gough categorized the thirty insurance claims that had arisen at that time for projects involving BIM into six categories in his presentation, "BIM Claims and Insurance Cover: A Survey of Recent Developments":

- **2D to 3D conversion**. Here, the contractor performs a 2D conversion and makes an assumption about design intent in the conversion process.

- **Versioning**. When firms "mix and match" versions of the same software, inconsistencies result between models of different versions.

- **Default settings**. When firms use the default settings of software, errors can occur.

- **Model reliance**. No surprise here, this issue is the most prevalent and occurs when someone over-relies on a model.

- **Interoperability**. Three claims have come about when conflicts occurred between design and

Figure 4.11   Assessing an acceptable level of risk for yourself and your organization.

fabrication models; these were primarily in structural steel.

- **Standard of care**. The most interesting claim by far comes from an arbitration that was resolved about two months ago, in the Midwest. The design professionals only created 2D documents (per their contract requirements). After the contractor did a 2D conversion, they published clashes to the architect, who "ignored them." The architect's argument was that they weren't paid to go above the standard of care. However, the arbitrator said that the architect should have resolved the issues, once advised. It was determined that the architect did not meet standard of care and the contractor was awarded several million dollars.[56]

As one commenter remarked upon seeing this list, "It would be interesting to know how many claims there would have been on these projects if BIM had *not* been used." (See Figure 4.11.)

Strategies: Making Collaboration Work

Does collaboration work? And if so, how does collaboration work? Do clients even want their architect to collaborate? Integrated design helps to make collaboration possible—and there are recent cases where collaboration has worked successfully. Some key strategies that help:

- Let go of ego and the idea of one team member as hero or individual contributor.

- Put the project first.

- Put the community and their needs right up there.

- Work on your *collaborative intelligence*.

On this last point, "BIM intelligence" or *collaborative intelligence* (as a proposed new type of intelligence), made up of a combination of social intelligence and technical intelligence, is a huge opportunity area for design professionals, where the big-picture thinking is coupled with granular detail; where one is able to zoom in and out of scales and recognizes when it is appropriate to do each. It is a way to measure a team's ability to work together—but also their comfort levels with groupware and other Web 2.0 technologies that encourage collaboration across teams.

Case Study Interview with Rich Nitzsche, CIO, Perkins + Will

Rich Nitzsche, CIO, Perkins + Will, registered architect and LEED AP, is responsible for the strategy, supervision, coordination, and delivery of all information systems and services firmwide.

What was the catalyst for P + W going over to BIM?

Rich Nitzsche: It is a process. When it comes to BIM, we've long been tracking BIM—I still have my pre-Autodesk Revit jacket. When I was with McClier, we bought in early. We actually did a building through schematic design using Revit—a maintenance building for American Airlines at JFK. P + W had Revit release 1 when I arrived here. We've been tracking BIM all along. Our feeling up to that point was that the product was not mature enough. Autodesk had recently taken it over. It had some limitations in its ability to scale and in its form-making capabilities. We were pretty cognizant if we were to make this a success, it had to be able to support most of what we're trying to do tectonically. Michael Masteller, P + W's corporate CAD manager, and I went to an executive briefing in November 2005 and came away thinking, from what we heard and saw, that it was time.

We worked hard to get to a place in early 2006, when we could mandate each office to do one medium-complexity, single-office Revit project. Not a multi-office collaboration. So 2006 was our pilot year. The mandate wasn't adhered to religiously—we had about 50 percent compliance. The point was to shake out some of the issues just on a stand-alone basis. A couple projects emerged that were multi-office projects. We started getting into the large-team workflow issues.

But then in 2006, Phil Harrison, our CEO said straight up in our leadership group meeting—to all our managing directors, all our global market sector leaders, the heads of finance and IT—we're going to be 100 percent BIM from this point forward. It was a bold statement, and that's what you'd expect the CEO to say. The reality is that we do have some asterisks on that statement. What we're trying to do now is remove barriers, get rid of those asterisks.

(Continued)

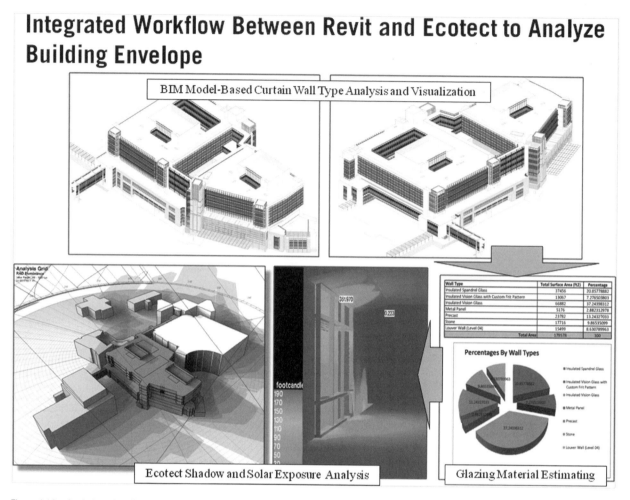

Figure 4.12   Analysis tools—Ecotect glazing study. © 2009–2010, Perkins + Will, all rights reserved

One reality is that you're not going to convert a project that's already well underway. Reality number two: if a client says you're going to do it in another program, fine. Reality number three is we didn't really have a platform that was facile enough for rapid deployment of stand-alone interiors groups. We didn't want to force-feed Revit to folks with the ramp-up time that's required.

Training is a whole other discussion. The real issue was human bandwidth. We just didn't have any. We're starting to roll this thing out and we're trying to recruit—we're still not 100 percent where we want to be with staffing of our overall BIM direction. Talent in this area has been very tough. So we've taken a couple of different approaches. (See Figure 4.12.)

The plan was to do your three days of training, then start your project just in time. That way you retain it and apply it. The thing is, three days of training doesn't give you everything you need. Where we fell down in that process is we didn't have enough support—troops—to go in with the team and be with them. A couple of years ago we instituted a program called Design

Technology Leaders (DTL). These are not IT people; they're architects or interiors people. It's an overlay. You overlay this role on top of your firm role—with the idea that there's some leadership credit toward your career. There's some extra compensation and some fairly defined limits on how much time is taken over by this kind of supporting role. The DTLs would field the easy to answer questions, help facilitate project setup. Again, something we mandated and haven't gotten 100 percent compliance on yet. We're working on it. The offices that have done this have become much more proficient, and the DTLs have created their own communities of practice. They're talking to each other, and we're starting to see a firm-wide community of practice between all of those who are doing their tour of duty as DTLs.

> *They want to be designers and architects first—they don't want to be technicians. But they recognize that they're good at it. [We] try to de-stigmatize it so we don't fall back on the old* CAD monkey *and* plot weasel *modalities.*
>
> —Rich Nitzsche

It's exciting because they're excellent users; they want to be designers and architects first—they don't want to be technicians. But they recognize that they're good at it. [We] try to destigmatize it so we don't fall back on the old *CAD monkey* and *plot weasel* modalities. I've had people in this office who have said that they are getting ready to quit because they're taking their architecture away and making them the BIM monkey. Hearing that, that's why we put a ten-hour time commitment cap per forty-hour work week. It's a leadership shift. If you want to advance, this two- or three-year tour is part of the deal.

IT is constantly changing. P + W is one of the world's largest architecture firms. How exactly do you turn a firm the size of an aircraft carrier around to embark on an entirely different IT direction?

RN: Sometimes you feel like you're in a dinghy pushing against that aircraft carrier, not making a lot of progress. We didn't do anything entirely different. Our implementation of ADT was pretty sophisticated. I'm not sure everybody was using all the sophistication baked into it. In many ways BIM was a natural evolution for us.

First of all, you have to have buy-in from the top. Phil Harrison had completely bought in to BIM. He was convinced that this is the future and this is what we need to be doing. Getting Phil on board was easy. Getting Phil and the rest of the executive leadership team on board with this—we were working from the top down and also started working from the bottom up. We could have done a better job on the bottom-up part. We're a bit savvier now about how to build buzz. We have to communicate in so many modalities. Not just once—we have to repeat ourselves, be consistent with the message, and approach it from a lot of different angles. You need to build momentum.

One of the things I've learned is we'd be sitting in an operations meeting with the guys who run our offices every day from a practical, bottom-line, and staffing point of view. One guy would grumble about how BIM is going. There's a great opportunity to find the people around the table who have success stories to tell, who have already done the labor to get there. You need to let them shine—and let peer pressure do its work. Not in a mean-spirited way—it's a way of saying, "This can be done." You've done it—why not have a conversation about what it took? Try and highlight the success stories.

That's something we're trying to do a lot more of in IT—focus on communication. I'm finding that peer pressure is one of the most effective tools to try and persuade other groups to move ahead.

(Continued)

P + W is a pretty young firm. Our people are doing the really heavy lifting on these projects, authoring and so on. They're going to care about the tools and use the tools. The people you call the mid-careerists—the project managers—they're not really using the tools so much. For them, they want to understand how to budget for it, what their people are doing, and how long it should take to do it. But they're not really hands-on so much. It is more important that they "get" BIM than that they use it. We have BIM for project managers training—BIM for principals and associate principals—for just this purpose. Just to acquaint them with the concepts and process. I personally haven't observed a lot of gray-hairs working in Revit side by side with the Revit jocks. (See Figure 4.13.)

Once BIM adoption and implementation were underway, what impacts, if any, did you see brought about by the technology on the workflow?

Figure 4.13 Analysis tools—Ecotect lighting study. © 2009–2010, Perkins + Will, all rights reserved

RN: What emerged pretty quickly was that large-team workflows were going to be a huge problem. P + W does 60 percent of its work between multiple offices. That's part of our go-to-market message. We have expertise all around the country—we don't necessarily have every expert in every category in one office. So if I have a nanotechnology lab specialist who likes living in San Diego, we'll build an office around that. We've done that—built offices around expertise.

The problem is, it's a fundamental principle of the firm that we collaborate. One of the things I was charged with in IT is to make it easier to collaborate. Eliminate barriers to collaboration. For example, our phone system here is the same in every office: four digits to call anyone. Other systems are equally standardized. With the large-team workflow we ran into some really serious limitations with BIM. That started to uncover issues with the network and the hardware platform. This challenge has us looking into some computing solutions that a couple of years ago we didn't anticipate we would be moving toward so aggressively.

We're very aggressively moving into cloud computing. We've already virtualized most of our server inventory. We're waiting for desktop virtualization to mature for heavy graphics use. One way we're defeating this problem is through clustering of resources, which plays into some green strategies as well. There are a lot of synergies there. We're also doing things like collocation strategies with other offices, where we have our people, all of the consultants—sixty to seventy people in all—collocated on one floor of one office using our equipment on our network to mitigate some of the distance issues and the intra-company model-sharing issues.

What BIM has done for us as a firm is that it has energized a lot of people in terms of the focus on the architecture again. Working in BIM is a lot more like doing architecture than being a draftsman.

—Rich Nitzsche

How would you describe P + W's firm culture, and what impacts, if any, has working in a BIM environment had on that culture?

RN: As collaboration is a core value, it has been a little stressful on the collaboration ethic. What BIM has done for us as a firm is that it has energized a lot of people in terms of the focus on the architecture again. Working in BIM is a lot more like doing architecture than being a draftsman. Even though we've had our struggles with Revit—it wouldn't have mattered if it was Revit or ArchiCAD—I ask everyone if they'd rather go back to ADT, and every time they say no, we don't ever want to go back—this is the way we have always wanted to do it.

It always comes down to speed and simplicity. Model management is a pain in the neck. It's a nightmare and requires a lot of upfront planning. If you're doing a K–12 project in the Chicago office with just Chicago people—that's easy. But if you're doing John Hopkins with L.A., Atlanta, Washington, and Chicago all in collaboration—that's a much more sophisticated, complicated problem. It depends on the building type, the scale of the building, and the team size to determine how easy it is to do things.

We had senior people in house who got freaked out by how little they saw on the sheets and they couldn't believe there was progress being made. And of course it was like pulling the rabbit out of the hat when it came time to produce the drawing set—magically, results start to appear. It took a while for there to be a comfort level. It's a perception thing. They'd ask for a printout of a set and they'd look at it and just freak out. But the team knew that the information was in there. They just hadn't revealed it all yet.

Another thing we learned is that there are different audiences for the BIM process. There are the technical coordinator types who are looking to see if the set is complete. Have we documented what we want to document about the building? But in the earlier phases, the designers want to see something completely different. The designers got a bit ticked off because we hadn't really thought through our project process and setup of views that designers want to see in order to make design decisions. Make sure you're communicating with the design team so that they are seeing what they want to see. When a designer says, "I want to see a set," that's different from when a technical coordinator wants to see a set. Its two different outcomes from the same model, making sure you're taking into account all the players. The designers are stakeholders, but so are the technical people who are responsible for the documents. They have different agendas.

Had the firm ever seriously considered not working in a BIM environment? Holding out until all of the interoperability, legal, and liability issues were ironed out?

RN: No, never.

IPD is seen as a process both driven and enabled by BIM technology. Has P + W worked on any IPD projects? Are you seeing owners enquire into it? What do you see for IPD's future as a delivery method?

RN: We have just barely put our toe in the IPD waters. We have a couple proposals out there with the IPD approach. As a firm, we're absolutely committed to IPD. We're calling it *Innovation in Project Delivery*. It's not going to be easy to take a design-bid-build culture and transform it to this. I come from a design-build culture with McClier, so I'm already sold on it. To me it makes complete sense.

(Continued)

It does clash a bit with this idea that we are a design firm. There's a little tension between being a signature design firm and getting into the trenches with IPD. IPD is the future. We're at a crossroads in the profession. The architect's role in the AEC industry is up for grabs right now. We have two things in our favor right now: BIM—we're not ahead of the contractors, but some of us are keeping up—and sustainability. And for me these two things create a perfect storm for us to have a conversation with clients about the project lifecycle. IPD enables you to talk about the whole supply chain. What does that mean? Design-assist? In terms of sharing the model? Issues of right of reliance? How do we do that? And then seventy to eighty percent of the building's life-cycle cost is in the O&M. That's a much tougher conversation to have with our marquee designers in the room or folks who don't focus that much on facilities management and think that it sullies the brand. How do we deal with that? In the meantime you have contractors or property managers—they're happy to have a conversation with the owner about services like that. Those maintain relationships; they generate revenue.

As architects, our fate is in our own hands. But we have to seize this moment with BIM and sustainability as our opportunity to have a deep discussion with the owner about our value proposition, being able to do things that constructors can't do or have not done. The danger right now is that constructors are hiring more architects than architects are, and we're getting co-opted there. I don't think it is malicious and feel that the adversarial view of them is wrong-headed. Constructors are taught to focus on their client. And our client needs these things. And if no one's going to provide it, contractors are going to do it. And if that means architects aren't there to compete for that and serve our clients, then somebody's got to do it. I can't fault the contractor for doing that. It means that if we want to remain relevant to the owner, and be an equal partner with the constructor, then we've got to step it up and focus on our client. That's where I see sticking one's head in the sand about BIM and IPD is not a survival position. How can you feel you are fully informed about your design decisions if you aren't talking to the people who are going to build it? (See Figure 4.14.)

Everyone today is trying to do more with less. Meanwhile, it seems like some of the programs design professionals are using pack in more with each release—in other words, try to do more with more. How do you work with the growing, and some say needless, complexity of some of the technology you work with?

RN: It's a real challenge. If you look at the entire spectrum of things we have to put out there—it's everything. We're going to laptops with Bluetooth headsets. Rather than being tethered to a workstation or office, you can go anywhere. The problem is, how much change can we inflict on our users in a given time span? How much can they absorb without insurrection? That's really what it boils down to. What our users really want is things to be simple, reliable, and fast. If we can just get software developers to focus on simple, reliable, and fast, we'll have a lot happier users. This is the real dilemma for us. We invest in these enterprise agreements because they represent a certain amount of value and simplify licensing for us. A new release of software comes out. We look at it and say, we just changed that a year ago. You look at how much value there is in the change and say—maybe we shouldn't do that. You start skipping releases, and what happens is you start to lose value. From a financial standpoint, every time I don't put out a [revision], I've lost value.

With reference to BIM and other related technologies, how do you—in your role—create and communicate value for a firm as large and diverse as P + W?

RN: The value proposition for BIM is that it has multiple facets. The way we sold it originally was based on anecdotal information about smaller team sizes, reduced effort to produce the same body of work—they were compelling enough to get Phil's attention. We've had some instances where this has been realized, on projects that have achieved real economies. But these

Figure 4.14   Exterior photo of the University of Minnesota medical biosciences building.

aren't those complex multiple-office, large-team projects. Competitiveness is another proposition. There's not an RFP that crosses our threshold that doesn't have BIM as a requirement. And now we're starting to see IPD show up. So if we're going to compete with what we consider to be our peer group—and even with people who are smaller than us—we've got to be ready on all of these levels. So we've got to go in with a great BIM story and not only a great sustainability story but a leadership story about sustainable design. We have a green operating plan, and green IT is part of the green operating plan. We've done a pretty good job of that. My goal this year is to get us into a leadership position about BIM and IPD—in the eyes of owners and our peers. Because we all measure ourselves to some degree in terms of how we measure ourselves in relation to our peers. And I would say we're on the front edge when it comes to those two things.

With the economy in the state it is in, some firms have seen their IT people take on more project work to account for a greater percentage of billable time. Has this been a trend you have observed?

RN: Our IT people don't do a lot of project work. I like the idea of doing project work because it gets our people closer to what's happening in the office. I personally would love to spend time on a project, seeing where their struggles are, seeing where things are great. I ask people to spend more time—if they can—closer to the projects for this reason.

(Continued)

This next question is on the strategic role of CIO. The CIO role historically was seen as a back-office position. In the last several years, CIOs have become much more visible, with several moving into a CEO or vice-chairman position. What are some of the characteristics of your position—especially when it comes to working in technology—that have an impact on firm leadership and strategy?

We CIOs have to wear a lot of hats. I care about marketing, and I care about data conversion. To be effective as a CIO you have to think holistically. You have to think about operations, communications, and leadership. The number one thing is having good people to delegate to.

—Rich Nitzsche

RN: Phil's always hammering on me to be more strategic. We CIOs have to wear a lot of hats. I care about marketing, and I care about data conversion. To be effective as a CIO you have to think holistically. You have to think about operations, communications, and leadership. The number one thing is having good people to delegate to. With respect to marketing, I love opportunities to talk to clients. To talk about BIM, IPD, things that matter to our clients. Having us in the room gives the client confidence to go ahead with their project.

What are some of the challenges facing an IT leader of a major architecture firm on a personal and professional level?

RN: Talent. Especially on the design app side.

Do you see BIM ultimately as a tool that leads to collaborative work processes or just a step up from CAD?

RN: Someone asked me: Do you need BIM to do IPD? No. You can do IPD without any of those things. BIM enhances collaborative work processes. BIM takes it to another level. But I don't think it's foundational. You have to have a will to collaborate. If you don't have a will to collaborate, you're not going to—and I don't care what technology you throw at it. When we hire, we talk a lot about chemistry, with IT people as well as with the local office. We don't always get it right. It's not always about collaboration, but if there's not good chemistry, the likelihood of good collaboration is pretty low. (See Figure 4.15.)

How did you know Revit was right for P + W?

RN: Revit and ArchiCAD were on par until the most recent release of ArchiCAD. Now ArchiCAD, with Release 13, is ahead. If ArchiCAD 13 was available when we made the decision to go with Revit, it could have very easily gone that way. It wasn't, so we leveraged our existing investment and went forward with Revit.

We have folks who insist that they can't design in Revit. And I have other designers who are just now emerging who say that they can accomplish 95 percent of what they need to do in Revit—designers who have taken it on as their personal mission, who say that they're going to wrestle this beast to the ground and bend it to my will as an architect. As these people emerge, we'll do the peer pressure thing. That said, we can't get stubborn about it and say we can't use these tools—SketchUp and Rhino—to author your design idea. We would have open revolt.

Looking back on your career, was there any technology or software that you invested time and resources in that didn't give you the results you anticipated in the end? (Autodesk Architectural Desktop is sometimes cited, with

Figure 4.15   Exterior rendering—U.S. Coast Guard headquarters.

regrets, as a dead end.) And what are the chances your current investment in BIM might have similar results—or the lack thereof?

RN: Everybody's got their shelfware stories. We've been pretty good stewards of the technology portfolio. Part of the proposition of having software is having someone use it. Sometimes IT gets ahead of itself and tries to put something in place where there's not really a demand or an audience ready to receive it. We had these functionalities but didn't have a constituency that was really driving it. We finally have leadership in place that is driving these decisions. Certainly there's a lot more dialogue about how much is it going to cost, why are we doing it? And that's healthy too. For years IT was pushing—"We know what's best for you." Now we have the kind of leadership in place that's demanding and pulling—and that, for me, is a much healthier proposition. That's emerged in operations, in finance, in the design and technical communities.

How much of IT is about technology and how much is about communication? Is IT really about technology, or is it about something else—greater productivity, project delivery, ROI, or business results, to name a few?

RN: It has been too much about technology for too long a time. We don't do that great a job of communicating. I feel I need a PR department for IT sometimes. Most people don't know that we have an 800 number—so if they're out in the field and need

(Continued)

to, they can reach us. We need to do a better job of communicating what's possible, communicating what we have. IT has a long way to go in terms of communicating our message more effectively.

With so many firms taking on BIM and integrated design for their competitive advantage, they seem to cancel each other out. While P + W has certainly felt some of the effects of the economy, it seems to have been affected to a much lesser extent overall. What is P + W doing to truly differentiate itself from the competition?

RN: We're pretty well differentiated by the fact that we're well diversified. We're more global than we've ever been. Our partner Dar is a huge factor in our ability to weather this storm. We're focused on design excellence, on expertise, on quality and innovation. We bring in people who are going to drive these goals, and it is up to IT to respond to these things. (See Figure 4.16.)

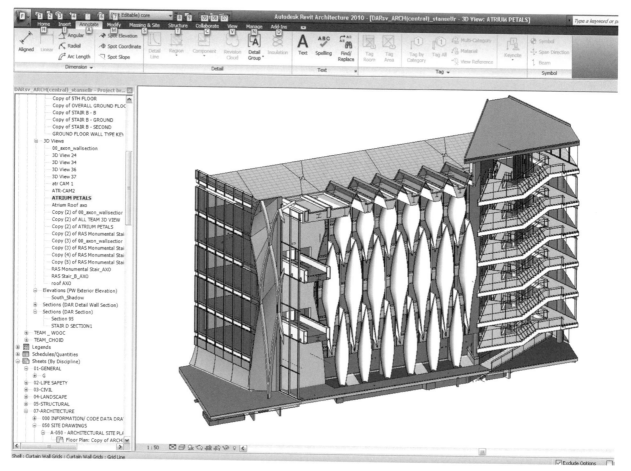

Figure 4.16   Interior atrium section study—DAR headquarters. © 2009–2010, Perkins + Will, all rights reserved

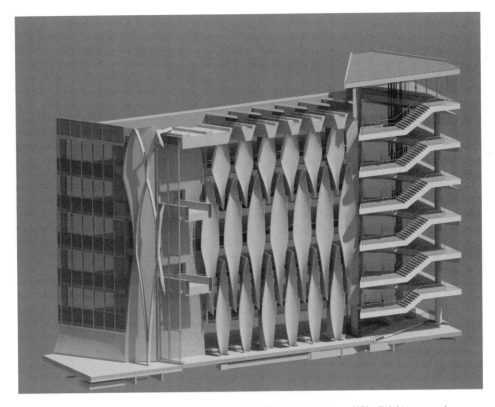

Figure 4.17   Interior Atrium section study rendering—DAR headquarters. *© 2009–2010, Perkins + Will, all rights reserved*

Unlike CAD, BIM requires that the operator understands how to put a building together piece by piece. As a design firm, what sort of concerns, if any, does this bring about? Is there concern that the firm might be light on building technologists—or, from a firm-culture standpoint, is BIM seen as something that might stifle design at P + W?

RN: When I joined the firm nine years ago, we were tending a little toward a boutique approach. We were not fully where we wanted to be with the technical side. This had already been recognized and there was already an initiative addressing this before I came on board. I would say now we always talk about full services. That doesn't mean we don't take projects through SD and then hand them off—we still do that. But we prefer full services—there are revenue reasons for that, but also for keeping your technical prowess, your technical chops as an architect. We don't really see a division between technical architecture and design. If anything, if there are barriers, we're trying to knock those barriers down. The things that are interesting to our designers are also interesting to our technical teams. We want to make sure that we don't silo these things. That would be antithetical to what we're trying to achieve. Being a boutique firm is not a survival strategy in these times. There will always be a few—but there aren't enough projects in the world to make being a boutique firm a viable business strategy. We have a much more holistic view of what it means to be a designer and an architect. (See Figure 4.17.)

(Continued)

In 2006, after attending the Construction Users Roundtable (CURT) National Conference, you wrote, in "Some CURT Remarks," that you came away with the realization that the architect-centric AEC world you inhabit seems very small in the larger sphere of construction and that it's easy for architects, yourself included, to imagine that most of the built environment involves us. "It does not, and not by a wide margin," you wrote. Similarly, construction industry attorney Barry B. LePatner has stated, "Architects currently design less than 5 percent of America's construction projects—a depressing statistic and a telling symptom of how marginalized the profession has become." Do you see architects' use of current technology tools and integrated practices as a way for them to become more relevant and central to the entire construction process? Do you see digital design tools as being closer to achieving these goals today than when you first made these observations?

RN: To the first question, yes. Emphatically yes. The second question, yes, but only incrementally so. The digital design tools still have a ways to go. One of the things we're focused on is auditability. I want to be able to audit the model. Auditability gets to the point of right of reliance. What can I reliably state about the model? Getting back to the idea of a building data lifecycle. If I want to hand off a model instead of drawings to a contractor, what can I reliably tell the contractor that they can expect from that? What would I be willing to contractually say about that proposition? We're looking real hard at how do we build auditability into the BIM environment? Taking it beyond clash detection. You talk to contractors about your model today—no matter how good you say it is—they're going to throw it away. As far as they're concerned, your model is not worth the bytes it took to make it. They're just going to build it from scratch. They want a model constructed in a way that responds to how they build the building. So if we continue to make columns that are twenty stories high, they're going to continue to say our model is junk. So we have to talk with the contractors and find out how they're going to make the building. It means we have to think a little differently about how we put the model together. We don't want it to be an impediment to design, but if we are delivering a model, we need to figure out what does it need to be? IPD would allow this to happen. (See Figure 4.18.)

Figure 4.18   Interior rendering, University of North Carolina School of Medicine imaging research building.

Among P + W's competing priorities, where does IT stand today compared, say, with ten years ago?

RN: We're trying to get IT to be less the necessary evil and be more of a competitive advantage in some form or fashion. We're trying to get that perception behind us. It's an uphill battle. The closer we get to projects and project teams, the more relevant IT starts to be to the folks doing the work. When you look at the IT team, how many people are taking care of the plumbing, and how many are taking care of the users and the apps that they're using? It's been disproportionately weighted toward the plumbing for years. We've been slowly shifting the focus to the end users, the applications, empowering and enabling people.

What are some of the current and upcoming trends and innovations you are paying attention to that will potentially make a difference to P + W and the way it practices and operates?

RN: This is what is going on in IT. This is what I'm listening to, hearing about, and paying attention to.

There's cloud computing—building a private cloud or multiple private clouds, [deciding] what's in the public cloud. Virtualization. Desktop virtualization. How's that going to impact your new office when you move down the street? What does it mean for applications? Green IT—speaking to the green issues, how we're able to get more utilization out of one box. There are some capacity issues that I am starting to get nervous about. People building up huge data centers. They don't know how they're going to power these facilities. Convergence. What's commodity versus what differentiates us? We believe it is the design applications space that differentiates us. Trying to find a way to get iTunes in-house without making the security guy go nuts—so we have a more facile way of delivering podcasts. High definition. We need to communicate better and cut down on travel. Social media. How do you control your accessibility? How do you manage that? Going completely wireless. The security question—especially for office guests. And lastly, video games as the paradigm for the future.

NOTES

1. James Vandezande, AGC BIMForum Review, October 8, 2008, allthingsbim.blogspot.com/ 2008_10_01_ archive.html.
2. *BIM Journal,* "BIM Explained", February 1, 2009, www.bimjournal.com/2009/02/bim-explained/.
3. Lachmi Khemlani, "AIA TAP 2007 Conference" December 11, 2007, www.aecbytes.com/newsletter/2007/issue_31.html.
4. Phil Bernstein, interview with the author, October 15, 2009.
5. Lance Hosey, "All Together Now Collaboration is the Key to Innovation," *Architect,* October 6, 2009, www.architectmagazine.com/sustainability/all-together-now.aspx.
6. Dan Hill, "The New Engineering: A Discussion with Arup's Tristram Carfrae March 31, 2008, www.cityofsound.com/blog/2008/03/this-discussion.html.
7. Khemlani, "AIA TAP 2007 Conference."
8. Aaron Greven, interview with the author, August 25, 2009.
9. Kristine Fallon, "Interoperability: Critical to Achieving BIM Benefits", April 2007,aiawebdev2.aia.org/ tap2_template.cfm?pagename=tap_a_0704_interop.
10. www.wikipedia.com.
11. BIMManager, "Five Fallacies Surrounding BIM," July 1, 2009, www.bimmanager.com/2009/07/01/five-fallacies-surrounding-bim-from-autodesk/.

12. *McGraw-Hill SmartMarket Report 2007.*

13. Bradley Beck, interview with the author, November 10, 2009.

14. Patricia R. Olsen, "For Writing Software, a Buddy System," *New York Times* (September 19, 2009), www.nytimes.com/2009/09/20/jobs/20pre.html.

15. Joann Gonchar, "Transformative Tools Start to Take Hold," *Architectural Record* (2007), construction.com/CE/articles/0704edit-1.asp.

16. Beck, interview.

17. Ibid.

18. www.aecbytes.com.

19. "From the Editors", September 15, 2007, www.di.net/news/archive/from_editors/.

20. Mimi Zeiger, "Role Models: A Digital Design Guru at SOM Looks to the Future of BIM," *Architect,* January 17, 2009, www.architectmagazine.com/bim/role-models.aspx.

21. Edgar Schein, "Organizational Culture and Leadership," in *Classics of Organization Theory* (Fort Worth: Harcourt College Publishers, 1993), 373–74.

22. Patricia Williams, "Managing Cultural Change Poses Challenge as BIM Gains Traction," OGCA Symposium, May 8, 2009, dcnonl.com/article/ id33677.

23. Steve Watt, "BIM Ushers in a Culture of Collaboration," October 20, 2009, www.reedconstructiondata.com/construction-forecast/news/2009/10/bim-ushers-in-a-culture-of-collaboration/.

24. Ibid.

25. Laura Sherbin and Karen Sumberg, "Bulldoze Your Cubicles for Better Collaboration," August 20, 2009, blogs.hbr.org/hbr/hewlett/2009/08/bulldoze_your_cubicles_for_bet.html#.

26. Yanni Loukissas, "Keepers of the Geometry: Architects in a Culture of Simulation", First International Conference on Critical Digital: What Matters(s)?, 18-19 April 2008, Harvard University Graduate School of Design, Cambridge, MA.

27. Yanni Loukassis, interview with the author, October 15, 2009.

28. Ibid.

29. Khemlani, "AIA TAP 2007 Conference."

30. Steve Carroll, comment in response to "BIM When Will It Enter 'The Ours' Zone," July 24, 2008, http://www.aecbytes.com/viewpoint/2008/issue_ 40.html.

31. Jim Foster, "Labor Productivity Declines in the Construction Industry: Causes and Remedies," June 10, 2009, frombulator.com/2009/06/labor-productivity-declines-in-the-construction-industry-causes-and-remedies/.

32. Khemlani, "AIA TAP 2007 Conference."

33. Beck, interview.

34. Ibid.

35. Ibid.

36. Mike Whaley, "There is No I in IPD!" May 20, 2009, www.aecbytes.com/viewpoint/2009/issue_45.html.

37. Ibid.

38. Elizabeth A. Chodosh and Gary T. McLeod, "Collaboration and Large Project BIM Imple-mentation with Revit," (Autodesk University, Decemmber 11, 2008), au.autodesk.com/?nd= class&session_id=2763.

39. Lauren Stassi, "Extreme Collaboration Interns in a BIM World," Texas Society of Architects/AIA, September 22, 2009, texasarchitect.blogspot.com/2009/09/guest-blog-extreme-collaboration.html.

40. Beck, interview.

41. Greven, interview.

42. Joanne G. Linowes, "BIM: New Era for Design = New Era for Communications", (presentation, AIA Convention, San Francisco, CA April 30, 2009).

43. Patrick Aragon, "Reinventing Collaboration across Internal and External Project Teams," September 14, 2006, www.aecbytes.com/viewpoint/2006/ issue_28.html.

44. Inga Saffron, "City's Green Groundbreakers," *Philadelphia Inquirer,* January 17, 2010, articles.philly.com/2010-01-17/news/25210169_1_design-firms-celebrity-architects-architects-focus.

45. David H. Hart, "Developing Trusting Collaborative Relationships," October 25, 2007, blog.aia.org/aiarchitect/2007/10/developing_trusting_collaborat.html.

46. Nadine M. Post, "Integrated-Project-Delivery Boosters Ignore Many Flashing Red Lights," May 6, 2010,

archrecord.construction.com/news/daily/archives/2010/100506ipd-2.asp.

47. Jarrod Baumann, "How to Play Nice: Sharing Revit Models," April 22, 2009, www.designwesteng.com/blog/?p=54.

48. Ibid.

49. Brad Hardin, "Composite Model Strategy," March 21, 2009, www.bimcompletethought.blogspot.com.

50. Mark Sawyer, "One versus Multiple Models –or- Should We PolyModel-Doodle-All-The-Day?" October 10, 2008, www.vicosoftware.com/blogs-0/the-agenda/tabid/84418/bid/6919/2-One-versus-Multiple-Models-or-Should-we-PolyModel-Doodle-All-The-Day.aspx.

51. SmartMarket Report on Building Information Modeling (BIM) McGraw-Hill 2008, www.construction.ecnext.com.

52. Nigel Davies, "(Mis)understanding BIM," March 26, 2007, www.biscopro.com/index.php/interesting-information/interesting-articles/33.html.

53. Gonchar, "Transformative Tools Start to Take Hold."

54. Paul Doherty, "Technology Back-to-Basics Advice," www.di.net, 2009.

55. Patricia Williams, "Managing Cultural Change Poses Challenge as BIM Gains Traction," www.dcnonl.com, 2009.

56. Laura Handler, "BIM Claims," January 18, 2010, bimx.blogspot.com/2010/01/bim-claims.html.

chapter **5** BIM and Integrated
Design

Figure 5.1   Results from the use of a blender in a non-industry-standard workflow, imported into Revit to make quantifiable. *Zach Kron, www .buildz.info*

Professionals in the building and construction industry have been slow to jump on the integrated design bandwagon. One goal of this book is to rectify this situation.

Before one can suggest and promote the integrated design process to owners, they need to thoroughly understand what it entails. If the best way to learn is by trial and error, this book aims to keep the mistakes—and associated pain—to a minimum. This chapter serves as a brief but incisive overview of integrated design.

BIM and Integrated Design

Why BIM *and* integrated design? Isn't BIM a large enough subject that it doesn't need to be qualified or adjoined by another, equally enthrallingly complex subject? BIM has one culture—growing out of IT, out of CAD and design—while integrated design comes from another: together, they form a culture of collaboration. Integrated design has a different culture from that of BIM—one concerned with the environment, creating high-performing facilities, streamlining, paring down and going lean; a culture of efficiency and fluidity; a culture that wants to do more with less and do well for—and good by—the owner.

BIM and integrated design are both processes, and once not only learned but experienced, it becomes apparent that they are made for each other. BIM technology enables—and is therefore the perfect accompaniment to—integrated design.

Just as "everything that rises must converge," over time BIM and integrated design will converge and the two areas of focus become one—interdependent, redundant, and indistinguishable from one another. When that day comes, integrated design will become integral to the BIM process.

Integrated design teams are guided by trust and information sharing, collaboration and transparency, where team success is equated with project success. They also make full use of existing technologies for the benefit of the project. (See Figure 5.2.)

Integrated design doesn't just follow BIM adoption, but evidence of having the capacity already in place to collaborate with others predicts the successful adoption of BIM.

As Phil Bernstein has written, "Evolution of BIM implementation came in parallel with willingness to collaborate and share project information, the move toward integrated practice that is much talked about in the industry."[1] This ability to collaborate is not only a talent and skill but also a mindset and an attitude.

BIM the Enabler

The fact is that BIM and integrated design go together. One enables the other—the technology enables the process, makes it likely, possible, and even necessary. There is a need for building simulation and

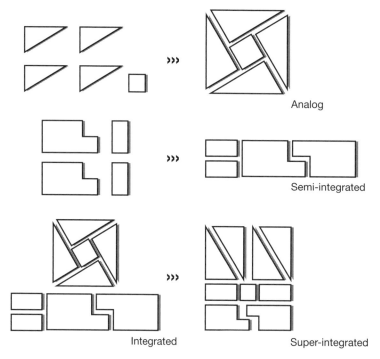

Analog

Semi-integrated

Integrated

Super-integrated

Figure 5.2   Toward a more complete integration. After Bryan Lawson, *How Designers Think*, 4th ed. (Architectural Press: Oxford, UK, 2006), 226–27. The terms *semi-integrated* and *super-integrated* are from "Preparing for Building Information Modeling," *Guidelines for Improving Practice* 35 (2).

BIM-Enabled Integrated Design

Building information modeling technology allows for integrated design to flourish, encourages—and provides a vessel and conduit for—the sharing of information between the design and construction team.

> Anyone attending a seminar on integrated practice/project delivery is exposed to a diagram showing a building information model (BIM) in the center of a circle of transactions. The diagram is emblematic of a new business process, and the model is a repository for all the data produced for or required to operate the building. The model receives and distributes information to a huge cohort that includes professionals, tenants, maintenance workers, emergency responders, and others. The diagram describes a hypothetical place with characteristics of an integrated manufacturing process superimposed on construction industry activities. The design tool, BIM, replaces the project lifecycle management software that lies at the heart of an integrated manufacturing process.*

*Barbara Golter Heller, "Red Business, Blue Business," May 30, 2008, http://www.di.net/articles/archive/red_business_blue_business/.

performance tools to enable the collaborative work processes. Together, BIM and integrated design help design professionals achieve their ultimate goals: well-designed buildings that function well, delivering anticipated results to owners, and high-performing buildings that benefit all involved, including future generations that are not represented in person at the table. Some go so far to say the integrated design process is a prerequisite to the creation of high-performance buildings. Because key participants are engaged and involved early, integrated design assures that everybody is on the same page, at the same time, with the same goals, working toward the same results.

BIM provides the integrated team with the ability to visualize the project, analyze design performance and code compliance, check for building system interference, conduct quantity take-offs, and implement phase construction; and for the owner to maintain and manage their facility through lifecycle modeling.

Defining Integrated Design

Terminology can admittedly get confusing. There is integrated design, integrative design, integrated buildings, integrated design process, integrated practice (IP), and integrated project delivery (IPD). To understand the difference between IPD and the subject of this book in its simplest terms, one, IPD, is a delivery method; the other, integrated design or ID, is a larger concept and process—free of its contractual identity—that contains IPD.

Integrated design can be understood as "a collaborative method for designing buildings that emphasizes the development of holistic design."[2] The only problem with this definition is that it defines one term by substituting another—holistic design—which at the time of this writing does not have a readily accessible definition. The implication is clear: integrated design is holistic in that it involves all stakeholders from the earliest stages, each having input into what goes into making the decisions that will lead to the completed project. It is holistic in that it takes every team member's point of view into consideration. And it is holistic in that these decisions are made with all the information shared at one time, up front—and not in the more traditional linear fashion, each entity maintaining and controlling the distribution of its own locus of information.

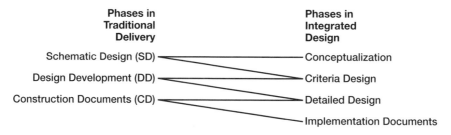

Figure 5.3   Phases of traditional project delivery renamed in integrated design.

Working simultaneously—as design teams did at City-Center in Las Vegas—is not collaboration. Working simultaneously means the work is occurring at the same time—period.

To integrate means to combine or coordinate separate elements so as to provide a harmonious, interrelated whole, organized or structured so that constituent units function cooperatively.[3] (See Figure 5.3.)

Multidisciplinary teams should not be confused with—or substituted for—the collaborative process of integrated design. In this context, to integrate means to

- Combine or coordinate separate elements to provide a harmonious interrelated whole.

- Organize or structure so that constituent units function cooperatively.

Crowdsourcing Design and Construction

The opposite of integrated design is working solo, isolated, in silos. If, as Ernest Boyer said, *"the future belongs to the integrators,"* then the past belonged to linear thinkers, the present to those who can think laterally and concurrently.

The integrated design process invites all affected parties into the planning process from the start encouraging—in fact requiring—multidisciplinary participation from all stakeholders. Further, integrated design

- Avoids handoffs from owner to architect to contractor by having all present at the table from the earliest stages.

- Takes into account each party's needs, expertise, and insights.

- Allows each participant to comment on and influence all areas of the project—each wears multiple hats.

Having everyone at the table from day one means that incompatible design components or systems—including clashes—are discovered earlier, when it is easier to respond and changes have less impact on schedule and cost. You could think of it as crowdsourcing your project.

Integrated Design as a Delivery Method

Integrated project delivery was developed in 2007, with initial case studies collected and disseminated in 2010 and 2011. What few understand is that integrated design is as much a mindset and attitude as a process and delivery method.

Architectural projects can be executed through a variety of project delivery methods. Prior to the twentieth century, there was a single project delivery method—the architect won a commission, produced drawings for design and construction, pulled labor and materials lists together, and oversaw the building of the project. As architects moved the discipline towards a profession and away from a craft, different project delivery methods developed to accommodate the changing relationship between architects and craftspeople. Currently, three project delivery methods dominate in the United States: design-bid-build, design-build, and construction management.[4]

While many contractors and construction managers will suggest an integrated design approach to owners, some owners aren't familiar with this approach. In these cases, the architect needs to inform the owner of the benefits of integrated design.

Phases of the Integrated Design Process

In IPD, the AIA phases (SD, DD, and CD) of the practice of architecture become Conceptualization, Criteria Design, and Detailed Design, with Implementation Documents and Project Buyout. *There are eight main sequential phases to the integrated project delivery method:*

- Conceptualization phase [expanded Programming]
- Criteria Design phase [expanded Schematic Design]
- Detailed Design phase [expanded Design Development]
- Implementation Documents phase [Construction Documents]
- Agency Review phase
- Buyout phase
- Construction phase
- Closeout phase

Source: "Integrated Project Delivery: A Guide," The American Institute of Architects 2007, version 1, http://www.aia.org/ipdg.

Design-bid-build is being supplanted by several other, more integrated building delivery methods.

An expected trend regarding project delivery, noted by Mark Zweig, founder of the AEC management consulting firm ZweigWhite, is that even though traditional design-bid-build is still the most dominant method—accounting for 60 percent of firm billings—it is slowly being superseded by other methods. It has declined 5 percent since 2002. While design-build receives much attention as the delivery method that will replace design-bid-build, it was construction-management-at-risk that made the greatest gains, increasing from 6.9 percent to 10 percent. Conventional construction-management accounts for 13.5 percent, and contractor-led design-build grabs about 9.6 percent. For the first time, architect-led design-build has been called out separately, and represented a scant 3.9 percent of all firm billings.[5]

There is a growing movement by owners, architects, and contractors away from the design-bid-build approach to the integrated design or integrated project delivery (IPD) approach.

What Drives Integrated Design?

There are several interrelated trends that are driving the move to integrated design:

- Greater accountability on the part of design professionals and constructors. According to Andy Stapleton of Mortenson, "The market is far more competitive than it was ten years ago, only partly due to the economy. Delivering a quality project on time and on budget is no longer a differentiator. Because of the increased competition, margins are even tighter and there is less room for error.

Planning the work more effectively through the use of BIM helps to mitigate the risk associated with our business and offers new opportunities to differentiate ourselves from the competition."

- Increasing complexity in buildings, building systems, team makeup, processes, and technology.

- Inefficiencies inherent to the design and construction process. A desire for less waste and improved efficiencies.

- The demand by owners for fewer conflicts, less resistance, and a reduction in adversarial relations.

- More job satisfaction.

- Addressing stringent energy, security, and other project requirements and goals.

Better results, lower cost, fewer claims, and reduced timelines. And improved information sharing and communication: "A NIST study calculated a yearly loss of $15.8 billion dollars in the construction industry due to a lack of information sharing and process continuity."[6] (See Figure 5.4.)

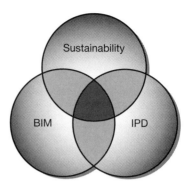

Figure 5.4   Integrated design occurs at the intersection of BIM, IPD, and sustainability.

Who and what drives the process is another matter. Who drives integrated design and is most frequently behind all of these drivers is the owner. When Howard W. Ashcraft Jr., a fellow of the American College of Construction Lawyers, was asked: *Can the IPD process work without a committed owner?* He responded:

No. It is designed to have an owner who is intimately involved with the project. If you go back to Construction Industry Institute

Challenges to Practice: Drivers for IPD

What are the industry issues that are fueling the integrated project delivery trend? A convergence of forces seems to be moving the AEC industry in the direction of integration—based on economics, productivity, and nature of current owner design requirements. These issues include the following:

- A shift toward globalized work processes: The building product supply chain is becoming heavily globalized,

making cost predictions more complex and demand for building materials more unpredictable. Outsourcing and shifting demographics are globalizing the workforce as well—fueling the need for new competencies relating to collaborative processes while simultaneously creating a new set of potential competitors worldwide.

- The need for increased productivity and low margins: Declining construction productivity is diminishing the ability to execute building projects reliably and profitably—and studies, most will indicate that the owner is the biggest factor in project success. Getting an owner who is active is a major thing, for IPD but also for delivering a better project overall.[7]

All in all, it is best to consider owner-driven integrated design a top-down process, while one that does not require the owner to drive the process could be considered bottom-up.

Prerequisites for Integrated Design

Prerequisites for successful integrated design include the following:

- Cooperation on the part of all team members and stakeholders.

- Trust—unconditionally, from the start.

- Sharing information with a goal of total transparency.

- Mutual risk and reward.

- Emotional and social intelligence, including managing destructive emotions and negotiating team dynamics.

- Monitoring organizational behavior.

Tenets of Integrated Design

> Keep it simple and keep it real.
> —Finith A. Jernigan, "BIG BIM, little bim"

More design time means less construction time.

Sometimes short phrases are easier to grasp and recall later—when you need them—than either lengthy testimonials or involved explanations. They represent the essence of integrated design.

Here are a few others to have in your arsenal when the opportunity arises:

- Less construction time results in less cost.

- All parties work together for the good of the project.

---

is frustrating the demand for more controlled building outcomes.

- The demand for sustainability: Sustainable building design hinges on the ability to gain insight into construction outcomes through analysis, prediction, and optimization of the design to lower environmental impact through reduced energy consumption, smaller carbon footprint, and the use of fresh water. As a result, sustainable building standards are expanding and evolving to address performance-based assessments that encompass a building's entire lifecycle.

- The increasing complexity of buildings themselves: Building projects themselves are increasingly complex endeavors, driven by ever more dramatic building forms, complicated supply chains, new project delivery standards, regulatory restrictions, project interactions amongst large teams of project specialists, and owner demands.

Source: Autodesk whitepaper, "Improving Building Industry Results through Integrated Project Delivery and Building Information Modeling," Autodesk, 2008.

- The project comes first.

- Results before ego.

Here are a few concepts to keep in mind when first starting out in integrated design:

- Architects must learn to become comfortable with some risk, and must move in the direction of accepting some risk every day if they are to thrive in this environment.

- Architects will have to become comfortable sharing the design role with others.

- An executive party functioning as the project's default board of directors—including, at minimum, the owner, architect, and contractor—makes decisions by consensus, not command.

- There are no *untils*.

Integrated design is a nonlinear process. In past delivery methods, where the electrical engineer balked at showing conduit below grade *until* caissons were located, with integrated design, there are no *untils*. Integrated design is coordinated because it operates—and decisions are made—simultaneous with others.

Architects have always designed in a nonlinear manner. The design process itself is integrated—however diagrammatic the process was taught, no architect can afford to design in a linear fashion. Design architects have to keep all the balls in the air for as long as possible—whether designing a house or high-rise—attending to building orientation and siting, budget, political interests, code requirements, firm orientation, style preferences, client's inclinations, elevator number and location, all of which must coordinate with roof penetrations above and parking below.

Breaking Integrated Design Down to Its Constituent Parts

To begin to understand the components of integrated design, you must first identify the basic principles of integrated project delivery. The basic principles of integrated project delivery are

1. Mutual respect and trust

2. Mutual benefit and reward

3. Collaborative innovation and decision making

4. Early involvement of key participants

5. Early goal definition

6. Intensified planning

7. Open communication

8. Appropriate technology

9. Organization and leadership

Again, these are the basic principles—self-evident and hard to argue with. Beyond these basic principles of IPD are basic principles of integrated design, decision-making protocols, and overall project objectives determined and agreed to early in the design process. Involvement of key participants—including stakeholders and design professionals—needs to occur early on, when they can have the greatest impact to deliver the most efficient building.

While contracts remain a necessary part of the process, they are a last step to something that is first and foremost relational in nature: trust is built prior to drafting contracts that serve to make official the already inherent relationship of team members (see Figure 5.5).

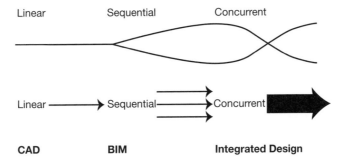

Figure 5.5   Moving toward a project team workflow—one that supports collaboration in BIM and integrated design.

Open and *enhanced* communication: communication by all team members—no matter their location or position—must be easy to access and use. "Increasing communication is important to get information directly flowing in both directions. Decision making takes it to a whole different level, because in IPD we're asking people to assume certain risks: scheduling costs, quality, etc. It's difficult to do that without giving people control over that risk, and that means joint decision making."[8] Whereas BIM team selection relies more on prior BIM experience than on relationships, integrated design agreements arise out of preexisting business relationships based on mutual experience, familiarity, and trust.

Some additional recommendations:

- Establish the owner, architect, and contractor as the heart of the core team; this eliminates the traditional roles of design architect and architect of record. In the integrated design process, while working in BIM, the architect's role shifts from exclusively that of design originator and independent expert to strategic orchestrator of data, information, knowledge, and work processes.

- Make not technology, but the appropriate use of available technology, your goal.

- Optimize effectiveness and efficiency throughout the project lifecycle.

- Keep the team intact from project conception through construction (and beyond).

- Align each team participant's incentives with overall project outcomes and success.

- Aim for continuous process improvement.

- Select team members who express a willingness to collaborate and share project information.

Expected Results from Integrated Design

Why collaborate? Why not go about doing things the way you've always done them? Besides the fact that the old way didn't deliver the results that were expected by building owners, working collaboratively in integrated design

- Increases the likelihood that the owner's project goals will be met.

- Optimizes the schedule and project time frame, eliminating schedule waste and time overruns.

- Lowers project costs through schedule optimization and systems coordination, reducing changes made in the field and eliminating the need for rework when costliest and most prone to error.

- Improves delivered project quality due to shared goals, especially with trades.

- Streamlines sharing of information between design and construction.

- Increases team communication, collaboration, and cohesion.

- Provides for input and information to be exchanged when most effective to do so.

- Increases productivity of the design and construction team, providing the right and best information when it is needed.

- Mitigates conflicts and eliminates adversarial relations between architect, contractor, and owner.

- Creates a safer jobsite through better understanding of workflow by all.

- Integrates building components into a synthetic whole.

Goals of Integrated Design

Overall project goals

Accessibility goals

Aesthetic goals

Cost-effectiveness goals

Functionality goals

Renovation/restoration/preservation goals

Productivity goals

Security goals

Sustainability goals

Perhaps most important, the combination of BIM and integrated design results in the likelihood of achieving a high-performance building, a goal shared by most project stakeholders and team members. Fortunately, BIM enables the process—integrated design—that will get you there, for high-performance building design is created through an integrated design process.

Many claim that the single most important aspect of green building is integrated design, the interactive process of bringing together all the right team members at the right times to address the right questions. This fundamentally differs from the conventional approach, in which the architect first creates a concept and then asks consultants to work with (or around) it, resulting in familiar horror stories about engineers shoehorning equipment into impossibly tight spaces. Truly changing the process means more than just letting more people join the conversation; it demands that architects fundamentally alter their role. But giving up control goes against everything architects are taught.[9]

Overcoming Impediments to Integrated Design

The owner has requested or required integrated design. *What now?*

Work with people you know. To reiterate, whereas with BIM it is more important that those you team with are familiar and comfortable working with the technology, with integrated design it is more important that you trust team members and work with those you know. *How you go about reconciling these two seemingly contradictory inputs will go a long way to determining your success in the process.* (See Figure 5.6.)

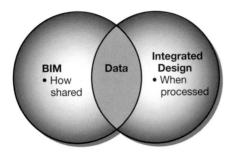

Figure 5.6 BIM changes how data is shared. Integrated design changes when data is processed.

Professionals in the building and construction industry have been slow to jump on the integrated design bandwagon. Why? What are the obstacles?

- Communication. Start with a design charrette.

- Potential liability for use of the information in your model.

- Define metrics for quantity, cost, quality, and timeliness of the work.

- Transparency—your comfort level with working open-book and baring all to team members.

- Working at cost for the length of the project—until potential profits, if any, are divvied up at project completion. Initial work up front is usually undertaken at cost and pays for itself in the end—that is, *if* the project moves forward (the nature of go/no-go projects) a risk some developers aren't willing to take.

- Hammering out an unfamiliar contract starting on day one—in lieu of working on a project design while the attorneys volley the contract back and forth, signing off just prior to issuing permit documents.

- The acceptance by designers of an unfamiliar standard of care.

- Leaving behind the long history of comfortable and familiar adversarial relations to act in a more enlightened, and thus challenging, way.

- Collaboration itself—working cooperatively with others on the team—is an obstacle, in that while most have worked on teams, few know what it means to truly collaborate, much less to be *required* to do so. It is well and good that one is expected to collaborate—but when in a design professional's training or a constructor's experience does one learn to do so?

- Likewise for trust: you are told to trust, but how is this accomplished? New roles serve to threaten our identity, especially after so many years of adversarial relations.

- Sharing information, interoperability, and maintaining transparency.

- Liability and responsibility.

When Howard W. Ashcraft Jr. was asked, "Is the U.S. legal system ready for IPD and BIM?" he responded by saying,

> The contracts are still evolving. We need to get the contracts optimized for use in BIM and IPD, and that will take care of the legal structure. There are some subsidiary issues having to do with professional licensing, third-party liability, and insurance that have not yet been nailed down, but I don't think those are huge impediments to adoption of IPD. The bigger impediment is that people have been used to doing things, in terms of contractual relationships, a given way for a long time. They have to unlearn a lot.[10]

When asked, "Do architects and engineers need to 'own' their risk more often?" Ashcraft noted,

> The needle has swung too far in the direction of insulating oneself from liability and separating oneself from the other parties in the construction process. That really has not been a

Integrated Design and Systems Thinking

In integrated design, buildings aren't seen as one-off, independent entities made up of separate building systems and isolated from their surroundings—but instead as part of a holistic process, an interdependent, living part of the environment into which it is placed and belongs.

The ultimate goal is for all the systems to work harmoniously, effectively, and synergistically—where each is made stronger and not in any way compromised by the presence of the others.

Decisions are made in reference to flows—having consequences that impact both upstream and downstream.

successful strategy. The needle needs to swing more toward accepting responsibility for the entire process and making sure that the bad events—cost overruns, failures, and the like—don't occur.[11]

BIM and Integrated Design FAQs

Q: Why integrated design? Why not integrated project delivery (IPD)? What is the difference?

A: Think of integrated design as the larger, enveloping category—including IPD contracts and delivery method but also workflow, social intelligence, mindset. IPD, with its emphasis on contracts and contractual relationships, is a subset of integrated design, which encompasses accountability of team members and workflow issues.

Q: What is meant by "integrated?"

A: Earlier processes were linear. Instead of being integrated, decisions were made inefficiently, in sequence. See the definition earlier in this chapter.

Q: How does integrated design differ from design-build?

A: Design-build is most often contractor-led and sometimes architect-led, while the integrated design core team is represented by the owner, architect, and contractor.

Q: Can you do BIM without integrated design? And can you do integrated design without BIM?

A: You can do one without the other, but BIM enables integrated design and therefore makes it possible.

Q: Does integrated design mean a return to the role of master builder?

A: Yes and no. Yes, in that the entire team—including the core members, engineers, subcontractors, and fabricators—together form a master builder unit. No, in that there is no one person on the integrated design team that plays this role. (More on this in the next chapter.)

Q: What gets integrated in integrated design?

A: People—their talents and insights, systems, business structures, and practices. Elsewhere, "integrative" design is sometimes used by others to connote an ongoing process that is never resolved. While integrated design focuses on the process, there is never any doubt that the end result is a design that integrates the input of all stakeholders, team members, and technologies.

Q: Who benefits from integrated design?

A: There's a perception that all sacrifice for the owner—that the owner has the most to gain, then the contractor, and lastly—if at all—the architect and others on the design team. In fact, given time, trust, transparency, and not a little effort on everybody's part, all benefit. The more who participate, the more who benefit—and the more benefits there are. With integrated design, the focus is on the owner—the owner's needs—and the end result, the completed building, optimized for greater value and reduced waste.

Q: At what cost?

A: Architects have to give up a bit of freedom, in that they are sharing their design role and responsibility with others. Everybody gives up a little by playing not only their role but to some extent that of others, insofar as they are willing and able to see the project—and make decisions—through other's eyes and priorities. If they are able to do this, then there is not only no cost but a great deal to gain.

Q: What relationship does integrated design have to sustainability?

A: The integrated design process increases the likelihood of a sustainable outcome for the project. Because the stakeholders are together from the earliest project stages, decisions can be made—from siting and orientation of the building to the specification of green components—in a proactive and coordinated manner. The integrated design process provides strategies to achieve sustainable building design through early intervention and the bottom-up consideration by stakeholders in how the orientation and siting, building program and design, materials and systems, and components and products of a building impact each other. In lieu of engaging sustainability specialists working independently, integrated design implies a holistic, collaborative approach engaging the insights and experiences of all teammates.

Q: Which party stands to benefit the most from integrated design?

A: While all stand to gain from working in integrated design, the owner usually stands to benefit the most financially, then the contractor, with the architect last. But architects also have other, more intrinsic ways to benefit from the process, which helps to balance things out.

Q: Which party is most at risk working in integrated design?

A: All parties are potentially exposed to new risks in multiparty agreements—but all parties also share in these risks.

Q: Why integrated design? What's driving the change in the industry and, by association, the profession?

A: Evolving technology is one driver. In a word? Waste. Owner's demand for better quality, less time, and lower cost (perfect, now, and free) services and construction.

Q: Isn't BIM alone enough to handle that you don't have to pile on it other demands? By introducing integrated design, doesn't it make it more complicated than it needs to be?

A: The integrated design process simplifies and streamlines working relations and decision making by removing the traditional roadblocks and obstacles to a successful outcome for all. In order to create a more coordinated and complete project in less time and for less cost, integrated design becomes the shortest distance between the two points of conception and completion.

Case Study Interview with Andy Stapleton and Peter Rumpf, Mortenson Construction

Andy Stapleton, director of project development at Mortenson Construction, helps lead Mortenson's effort in the development of virtual design and construction (VDC) and building information modeling.

Peter Rumpf, integrated construction manager at Mortenson Construction, is a licensed architect and frequent speaker at industry events. Peter leverages BIM and VDC for the advancement of technology in construction.

What are some of the firm-culture differences you've had to face working with others from other disciplines?

Andy Stapleton (AS): Mortenson is a builder whose core principles are based on collaboration and teamwork. The use of VDC in our company was a natural fit. Not every firm has those same principles at its core. Breaking down those barriers and fostering relationships based on teamwork has been a cultural difference we have dealt with over the years.

Peter Rumpf (PR): Mortenson has been using this technology for a long time, and therefore we understand its value. When working with companies that have not experienced the benefits firsthand, there can be some hesitation or reluctance to use the technology. Many people are afraid of changing the processes that they have used for decades. They understand the risks of doing things the old way. Part of our job is to convince them the risks will decrease with the proper use of this technology.

What does it mean to be a contractor today? How does it differ from even ten years ago? What would you advise someone thinking of going into the field?

AS: The market is far more competitive that it was ten years ago, only partly due to the economy. Delivering a quality project on time and on budget is no longer a differentiator. Because of the increased competition, margins are even tighter and there is less room for error. Planning the work more effectively through the use of BIM helps to mitigate the risk associated with our business and offers new opportunities to differentiate ourselves from the competition. For someone considering entering the field I would tell them that it is extremely competitive. The fees are very tight—you really have to be on your game.

PR: BIM and VDC are truly a sea change to the industry. Clearly we are just at the beginning of the sea change, but I do not think it is an overstatement to say these technologies will revolutionize the way that buildings are built.

As a pioneer of model-based construction and virtual design and construction—VDC—Mortenson virtually does it all: design, construct, fabricate, envision. Can you imagine a future without the need for architects?

PR: As an architect, I would have to say I don't envision a world without architects. Mortenson, as a construction company, is a builder through and through. We're very good at leveraging technology to communicate the project's design intent to all stakeholders—but we don't want to define what that design intent is on any given project. It's a question of where our core competency resides. We have a number of architects on staff whose role is to integrate the process, not eliminate or replace design partners. (See Figure 5.7.)

AS: When we work in design-build, we hire an outside architect to perform the role of designer. One of the reasons I see the value in design-build is because we have the in-house expertise to manage the overall process. Mortenson in that situation is the contract holder with the owner as the design-builder, so we have a lot at risk. But then we assign certain parts of that risk to the appropriate members of the project team that are best qualified to carry the risk. This includes design firms and key subcontractors who are integrated in the project early on. If we tried to do everything in-house we'd lose some of the checks and balances and the value that brings. We reach out to find the best designers for each project type we build.

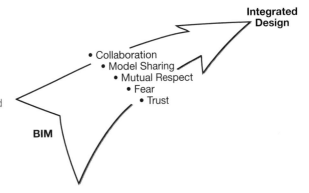

Figure 5.7   What stands in the way of moving your practice from BIM to integrated design?

There are many things you've had to learn to get to where you are. In order to work in the current technological—and perhaps economic—environment, are there things you've had to unlearn?

AS: Those firms who had not previously focused on collaborative relationships may have had to unlearn their ways. Mortenson has not found itself in this position. We've built some of the more complicated structures in the country. By nature we're founded on that quiet competency or can-do attitude where we say, *there must be a way to build it and we're going to find a way to build it*. It's in our best interest to find a solution and to do that together.

> *Those firms who had not previously focused on collaborative relationships may have had to unlearn their ways. Mortenson has not found itself in this position.*
> —Andy Stapleton

On any given day, what percentage of the issues you face are people problems or people issues—as opposed to technological or business issues? Have you seen a change over time?

AS: While it's an interesting question, I don't believe you can separate the two issues. Even when you have a technical problem, more often than not the technical problems arise from miscommunication between people: file formats, due dates, coordination of services, responsibility for tasks, etc. As a general rule, I would say that 80 percent of the issues are communication issues or technical issues that arose from miscommunication, and 20 percent of the issues are strictly technical issues without any associated people problems or people issues.

PR: This has been pretty consistent over time. BIM helps reduce miscommunication—it improves communication.

Beyond communication, are there any other people issues you've seen brought about by these changes?

AS: Because the technology is relatively new, one of the challenges we have is a lot of the people who have risen in the industry prior to the advent of BIM may not be exposed to BIM or comfortable with it—in a lot of cases there's resistance.

PR: I think acceptance and understanding of the technology is getting better and better. Massive communication efforts have been made in the industry, by McGraw-Hill, by Mortenson—giving presentations, trying to reach the general public. Still, there's

(Continued)

hesitancy by some people in the industry who are afraid of what they don't know. I would hear again and again, *prove to me the value*. It's nice to see a 4D model—*tell me it's going to make me money*. Show me the numbers that prove what you're telling me. Until we started measuring and demonstrating the value, and the McGraw-Hill report *The Business Value of BIM* came out, we didn't have a lot of objective data to verify the value.

Mortenson has partnered with McGraw-Hill, Autodesk—even, in a prize-winning collaboration, with Skidmore, Owings and Merrill LLP—on the "CANtilever with Souper Graphics" sculpture. What is your secret to successfully collaborating with others?

AS: Communication is key to any successful collaboration. Mortenson is very good at leveraging the latest technology to better communicate with our project team members.

How would you describe the most important attitudes and/or mindsets for team members to acquire and/or cultivate working in BIM and integrated design?

AS: The most important attitude is "Can do!" and a mindset that we are involved in a movement far larger than any specific task at hand. We might be stumbling over a couple of blocks here, but realize the long-term benefits to the company, the industry, are worth it. Realize that there's some real change that can take place, some real benefit.

PR: The construction industry has a reputation for being very conservative and risk-averse. Until the project team members understand how the new technology works and how it will benefit the entire project team, full collaboration and full commitment to new processes are difficult. Those that view BIM or VDC as just another contractual requirement to be "dealt" with miss the true value of VDC. The projects that will experience the greatest benefit from VDC are the ones that are willing to try new things. We want a team that is willing to innovate, to think outside of the box.

Breaking free of the silos of information between the architect, engineers, and builders that were common place in the industry for many years can be a challenge. Trust amongst team members is critical to a successful project. (See Figure 5.8.)

Figure 5.8   In terms of owners' expectations, all pieces of the puzzle are expected to be in place.

Is there anything, from a mindset standpoint, that you've had to change in yourselves to adapt to this new BIM and integrated design environment?

AS: Peter and I have both had to cross the fence and come over to each other's side a bit more. I've had to let Peter into the coordination side of things to ensure that he understands what I'm doing. Just because it may look easy to do in the model, it may not necessarily be the way we do it in the field. There's got to be give and take on both sides.

PR: Because I now have the contractor's perspective, this technology has better defined for me the roles and responsibilities of an architect. If I were to ever practice architecture again I will be a much better architect than had I not worked for a builder. I now understand what's important, what's not important from a documentation standpoint to a degree I could never have gotten to had I stayed on the architecture side of the table.

Is it possible for students to learn this in school—or the school of hard knocks?

PR: A very good architectural practice professor would be able to accomplish a lot of it. That said, where I learned the most was when I was creating drawings for the actual person who was pouring the concrete.

> *Where I learned the most was when I was creating drawings for the actual person who was pouring the concrete.*
>
> —Peter Rumpf

AS: Even the best professor or the best school program cannot replace the sense of urgency and stress you work under in a real-life situation. Someone could be incredibly proactive and perceptive as to what the needs are in the field. I still encourage schools to do all these things, but until you know you're liable, it's still theoretical. You got a B instead of an A, you didn't just cost somebody a million dollars.

Mortenson Construction has worked on over one hundred integrated practice projects—more than any other construction firm. What are some of your key takeaways? What advice do you have for others working in an integrated design environment?

PR: The tools provided through the use of VDC allow project teams to communicate in new ways. Using Navisworks and GoToMeeting, project teams can solve problems much faster. I would advise an integrated design team to make sure all team members (architect, engineers, builders, and owner) understand the technology and use it.

Mortenson has experienced improved collaboration with design partners and subcontractors on their projects. What are some of the other social benefits of BIM that you've experienced, as opposed to technical or business benefits of utilizing BIM?

AS: I believe that BIM has increased the mutual respect that the team members have for one another. Builders learn to appreciate the challenges design teams have when attempting to coordinate and complete a design prior to having all of the team members on board. Designers come to respect the level of detail and complexity involved with actually constructing a design in the real world.

PR: One unforeseen social benefit is the use of 4D models during public affairs events. 4D models are an excellent communication tool with owners and with the general public. We have used 4D models at "town hall" meetings with concerned residents to explain complex projects and how they will impact the community.

You make use of social networking sites, including YouTube and LinkedIn. Anyone can watch one of your contractors at a hospital construction site describing the project vision—or a project manager lead the press on a tour of the new Minnesota Twins stadium under construction. Peter has given talks at McGraw-Hill events. Have you found that BIM and integrated design—technology and process—have required you to be more extraverted, social, and communicative than you had to be in the past? Does it make certain demands on you that are new to your role and professional identity?

AS: Definitely. As I mentioned, Mortenson has a quiet competency—in this day and age, quiet doesn't cut it. We used to say our work speaks for itself. Now we have to make sure we're out there as much as anyone else—in fact, more than anyone else because we're the leaders in the industry.

(Continued)

PR: The role of BIM manager did not exist at all in the industry five years ago. This position demands excellent communication skills. Often the integrated construction manager has to work with all project team members, from construction executives to labor foremen, which requires a variety of communication skills. One aspect of the BIM manager position is *technology evangelist*. The ability to objectively discuss the risk/reward aspects of the use of the new technology is a very important and difficult skill for BIM managers to acquire.

> *One aspect of the BIM manager position is* technology evangelist. *The ability to objectively discuss the risk/reward aspects of the use of the new technology is a very important and difficult skill for BIM managers to acquire.*
>
> —Peter Rumpf

Would you describe your roles today as less about building buildings and more about helping people understand what is involved in the construction—requiring seeing the big picture and synthesizing a great deal of information from many disciplines, a role perhaps architects used to have?

AS: I don't think the two are mutually exclusive. Because we are brought in early to the process, it is about communicating the design intent. Helping the customer understand that is so fundamental to our building the project. Often, the questions we have about constructing the building are tied to understanding the design intent. Constructing buildings is all about communicating with people across multiple disciplines to focus our energy toward a common goal of erecting structures for society. I think this is a role that all project leaders have. Sometimes you find the most dynamic leaders are on the architectural side, and sometimes they are on the construction side. The best communicator is quite often the most effective leader.

How would you describe the leadership role in an IPD project? Who is normally in charge? Is it conventionally with client or owner in lead? Would you ever describe the team as center-less, where the team leads itself?

AS: The leadership role in an IPD project will vary by project and project delivery type. Our focus is more on the process and less on the contract type. In a design-build delivery method, which is very much an IPD process, the project executive for the design-builder would be the leader for the project. There are some contractual IPD projects that are neither integrated nor collaborative. While an executive team can be appointed to oversee a project, there will always need to be a point person to lead the overall process. This person may report to the executive team. I have never seen a center-less project work very effectively. Ultimately, you need to have a single point of contact.

PR: On the technological side, the leadership role in an IPD project should be the model manager. That role changes from design-intent model manager (BIM model manager), where the lead point is the architect of record, to the construction/fabrication model, where the model manager on the build side becomes that point person. Typically, the model manager has the responsibility of bridging between the design model and the fabrication model. For a true IPD project, the architect, owner, and contractor have to work in concert. Each maintains their base responsibilities, but everyone works together to make sure all aspects of the project are a success.

BIM forces architects to access their inner contractors—to think more like contractors from the early phases. Would you say the same for contractors—that BIM encourages contractors to think more like an architect? Or was that always the case?

AS: BIM/VDC forces both architects and contractors to deal with construction realities. It has forced architects to think more like contractors than contractors to think more like architects. It has increased the practical awareness of construction. It hasn't forced contractors to participate in the aesthetic aspects of design. That's not to say that isn't the next step. I can see it eventually heading down that path.

When the project team can evaluate a true digital prototype for an entire building, everything has to be considered. In the past, a large part of a project was figured out in the field. Today it is possible to create a digital prototype of virtually an entire project, which forces both architects and contractors to consider many more situations than a typical 2D paper documentation effort would allow.

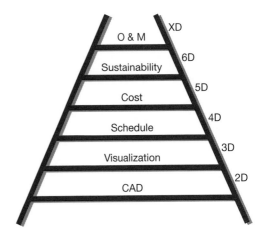

Figure 5.9   Climbing the BIM ladder. How can you make the model work for you on multiple levels?

PR: Because communication is so much better due to improved project visualization, we as builders are able to achieve closer to what the original design intent was meant to be than before we made this technology change. In the past, design intent wasn't met not because it couldn't be met but because it was misunderstood. Now, with the level of communication and understanding as high as it is due to these technologies, it's a lot easier for us to truly dissect and build to the design intent. (See Figure 5.9.)

Ten years from now, who do you think will be leading the process—architects, contractors, some kind of combination?

AS: Ten years from now we hope the project team evolves toward qualification-based collaboration where architect, engineer, and contractor are selected at the same time as part of a single team based on their qualifications and ability to deliver superior projects.

PR: A super team that's put together to execute a project.

AS: You might not be the same entity—it may not be IPD from the standpoint of creating an LLC. Even though it may be an integrated team, I'd still go to the separate entities for their area of expertise.

Mortenson has received many awards for its work in BIM and integrated design. The Edith Kinney Gaylord Cornerstone Arts Center and Aurora, Colorado, Research Complex II come to mind, among many others. Just as BIM makes architects better architects, do you feel BIM makes you better contractors?

AS: Definitely. VDC gets us to understand the interconnected and coordinated components of the project far more effectively than 2D drawings. 4D also lets us better manage a schedule. As far as quantity take-offs in BIM—as an industry we're still in the

(Continued)

early phases of 5D. Estimating is still more of an art than a science. It's not as objective as everyone would like to think. It's not just about knowing how large or how high or how many corners a masonry wall has, but whether it is being done for a basement, the ground floor, or ten stories up in the air. How to do you get access to it? All these things need to be factored in.

PR: The ability to build a digital prototype allows for a much higher-quality project. (See Figure 5.10.)

It is said that mutual respect, trust, sharing of information—all human factors—are critical for successful integrated design. Others have said if necessary, you just force everyone to conform. IPD can be idealistic—it can be tough getting everyone to cooperate. Do you sometimes have to resort to force?

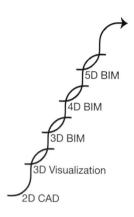

Figure 5.10   Progress in BIM and integrated design can be seen as a succession of sigmoid curves.

AS: All of the factors you note above are critical for any project. Mortenson maintains IPD is a process independent of contractual delivery method. CM at risk and design-build delivery methods can both successfully serve as IPD contracts. The key is to have respect, trust, and commonality of purpose. At the end of the day, yes, sometimes we do need to resort to contractual language or "force" for the good of the overall project. That is even more dangerous with VDC. When everyone participates in the modeling process, you truly are only as successful as your weakest link: the team member that inputs information flat-out incorrectly, or is behind in the schedule, or keeps changing their input—in all of these cases it affects everybody negatively.

PR: On some of our early projects it was commonplace to run into resistance from some of the project team members. However, in almost every situation those that might have resisted the technology at the beginning are enthusiasts by the end.

It is sometimes said that the biggest impediment to a successful collaboration is that the contractor can't trust the architect's model—their data, their information. Would you agree?

AS: No.

PR: Right of reliance on the design models is an issue the industry needs to address, but Mortenson has had very successful IPD projects where the architecture model was created in-house by Mortenson. The ability to rely on the design models allows Mortenson to focus on other areas of the project and leverage the technology in new ways and will increase efficiency.

Right of reliance is a hurdle the industry needs to address. Would I say that it's the biggest impediment to a successful

When everyone participates in the modeling process, you truly are only as successful as your weakest link: the team member that inputs information flat-out incorrectly, or is behind in the schedule, or keeps changing their input—in all of these cases it affects everybody negatively.

—Andy Stapleton

collaboration? No, I would not. I think the value of a BIM that includes a limited right of reliance, reliance on locations of walls, doors, ceilings, windows, et cetera, is much greater than a BIM that does not have a right of reliance. Resolution of this issue is part of the evolution of VDC. I also think informed owners would be willing to pay for the added time it takes to create a BIM that has a right of reliance.

If you are the BIM manager, how do you make sure all of the trades are doing what they are supposed to do for the BIM?

PR: Managing the master coordination model is very challenging. All trades need to model their scopes of work, including hangers and access zones to all of their equipment. The entire project team (superintendent, project engineer, quality engineer, VDC manager) all share in the responsibility of ensuring the model is complete.

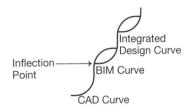

Figure 5.11 Successive sigmoid curves. The secret to continual growth is to start on a new curve before the current curve comes to an end. How do you know when an inflection point occurs?

It is sometimes said architects want one thing—design excellence, control—and contractors another—make a profit, get in and out—and the idea of their collaborating is unlikely at best. What are your thoughts on this?

AS: We feel both architects and contractors want a satisfied customer more than anything else. We also feel that a successful project is both beautifully executed and profitable. (See Figure 5.11.)

Architects were the early adopters of BIM technology. More recently, contractors have been picking it up. What do you make of the construction industry's current interest in BIM? Do you feel it is mainly due to the fact that contractors have the most to gain from the technology? Is it because contractors have the resources to acquire these tools? Or is it something else?

AS: Mortenson has been using VDC since 1999. Over the years we have come to understand that using BIM improves our bottom line, and we plan for it accordingly in our proposals. I believe that architects have a lot to gain from VDC (less RFIs, minimal redesign due to misinformed client needs, lower CA costs, etc.), but they are still struggling to identify and quantify these benefits. Contractors have adopted the new technology because the tools allow us to build better, faster, and safer. Adding information to the model helps the contractor better understand risk, and ideally helps the contractor save money. Most importantly, VDC allows all of us to provide a better experience and facility for our customers.

PR: Do I think builders have more to gain from BIM? Yes, I do. The more time an architect spends in a BIM model, the less money they make. Architects are paid to document design intent as quickly as possible. The more time a builder spends in a model, the more value we can extract from it and potentially the better the facility we can provide for our customers.

AS: To me, visualization benefits the architect in working with end users and clients because it streamlines the review process so that architects aren't spending as much time in front of the computer remodeling it per the owner's remarks. If architects can help those who otherwise can't read plans and documents speed up their understanding and the review process, this is where there is a lot of value for the architect. This is where I see a potential opportunity for the architect.

Case Study Interview with Jonathan Cohen, FAIA, Architect and Author

Jonathan Cohen, FAIA, is an architect, vice president at Brookwood Group, and author of Communication and Design with the Internet: A Guide for Architects, Planners and Building Professionals *(Norton, 2000) and* Integrated Project Delivery: Six Case Studies *(Mc-Graw-Hill). Jonathan is a past chair of the Integrated Practice Steering Committee of the AIA California Council.*

Do you recall what your first exposure was to integrated project delivery—and what your reaction was?

Jonathan Cohen (JC): A group of us were theorizing about this quite a while ago, when we looked at the radical transformation of manufacturing with technology and started wondering how that process and technology might be applied to construction. We first started to look at this in the late 1990s. We didn't have a wholly formed idea of it or the term *integrated project delivery* yet. I was invited onto the AIA California Council integrated project delivery task force and served as chair of the AIACC IPD 2007 committee. There was a group of thought leaders in the industry who were kicking the ideas around. One important group to be acknowledged is the lean construction—as well as the Toyota manufacturing system. That's not the whole IPD process—but it's an important forerunner. The 2010 case studies are the first opportunity I have had to learn about completed IPD projects, and consider it a validation of some of our early thinking.

Do you see your involvement with integrated design as something that grew out of your earlier focus on IT? How, if at all, are they related?

JC: Yes, certainly. It started with IT, but I was never interested in technology for its own sake. I was always looking for its application for architectural practice and the building industry. I saw two transformative technologies, one being the Internet and the other being BIM. They don't solve the problem, but they point out just how disconnected and fragmented our current system of designing and building is. I knew that both of them would be key enablers of process change, but in and of themselves they don't really do anything. Designing and building have always been a group undertaking involving a lot of people, so communication is always important. We have these great tools—why aren't we using them to cure the fundamental problems facing our industry? It starts with IPD, but it certainly doesn't end there. I would underscore that BIM does not equal IPD, even though the software vendors would like you to think so. One is a tool, and the other is a process. BIM can support IPD, but I know of a lot of design firms that are using BIM just for internal use, with no sharing. (See Figure 5.12. Note: The accompanying figures are for illustrative purposes and do not represent the work of the interviewee.)

What role—from what you could learn from your observations of the integrated design teams—did force play in getting everyone to cooperate? Do you believe integrated design could work without the contractual agreement? Or would human nature get in the way?

JC: In terms of the project teams, I didn't really see any force or coercion. I do think these things have to be carefully planned and set down in writing. There has to be the commercial alignment of the parties. Because in the typical old-fashioned design-bid-build process, everyone's goals are not in alignment, leading to information hoarding and all kinds of behavior that doesn't contribute to the success of the project. People are not going to be incentivized to do anything that is contrary to the overall project good. That may sound utopian, but this is not a handshake thing at all. It does require an agreement. It requires financial transparency and open books: trust and verify. It's not holding hands and singing "Kumbaya."

Figure 5.12   "Advanced collaboration rooms"—rooms within their many offices dedicated for use of collaboration technologies—allow HOK employees to bring their best creative minds together. Photo courtesy of HOK

It's setting up the roles and relationships, incentives, and aligning commercial goals. The single most important thing is to make it project-centered.

When we were looking at how manufacturing transformed itself—it had to because there was global competition. They didn't do it just for the fun of it. They needed to survive. What's fundamentally different between manufacturing and construction is that in manufacturing you have a central management. You have a design department, a production department, a marketing department—but they're being centrally directed. Individuals have different roles to play and things to accomplish, but somebody's directing the whole process. Since you don't have that in construction, what can you do to substitute for that? This collaborative three-legged-stool setup does exactly that. It takes the place of the central management that you would have in a manufacturing process.

Some see integrated design requiring one to "gamble on the other guy not screwing up." What might be another, more helpful or productive way you might suggest that they look at the situation or opportunity?

JC: It's not a gamble; it's the opposite. There's less risk because there's more transparency. That gives everyone more control. From an architect's point of view, you're not gambling on the other guy not screwing up. You're helping the other guy not to screw up. And he's helping you not to screw up. Instead of looking at your drawings and looking for change orders,

> *From an architect's point of view, you're not gambling on the other guy not screwing up. You're helping the other guy not to screw up. And he's helping you not to screw up.*
>
> —Jonathan Cohen, FAIA

(Continued)

he's looking for things that need to be corrected, so all can benefit. In a design-bid-build project you don't even know who the builder is going to be. That's a huge gamble—you're really rolling the dice there. So I see this as reducing risk and making it less of a gamble.

Our recent case studies were important because they examine real projects after they are completed. Many of the participants felt that the risk is better understood—and therefore there is less of it. The risk of doing something new as a reaction to change is psychological. With IPD—at least where it is now—teams should be self-selected on the basis of trust, previous relationships, and projects. Architects and builders should also be working to figure out how they are going to work together. The way to reduce the real or perceived risk is by becoming proactive and forming alliances before you get the project, then to be able to come in as a team and show an owner that you have already worked out how you're going to work together. That will be a huge selling point. With BIM there's a need to know whom you are exchanging information with and how you're going to do that, that you are BIM-compatible. With IPD, the relationship is an important determinant of success.

Through your work—and reporting on integrated design—you have had as much exposure, if not more, to this new delivery method in action. How would you describe integrated design's current state: robust, healthy, wait-and-see, or on life support? Why?

JC: Very robust, especially in health care. There is a lot of inertia to overcome in the industry, especially among owners. IPD has to be driven by the owners because they are the principal beneficiaries. Builders and architects are secondary beneficiaries. These case studies and others are a proof of concept. It is just going to be a slow process of owners looking around at their competitors. What's happening in health care is that other competitors are looking at Sutter [i.e., Sutter Medical Foundation Medical Office Building, Fairfield, CA], and they are seeing the great success that they're having. A comparable project using design-bid-build is not doing as well. So within health care I see it spreading from Sutter to other healthcare providers, and that's going to happen in other areas. IPD is ideal for institutional owner-operators, so the next series of projects might be in higher education and scientific laboratories. (See Figure 5.13.)

IPD supports the idea of nimble teams that are able to react to change. Even though healthcare projects take a long time and are heavily regulated, nobody wants to open a hospital that doesn't have the latest in technology and latest in thinking. One example is the St. Clair project. They changed patient rooms from back-to-back to same-handed while steel was being erected—an incredibly late, major change. The IPD team was incentivized to react to that much faster than a traditional team would have. Traditionally, the owner wants to make a late change; the builder starts rubbing his hands, thinking juicy change-order; the actual designers are long ago dispersed onto other projects; and there's no incentive to move rapidly or completely. IPD lends itself quite well to complex projects that are likely to have late changes. If it works in health care, it ought to work in a variety of projects.

Those that work in the AEC industry are primarily conservative and risk-averse when it comes to money, their business, and learning new technologies. The construction industry is conservative to begin with and in an economic down-turn is all the more conservative, falling back on traditional methods for project delivery. What role, if any—positive or negative—do you see the economy playing in the adoption of integrated design by the AECO industry?

JC: With fewer projects being built, the pace of innovation is going to slow. I have heard anecdotally, "Let's go out to bid because we can get low bids now." That might be a false economy because when you look at the process, IPD enables owners

Figure 5.13   HOK's collaboration tools are used for training sessions and coordination meetings, and to help hundreds of employees around the world collaborate on design. Photo courtesy of HOK

to lock in the lower cost during design rather than waiting until the construction documents are complete. If you want to take advantage of the current environment, you're not giving up anything with IPD. Say with a subcontractor what you're locking in is their fee, which they'll keep as low as possible if they're looking for work. The other hard costs, labor and materials, they are what they are. With open books, if construction costs are low it's because material costs are low and labor costs are perhaps lower. That's true across the board.

In the 2010 report, each integrated design team had its own lessons learned—with some overlapping experiences. What would you say are the one or two major hurdles that integrated design has to overcome to become the go-to delivery method for the industry?

JC: It has to get through and come from the owner organizations. It is a conservative industry. Building is seldom the core business of any enterprise. It is hard to get them to focus and learn. It is just going to be a long, bubbling process working its way through organizations.

Everyone needs to make a living. But historically architects have it drilled into them that they shouldn't be in it for the money—that the rewards, when they come, are more intrinsic. Many would admit that they enter the profession as a higher calling, and money isn't even part of the equation. Integrated design seems to make money a deciding factor in its success. Is this solely due to the fact that the integrated design team has to invest so much time, design energy,

(Continued)

and thought up front, and historically only sees monetary gains in the later phases?

JC: The idea with IPD is that at the beginning, everybody is working at cost with no profit. The profit depends on the successful outcome of the project. What I've heard from architects that have worked on these IPD projects is that they receive a lot of intrinsic satisfaction from a happy owner, a less contentious process, less friction, less yelling at each other in the trailer. They all felt more personally fulfilled, and personal fulfillment is part of what architects want. I think they're going to get it from IPD. Their role in IPD is going to be different. It's really about getting value for the owner. That's what it's about, while getting fairly compensated ourselves. Architecture is still a profession with ideals—that is valid. I hope that doesn't go away. I don't think it will. I do think it is in danger of losing a lot if it is unable to adapt. (See Figure 5.14.)

What are some roles that integrated design teams require that didn't exist even five years ago? Can you describe the role a facilitator plays on an integrated design project?

JC: A facilitator, for one. I do believe there's an unmet role called the IPD facilitator/coordinator. I've actually built a business concept around that, spelling out nine services. Basically, it's a process design, and you're assisting the owner in helping to sell the IPD process internally and externally. You're helping

Figure 5.14   Videoconferencing helps keep multiple offices connected and remotely located employees stay in touch, and helps to cut travel time, expenses, and carbon emissions. Photo courtesy of HOK

in the selection of the team. I haven't seen, in any of the projects I studied, their bringing in an outside person with the exception of people from the Lean Construction Institute, to put on seminars. Someone might have been brought in to evaluate and compare, to benchmark projects with respect to design quality, as in the case of Autodesk. But these aren't what I mean by the facilitator-coordinator role.

Whether this facilitator role is filled in-house or is an outside consultant, it has to be filled. It's very much a possibility that construction managers will claim this role. It has to be an independent party.

The projects I studied all had sophisticated owners. What I have heard from some owners, particularly in the public sector, is that they don't perceive themselves as having the resources to do this. If they don't have the resources in-house, then perhaps they should bring someone in to facilitate. This someone gets involved at the very beginning and even has a hand in criteria for selecting the team. You're helping with establishing a legal framework. You're helping to establish project goals and expectations. This is a very important step that you have to do with IPD. Not just cost and schedule but design quality, operational efficiency, and sustainability goals. These goals would require an independent entity, such as a facilitator-coordinator, to evaluate. These are the goals we'll have to attain to call this a successful project. Any financial incentives are going to be paid as a result of meeting or exceeding these goals.

The challenge comes from the way we're trained. When we go to architecture school we're made to think we're little gods and that it isn't a collaborative process, when in fact it always was.

—Jonathan Cohen, FAIA

Architects—generally introverted by nature—must communicate and collaborate at all times on all projects working in BIM and integrated design. What challenges do you think this will have for the architect, and what recommendations would you make?

JC: The challenge comes from the way we're trained. When we go to architecture school we're made to think we're little gods and that it isn't a collaborative process, when in fact it always was. I hope architectural training changes to emphasize collaboration and teamwork. If you're not willing to share, this isn't going to be a good process for you. I see it as imperative for the profession to survive.

AIA named the collaborative delivery process "integrated project delivery"—IPD. Any signs that it will go by a different identity, especially if another organization or entity takes it up and runs with it?

JC: When you say IPD, people seem to know what you're talking about. Interestingly, the name is copyrighted or trademarked by the Lean Construction Institute.

Architects and contractors have historically had an adversarial relationship. BIM and integrated design require that they not only work together, but that they do so—with the entire team in place—from day one. What will it take for them to get along?

JC: In the projects that I studied, architects and contractors did get along. That was in part because they already knew each other and liked each other. There's an aspect of mutual respect. Architects owe contractors more respect than they give them. One of the most important changes of the past twenty-five years has been the professionalization of construction. These are college-educated professionals. We need them and they need us, and we should respect each other.

How much of a successful experience in integrated design would you say is interoperability and a tight contract, and how much is attitude and mindset of the participants?

JC: I think you have to have both. One of the case studies—the one at Arizona State—they used a standard design-build contract because that is what the City of Phoenix required. The contract did not reflect at all the process that they followed, and that I wouldn't advise anybody to do. It's taking a big risk. In the event of a dispute there would be a lot of things that wouldn't be enforceable.

(Continued)

Integrated design requires greater flexibility, interaction, and a fluid work process involving team members stepping out of familiar roles. What is your impression of those in mid-to-late career learning a new technology such as BIM and also learning to work in a completely different—fast-paced, concurrent, integrated—way than they have been used to?

JC: In terms of the IPD case study projects, a lot of the people—including owners—were quite senior. Certainly the decision-makers and important players were all senior. So I don't think it is the case that older people are less willing to try new things. In some ways they have the self-confidence to try new things. Across the board, this is not a young person's exercise at all. Their experience served them well. Part of being senior is that they have all had bad experiences with the old way of doing business, sometimes really bad, and that became a motivator for trying something new. We already knew that the old process didn't work—we didn't need anyone to convince us otherwise. The only question is: will this new process work?

Your book, *Communication and Design with the Internet: A Guide for Architects, Planners and Building Professionals*, asserts that it's not about computers; it's about communication. Would you say the same about BIM and integrated design?

JC: One is a tool; the other is a process. Computers are a tool for communicating. BIM is a tool for enabling integrated project delivery. It's the process transformation that is the most important, and the adoption of the technology guarantees the process transformation at all.

When you wrote your book, did you anticipate cloud computing?

JC: I write about web-based project teams in the book. Web applications, not just storage in the cloud—at the time we were calling them extranets.

Who today drives integrated design? Is it the owner? And do you anticipate this will change over time?

JC: It has to be driven by the owner—they have to be prepared and set up for it. They have the most to gain. It has to start with them. I know that there are a lot of people trying to sell owners IPD, but I don't know if that is going to work.

When reporting on the integrated design case studies—in your interviews and visits to the project sites, in the conclusions you drew—was there anything you learned that surprised you?

JC: One was the quite remarkable enthusiasm of just about everyone for this collaborative process. There was a thirst for something they could feel good about as opposed to gnashing their teeth, getting into disputes, and having an unhappy owner. Every participant in these studies wanted to do it again. They didn't necessarily think it was appropriate for every project.

It's getting late and not looking good for the architect. And frankly, IPD could turn out badly for the architect.

—Jonathan Cohen, FAIA

A second was the creative variety of approaches I saw. People were trying things to see what works. I caution people not to be too inflexible about what the correct formula is for this. We're still learning. The level of creativity in approach was very high.

I was surprised by how successful these early projects were. There wasn't one failure. Considering that this is trying a whole new paradigm, that's pretty remarkable.

There was a lot of controversy about the financial incentives. People were very forceful on this note, both pro and con. We haven't necessarily figured out the proper way to do that yet. As Howard Ashcraft said, if not properly structured, the financial incentives could cause harm to projects. But properly structured, they help. This has to be very carefully considered. The shared risk and reward is a very important part of this. But it has to be very carefully considered how you do it. If you don't do it correctly, you could set up a situation where people are operating against the project, trying to get the payoff.

In the *Architect's Handbook of Professional Practice, 2004 Update*, in the chapter entitled "The New Architect: Keeper of Knowledge and Rules," when you wrote that "Information Technology will be a key enabler of process reform in the building industry, historically a laggard in productivity compared to other sectors of the economy," did you have integrated design in mind—even though it wasn't officially introduced for several years?

JC: I wanted the architect to have this role for the industry. It's getting late and not looking good for the architect. And frankly, IPD could turn out badly for the architect. I would say that the ones who are most at risk from it are the consulting engineers, because their work is all but thrown away now. Architects are going to do less detailing in fewer hours and make less money unless they can exert more leadership. So IPD could turn out to be not such a great deal for architects. I'm proud to be an architect, but I'm surprised and disappointed that the profession has not taken on a stronger role in this.

I, along with others, have been telling architects that they need to step up and exert leadership because they are the natural party to do that: because of their training, they know how to solve problems and they are typically involved in the project longest. I really thought architects were the ones to do this, but it hasn't happened so far and frankly I'm worried. Contractors have been discussing lean construction for fifteen years. Architects are great at the theoretical level—issuing documents, writing case studies, and writing books. The general contractor community has really been going strong with lean construction and has been out ahead of us. We have to admit this.

NOTES

1. Phillip G. Bernstein, "BIM Adoption: Finding Patterns for a New Paradigm," March 17, 2006, www.di.net/articles/archive/bim_adoption_finding_patterns_for/.

2. www.wikipedia.com.

3. www.dictionary.com.

4. Julie Gabrielli and Amy E. Gardner, "Architecture, AIA University of Maryland School of Architecture,

Planning, and Preservation," May 28, 2010, www.wbdg.org/design/dd_architecture.php.

5. Andrew Pressman, "New AIA Firm Survey Indicates that while Business Is Good, the Profession Itself Changes Slowly," March 2007, archrecord.construction.com/practice/firmCulture/0703AIAfirm-1.asp.

6. Dianne Davis "Lean, Green and Seen," Fall 2007, www.wbdg.org/pdfs/jbim_fall07.pdf.

7. Howard W. Ashcraft Jr., "IPD is Light Years ahead of Traditional Delivery," *Building Design & Construction,* 2009),

www.bdcnetwork.com/article/howard-w-ashcraft-jr-ipd-light-years-ahead-traditional-delivery?page=show.

8. Ibid.

9. Lance Hosey, "All Together, Now," October 6, 2009, www.architectmagazine.com/sustainability/all-together-now.aspx.

10. Ashcraft, "IPD is Light Years ahead of Traditional Delivery."

11. Ibid.

part III Leading and Learning

In this part, you'll learn how BIM changes not only the technology, process, and delivery but also the leadership playing field; how to shift into the mindset essential to lead the BIM and integrated design process in turbulent times; and how to become a more effective leader no matter where you find yourself in the organization or on the project team.

You'll discover how the introduction of BIM into the workforce has significant education, recruitment, and training implications, and review the most effective ways to learn BIM. A brief overview of three approaches to the topic of BIM and the master builder is offered, including arguments in favor of and against the return of the architect in the master builder role, and an argument for the composite master builder or master builder team.

In these chapters, you'll meet an architect and BIM manager who successfully made the transition from pencil to CAD to BIM of the greatest complexity; glean several significant insights from a regional director in the Office of Project Delivery at the General Services Administration (GSA); and hear from two educators—one an ethnographer of design and technology who brings a background in architecture, computing, and anthropology to the study of human-machine-environment interaction; and the other an educator and industry technology strategist with firsthand experience working in integrated design on a significant IPD project, who shares his perceptions of what is on the horizon for professionals, organizations, and the AEC industry as it concerns BIM and integrated design.

chapter 6 Leading from the Model

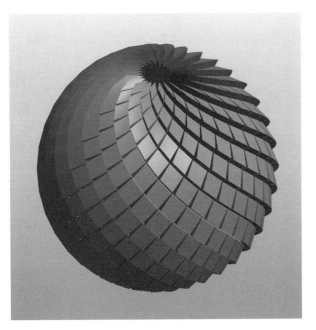

Figure 6.1 BIM provides architects with an opportunity to remain at the leading edge of practice. *Zach Kron, www.buildz.info*

Leading at any time is hard. Leading during turbulent times is even more difficult. Due to disruptive technologies and new ways of working together—the introduction of collaborative work processes—learning how to shift into the mindset essential to leading the BIM and integrated design process has become especially critical. This chapter will help you, working in a BIM and integrated design environment, to become a more effective leader no matter where you find yourself in the firm hierarchy or on the project team. For the goal of BIM and integrated design is nonhierarchical leadership—more and better leaders at every level.

BIM and the Return of the Master Builder

Leaders are those who assume, grab, or inherit positions of authority, whether within organizations or on project teams. At the beginning of projects, a great deal of jockeying for position always goes on. Architects will tell you that the person with the best understanding of the design and command of communication— verbal and graphic—will lead. Contractors, on the other hand, might identify the person who is familiar with all of the major issues impacting how the project is built and is the most assertive, or aggressive, as the leader. The owner usually doesn't care *who* leads, as long as *someone* leads the process.

BIM changes not only the technology, process, and delivery but also the leadership playing field. Although buy-in and support from senior management is critical, that is not the same as leadership.

While leadership historically has been top-down, working in BIM and on integrated teams changes all of that. Leading in BIM and integrated design is more similar to followership (being open, and having the capacity to follow someone in charge)—and having middle managers lead from within the organization. Thus with BIM, the top-down and bottom-up approaches converge where leading from the middle becomes leading from the model.

Enter the Master Builder

Master builders held all kinds of jealously guarded tricks of the trade—a vast inventory of knowledge about material selection, personnel management, geometrical proportioning, load distribution, design, liturgy, and Christian tradition. And make no mistake, those masons saw no clear boundary between things material and things spiritual.[1]

Etymologically, *architect* derives from the Latin *architectus,* itself derived from the Greek *arkhitekton* (*arkhi*, chief, + *tekton,* builder)—that is, chief builder.[2]

Leadership is an unwieldy subject—worthy of not only its own book or bookshelf but its own library. The focus of our discussion on leadership in the age of BIM will therefore be centered on the possibility for the architect to regain the role, if not the title, of master builder.

Without reiterating the long and storied history of the master builder, suffice it to say here that while design professionals are divided on whether once again to invoke the title or leave it for posterity, one thing is in

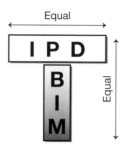

Figure 6.2   The ideal T-shaped teammate has equal wingspan and depth.

agreement: the term *master builder* implies an understanding of all facets of the design and construction of architecture. "Through antiquity, architecture and construction were united by the cultural intentions of a 'Master Builder,' who balanced art, science, materials, form, style and craft to achieve his vision."[3] Each member of the integrated design team, if they want to meet current and future user needs, must understand the impact their discipline has on each other and on the whole. (See Figure 6.2.)

Architect as Virtual Master Builder, Leader of the Design Process

The argument goes something like this: if architects are able to learn and navigate the mindsets, attitudes, and skills necessary to truly collaborate with others—and learn how to design buildings that are optimized to give owners, contractors, and other team members what they need of high quality and low cost, sustainable, delivered faster and with less waste—then they will be trusted, newly esteemed, and return to their rightful role of virtual master builder.

The greatest value of BIM to architects is the change in the relationship between architects, engineers, contractors, and owners and the collaboration it enables. And that change in relationship provides an opening for architects to once again lead the design—and, through the dictates of BIM, construction—process.

Excerpts from an Open Letter Written by Kimon Onuma

There is a romantic and nostalgic notion in the architectural community that we must be the master builders and that maybe BIM will allow us to do that. This will not happen with the current processes of architecture. BIM will not change that for us unless we embrace the change.

Onuma continues,

The process of designing and building a project is much more complex than the traditional notion of a master builder can handle. Just the systems alone in a building are exponentially more complex than they were at the time of the master builder.

He concludes,

The opportunity is clear for architects. Architects are positioned at the center of the design and construction process not as the "master builder" integrating and organizing all the disparate pieces of the building but now as the information and process builders and coordinators in this process.

Source: Kimon Onuma, "BIM Ball—Evolve or Dissolve: Why Architects and the AIA are at Risk of Missing the Boat on Building Information Modeling (BIM)" (open letter, www.bimconstruct.org, 2006).

One concludes that BIM provides a great opportunity for the architectural profession to regain the role of master builder.

Let's take a brief look at each of three stances to the topic of BIM and the master builder:

1. Arguments in favor of the return of the master builder.

2. Arguments against the architect as master builder.

3. Argument for the composite master builder, or *master builder team*.

Arguments for the Return of the Master Builder

Some professionals—primarily architects—believe that architects should become master builders again, and that newer technologies and increased communication are the natural catalysts for bringing this about. Take the case of the Philadelphia architecture partnership Erdy McHenry, whose founders, Scott Erdy and David McHenry, are attempting to identify lower construction costs and faster delivery by

resetting the relationship between the architect and the builder. They argue that the lack of communication between the professions is the real reason for the high cost of construction. Erdy McHenry believes it can save money and speed up the process simply by engaging in a collegial back-and-forth with the craft trades—steelworkers, carpenters, electricians—before construction. Those conversations would help fuse architecture and building so that the architects and contractors designed as a team. The goal, McHenry explained, "is for architects to become the master builder again."[4]

Likewise, BIM is often mentioned as a catalyst for bringing about the return of this role:

Rather than wait until a design is finished, he and Erdy start sharing computer models with contractors as they're developed. The builders, they argue, can spot mistakes early and suggest a more efficient way of accomplishing the same task.[5]

In the past it took many years of experience to become a master builder. Mastering BIM speeds up that process. Today, with education, training, and access to technology, becoming a master builder is within reach. But instead of years spent as an apprentice, architects just starting out on their careers can work toward this goal. The reason for this is that seeing oneself as a master builder is as much a mindset and attitude as a matter of experience. The mindset in particular is seeing yourself residing at the juncture of the trades, profession, and project stakeholders— and assuring yourself that the work you do comprises design with the intent to build. Practitioners of design for design's sake need not apply.

There are four ways in which the architect can regain master builder status in the coming years:

- Become a more complete architect.

- Take on more of a leadership role.

- Become an architect as virtual master builder.

- Become a constructor as master builder: architect-led design-build. (See Figure 6.3.)

More Complete Architects

Before BIM, architects were seen as being incomplete. Since the 1970s they had given up a great deal of responsibility to other professionals and with each passing year since have been seen as ever more

Figure 6.3 The T-shaped teammate: the ideal colleague working in BIM and integrated design has both the deep skills of a do-it-yourselfer (DIY) and the broad reach of someone who can work side by side (SxS) with others.

tangential to the design and construction process. BIM—in some people's view—allows architects to regain some of what they lost along the way. This is the return of the Renaissance-man architect. As architect Paul Durand explains,

> BIM has made us more complete architects. Gave us a tool and brought everybody to the front of the project with us to help us do a better job. In a more sane way. I have found architects all too prone to be traditional. They have a traditional image of themselves. They see themselves as misunderstood artists. The more that they feel they are misunderstood, the more they feel like they are an artist. What we want to be are better architects. More complete architects.[6]

More of a Leadership Role

In addition, Durand sees BIM as offering architects an opportunity to lead the process:

> BIM allows us to be better architects. It brings back the "master builder" model to our work where the architect is in control, masterfully bringing art and technology together. We lost control in our industry and are often considered a necessary evil while others have taken art and quality from buildings to build them simply, quickly, cheaply, and for greater profit. Today we are on the brink of a changing industry and there is more opportunity for architects to lead again and keep architecture and quality in the building equation.[7]

This is the architect as master facilitator. By working not only with but *through* others, we get the most out of teammates. This is the Master Builder as strategic orchestrator orchestrating people and the process. When asked what recommendations he has for what architects would need to do to recover a leadership role, architect-turned-BIM consultant Aaron Greven responded:

> My experience on the design-build side showed me just how far I believe architects have left the master-builder mold behind. Too often architects are washing their hands of knowing or commenting on anything to do with constructability, cost, schedule, operations, even energy. This is what added value most to architects' services throughout history—we knew better than anyone else how best to build. I think architects are marginalizing their own usefulness by not grabbing these responsibilities back—and knowing more about their design and the impact of their decisions. BIM gives us the opportunity to know more, anticipate more, and analyze more. I think too often firms are looking at BIM as a way of drawing better—but are missing the point. Architects have to reinvent how they deliver their services, beyond the paper sheet. Architects can focus less on documentation (because BIM tools will automate much of it, and builders will find less value in it) and more on analysis, and prototyping to improve the end product. Especially in a tight economic climate, owners are going to demand more certainty, and early in a project's life. Architects have the opportunity to do this by working with more data and sharing more information.[8]

Greven continued:

> The separation of architects from master builder—in my mind that's what I always thought architects were and should be, should aim to be and attain. My impression is that architects are migrating away from that role, the increasing gap between design and build. I think there is hope and I think some of that is an integrated design approach, where modeling information is shared, where it's not just sending architectural backgrounds to an engineer for them to execute their design. I think there's an opportunity for the architect to take more of the project leadership role.[9] (See Figure 6.4.)

Architect as Virtual Master Builder

Architects can achieve this leadership of the BIM process by taking on a collaboration mindset. The ability to collaborate and work productively in teams—historically subjects better left to psychologists and operations—will be the most critical skill sets design professionals will need to master if they are to survive the current professional, economic, social, and technological challenges. Especially with the growing use of BIM and integrated design–led projects, the need for collaboration—and utilizing collaborative skills—will be required of every design professional. If they are able to learn the mindsets, attitudes, and skills necessary to truly collaborate with others—and learn how to design buildings that are optimized to give owners, contractors, and other team members what they need of high quality, low cost, sustainable, delivered faster and with less waste—then architects will be trusted, newly esteemed, and return to their rightful role of virtual master builder.

All of these abilities distinguish the architect from the contractor—the only real competition, including the credentialed but overly focused engineer, for master builder status.

Constructor as Master Builder: Architect-led Design-Build

Architect-led design-build requires that one take on risk, and so one must have courage.

> For architects with the courage to branch out from their well-entrenched methodologies,

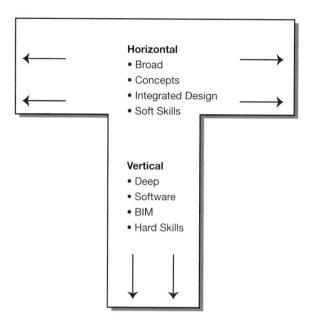

Figure 6.4   The T-shaped teammate has a variety of skill sets and resources in his or her arsenal.

tremendous opportunities for increased complexity, control, and economies of scale through digital fabrication lie ahead. Such endeavors permit industrious architects to focus design efforts and material explorations on specific areas of architectural significance (regardless of scale) and thus reassert themselves as master builders.[10]

Contractor-led design-build still requires the architect. I asked Andy Stapleton of Mortenson Construction if he could imagine a future without the need for architects. His reply:

> Mortenson does not deliver design services. However, we do see ourselves as a master builder and a major proponent of the design-build delivery method. We believe design-build is the optimal solution for many potential owners because it takes advantage of each team members' primary skill sets and allows sophisticated construction companies like Mortenson the ability to lead the design and construction process in partnership with architects, consulting engineers, and key subcontractors. I don't envision us ever not needing architects.[11]

This approach to returning to master builder status is through accepting and taking on design-build, which requires risk taking, industriousness, and courage.

Arguments against the Architect as Master Builder

Kimon Onuma, in his open letter "Evolve or Dissolve," quoted in the sidebar on page 161, addresses "why

The Digital Master Builder

Lacking at the start of the twentieth century was the information needed to effect real change in the way we build. Tools to represent and transfer information instantly and completely are with us today. They allow connections among research, design, depiction, and making that have not existed since specialization began during the Renaissance.

—Kieran Timberlake

Once, as "master builders," architects both designed and built structures. However, architects relinquished their direct role in the building process centuries ago and have instead relied on 2D drawings to describe their visions to specialized builders. Today this communication process is rapidly changing as a direct result of digital fabrication introduced in 1971 by technology developed at the French automotive company Renault. Drawings are being augmented—if not entirely replaced—by processes that permit 3D fabrication of complex forms directly from architects' data. In this context, the much-vaunted 1997 Guggenheim Bilbao, celebrated for its convoluted artful forms,

is far more groundbreaking for its use of innovative digital construction processes in which Gehry's office assumed responsibility for the accuracy of fabrication.

Although this is not in itself news, direct digital communication has reinvigorated the concept of master builder for a few architects. Repopularized some thirty years ago by the radical Jersey Devil architectural group, the design-build method means the responsibility for design and production are provided by the same party. Pedagogically significant since it opens up a fertile dialectic between design and tectonics, there is again tremendous interest in this model in academia—most notably in the revered Rural Studio, initiated in 1993 at Auburn University by the late Samuel Mockbee. Many other schools have adopted design-build in their curriculum. . . . The upshot of this is that more emerging practitioners are once again enthusiastic about possibilities inherent in varying levels of participation in the actual *making* of design.

Source: David Celento, "Innovate or Perish: New Technologies and Architecture's Future," Harvard Design Number 26 (Spring/Summer, 2007).

we are no longer master builders and never will be with the current mindset."[12] He continues:

At the urging of the AIA and the architectural community we have progressively, for the sake of limiting our liability, pulled away from being the master builder. Construction management filled that role for us since we were not able to manage it. We are now perfectly poised to reduce our relevance even further. The threat is clear, yet most architects prefer to ignore the BIM revolution and do not understand what this is all about, while passively waiting for things to happen. This will result in architecture and design

being marginalized and the 15.8-billion-dollar gap being filled by other members of the industry team. We romanticize about being the master builder once more. We must lead this change to make it happen.[13]

Architects as master builders made sense as leaders of building projects in simpler times. Today, when construction is more complicated and building projects more complex, has the time passed when the architect could return to a role as master builder? Or have BIM and integrated design made such a return more likely and possible? Call it the case for complexity. (See Figure 6.5.)

Figure 6.5   For those who remember constructing and drawing perspectives by hand, it's your lucky century. *Zach Kron, www.buildz.info*

The Case for Complexity

The case for complexity goes something like this: No matter how talented and well-rounded an architect is, no matter where they were educated or trained, what office they worked in, or who this person is, one person cannot—and should not—do it all.

Few architects can design and develop a building, let alone check for codes, coordinate, manage the process, and produce all of the construction drawings for it, and then see it through to completion, on time and within budget. And yet that is what it would take for one person today to serve as master builder. Some have spoken out against the idea that a single entity—no matter who it is—can possibly lead the entire design and construction process:

> Today, the required legal, technical, and cultural knowledge base has such breadth and depth

that it is no longer in the best interest of the project for one discipline to hold, implement, and be responsible for all building-related knowledge, as did the master builder of old. Professional malpractice concerns have led liability insurance companies to encourage, even implicitly force, architects to limit activities to design. For example, "construction supervision" became "construction observation," moving the architect further away from the risks associated with construction activities.[14]

In the book *Refabricating Architecture,* the authors state that no one individual could be expected to serve the role of master builder today. "While we cannot return to the idea of the master builder embodied in a single person, the architect can force the integration of the several spun-off disciplines of architecture . . . all with the aim of reuniting substance with intent."[15] Phil Bernstein agrees:

> I think in order to progress this dialogue in our business, we need to abandon the concept of a master builder. It's very romantic. Hasn't existed since Brunelleschi. And he had essentially an infinite supply of slave labor available to him. And he could take forty years to build his buildings. We're way past that, this whole master builder thing. The reason I endorse Stephen [Kieran] and James's [Timberlake] rejection of the concept is that it is just incompatible with the idea of a modern building. You need to know too many things for one individual to be in control. The whole master builder discussion is a proxy for a false argument. It's an uninteresting argument about who's in charge.[16] (See Figure 6.6.)

Andy Stapleton of Mortenson Construction also cited increased project complexity as a reason against the

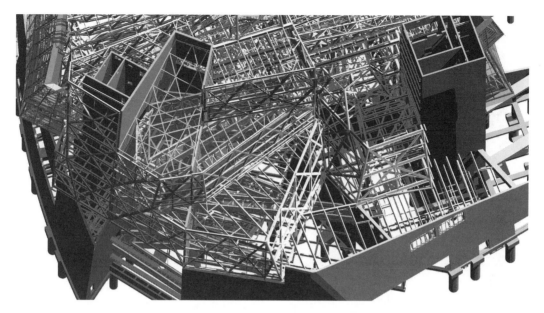

Figure 6.6   Bird's-eye view of structural model from north. *Canadian Museum for Human Rights; Smith Carter, executive architect; Antoine Predock Architect, design architect*

suggestion of one person leading the process. "The buildings we build today are so complex that no one person is the 'master builder'—the integrated team is now the master builder. I always want to have the strongest team to work with, bottom line."[17]

But if it is not the architect who leads the process—is there another design entity that might be better situated to do so? When asked why he used the title "designer" in lieu of "architect," Peter Rumpf of Mortenson Construction tellingly responded by saying: "In my opinion, a designer is more adept at big-picture concepts and provides a vision for the project. An architect is a master communicator and coordinator more adept at documenting, collaborating, and executing the design intent."[18]

Not to mention the implications of the title. The "master builder" moniker rings of *master,* of colonialism and of

control—the very opposite of the hallmarks of our age: decentralized, fragmented, and glutted with information. How could any one entity possibly claim to master it all? The advent of BIM and integrated design change a great deal about how architects operated in the past as well as the work they were primarily responsible for. Architects formerly responsible for coordinating and orchestrating the input of multiple disciplines during the design process now have BIM and add-on programs such as Navisworks to take care of this—as well as the contractor or whoever operates these programs. (See Figure 6.7.)

Argument for the Composite Master Builder, or *Master Builder Team*

The concept of the *composite master builder* is the brainchild of architect and planning consultant Bill Reed, co-author with the 7group of *The Integrative*

Figure 6.7   3D perspective from Level 04 looking northwest. *Canadian Museum for Human Rights; Smith Carter, executive architect; Antoine Predock Architect, design architect*

Guide to Green Building: Redefining the practice of sustainability (John Wiley and Sons, 2009). As described in a blurb for this exceptional book,

> With whole building design, the project team can be guided once again by a collective vision. This structure, along with the process by which the design team works together, has been termed by Bill Reed as the "Composite Master Builder." The term recasts the historical single Master Builder as a diverse group of professionals working together towards a common end. The intention is to bring all of the specialists together, allowing them to function as if they were one mind. The process avoids, as Mario Salvadori says, the "reciprocal ignorance" of the specialists in the design and building field.[19]

Phil Bernstein has his own take on the subject: "It's master building—not master builder. Yes, it's the team. The idea that one person can be at the center of the overall process—didn't we leave that behind with Ayn Rand? Buildings are just too complicated. I couldn't even do it on my own house addition!"[20]

The integrated project team would act, in this scenario, as a master builder team. The team—facilitated by an outside facilitator or team member as strategic

Figure 6.8 Exterior view of BIM model from north at 85% Construction Documents. *Canadian Museum for Human Rights; Smith Carter, executive architect; Antoine Predock Architect, design architect*

orchestrator—would meet early on to agree on team protocols, design criteria, and how often to meet and review project progress, and then continue to act as a collective throughout the design and construction process. Peter Rumpf of Mortenson Construction also believes that the master builder role is more team-centric than that of any one individual:

I think it is great when architects seize this opportunity to become more involved in the integral workings of their design. The new technology does allow for big-picture understanding of very complex projects, and therefore

the master builder role is held by the team. One master coordination model can contain information from every aspect of the project—architecture, structure, enclosure, mechanical, electric, plumbing, fire protection, medical gas, pneumatic tube, FF&E, civil, et cetera—allowing the model manager a complete picture of even very complex projects.

For me the term "master builder" is applicable to people with the ability to call upon their vast knowledge to iron out the details. Someone who has intimate knowledge of how things go together, which VDC requires.[21] (See Figure 6.8.)

Figure 6.9   Interior view from Garden of Contemplation looking north. *Canadian Museum for Human Rights; Smith Carter, executive architect; Antoine Predock Architect, design architect*

So, does integrated design mean a return to the role of master builder? Yes and no. No, not in that there is any one person on the integrated design team that plays this role. Yes, in that the entire team—including the core members, engineers, subcontractors, and fabricators—together forms a master builder unit. In the past we encouraged emerging architects to become CAD experts when they should have been focusing on how to put buildings together. Working in BIM integrates these efforts—learning a program while learning how to build. When I asked Yanni Loukissas if he believes that these tools offer the architect an opportunity to regain their position, role, or place as the master builder on the project, he replied:

> I'm not so interested in the idea of bringing back the master architect. Some will tell you that there

was never a master builder, that it is a myth that architects use now to claim a central position. In *Keepers of the Geometry,* there's a person that calls himself a techie-enabled architect, someone operating from the center, who's the translator, managing all of the information, bringing everything together. He doesn't even have a professional architecture degree. This vision—as a technological mediator—I don't know if it is even available for architects or to someone who is not technically skilled to the extreme this person was. This fascination architects have with being in the center—being the singular author—I don't know if it's so productive. There are other interesting ways of working that are about enabling other people—more participatory, collaborative approaches to design.[22] (See Figure 6.9.)

Case Study Interview with Bradley Beck, Architect and BIM Manager

Bradley Beck, project architect and BIM manager at FitzGerald Associates Architects in Chicago. For the Canadian Museum for Human Rights (CMHR), Brad was charged with the transformation of 2D Design Development documents to a complete 3D Building Information Model that is currently being utilized as an aid in construction.

Are BIM authoring tools ready for schematic design? If not, what's missing? What would need to change for architects to design in BIM?

Brad Beck (BB): They're not ready for schematic design. What they need—and what's missing from them—is flexibility, and an intuitive way to make changes within the software. A way for getting an intuitive change to happen within the software isn't quite there yet.

What do you make of the claim that BIM thinks the way that architects think? Isn't that intuitive?

BB: It is—if I thought that BIM thought the way architects think. But I don't think it does. It thinks the way contractors think. For a contractor it's either one way or another way; it's not a whole host of options. It doesn't have an "if/then" mindset, which is what the software needs. It's tough for software to have as much information as BIM needs and still be flexible enough to show different design options. (See Figures 6.10 and 6.11.)

Figure 6.10   Exterior view of BIM model from east at 30% CD. *Canadian Museum for Human Rights; Smith Carter, executive architect; Antoine Predock Architect, design architect*

(Continued)

Figure 6.11   Exterior view of BIM model from north at 30% CD. *Canadian Museum for Human Rights; Smith Carter, executive architect; Antoine Predock Architect, design architect*

Is the current ideal SketchUp through SD—then, once design is pinned down, moving to BIM in DD? Do you feel BIM is best used for DD/CDs for the interim?

BB: I do. Interim though implies that there will be a BIM tool ideal for SD. Because SD is so inherently fluid and intuitive it may not want to be part of BIM, because there are so many things that go into SD that are still in flux and not yet determined. BIM is a sponge for information. If you don't have that information yet, you're not fully taking advantage of BIM. And the software's not ready to not have the information in the model. Hand sketching and simple tools like SketchUp will remain for quite a while until BIM software makes a big leap. Because those things aren't determined in SD, the models get so large with so much information it's not advantageous during SD. In DD you have a better understanding of what the building is going to be. Especially the way we're going toward DD, which are essentially junior CDs.

What would need to change for BIM to be utilized to its greatest advantage?

BB: The answer depends on the industry's perception of BIM. And the current perception is that BIM increases your productivity and decreases your change orders. This perception is going to change, leading to a 4D thought process of how buildings will get built, especially concerning the fabrication of systems and building elements. BIM is going to lead to architects thinking more like designers and contractors, and less just like designers. So there's going to be a lot more understanding of construction techniques by architects. There's going to be a lot more thought in the design process having to do with constructability. (See Figures 6.12 and 6.13.)

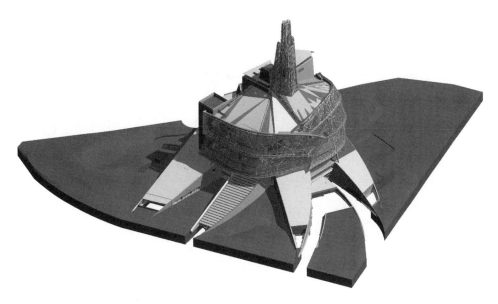

Figure 6.12   Exterior view of BIM model from west at 30% CD. *Canadian Museum for Human Rights; Smith Carter, executive architect; Antoine Predock Architect, design architect*

Architects have to make a greater move toward thinking like contractors than contractors thinking like architects.

BB: That's more so because of the roles each plays. Not so much because of BIM. Architects feel like they're getting the brunt of the liability for the buildings and none of the decision making or the responsibility that they want. Contractors don't want to make the leap to the architect—they find themselves in a good spot already. Architects need to take on a bit more and reach out more to contractors.

By filling in a dialog box you've just given tons of information to the entire model. And that feels not productive at all because you don't feel like you're creating anything. That's when you feel the least productive, but you're actually the most productive.

—Brad Beck

Figure 6.13   Site plan at 85% CD. *Canadian Museum for Human Rights; Smith Carter, executive architect; Antoine Predock Architect, design architect*

(Continued)

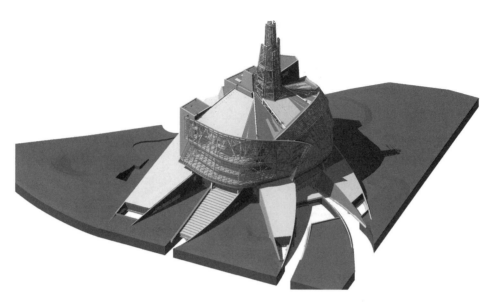

Figure 6.14   Exterior view of BIM model from east at 85% CD. *Canadian Museum for Human Rights; Smith Carter, executive architect; Antoine Predock Architect, design architect*

When are you most productive in BIM? When do you feel least productive?

BB: The answer's the same. You feel like you're the least productive when you are the most productive. When you're putting all of the information into walls and dialog boxes, putting in specifications—that is probably the most important thing you can do, because in doing so you're providing information for each instance of that one thing. By filling in a dialog box you've just given tons of information to the entire model. And that feels not productive at all because you don't feel like you're creating anything. That's when you feel the least productive, but you're actually the most productive.

So if you're a younger staff member working in BIM, you might be perceived by senior management not in the know to be working slowly—or not making adequate progress, having little to show for your efforts—when in actuality you're making a great deal of progress.

BB: There's also the issue that even though you are in DD, the design of that room is likely to change. You lose productivity just by placing the walls. If the wall moves, you lose that productivity—even though the information in that wall is still the same. (See Figures 6.14 and 6.15.)

Communicating with others—easier, harder, or different working in BIM when compared with how you worked before?

BB: Communication is probably the best-kept secret of BIM. It is something that is imperative to the building information model and is so subliminal that you don't even realize how much communication you need and how much you're providing. It's a huge benefit of BIM. In a lot of ways it's easier, but in some it's a little bit harder. Recently, on CMHR (Canadian Museum for Human Rights,) we received a sketch for a bathroom layout that looked fine—at the height its walls were cut. But right above that height

Figure 6.15   Exterior view of BIM model from north at 85% CD. *Canadian Museum for Human Rights; Smith Carter, executive architect; Antoine Predock Architect, design architect*

was a beam you couldn't see in the plan. It's hard to go back to a senior designer or senior team member and say, your layout doesn't really work. It has to happen, but it's a bit harder to swallow when the junior staff has to deliver the news that it doesn't work because of this, this, and this. The biggest difference between hand drafting, CAD, and BIM is this feeling of mutual mentorship that happens when you're sitting with a senior team member and they're watching what you're modeling and making decisions. You don't realize it, but you're both mentoring each other. And it's not something that's forced—like the IDP program, where you have to have a mentor. It's more organic. You can say to the person you're next to, "What about this?" Because you're working in 3D you can say, "This doesn't work because of this. Let's change what we're doing. How about this?" It fosters this mutual mentoring that you don't really get by redlining drawings and handing them off. You're mentoring up as well as down.

Describe your CMHR project's workflow. How did you work internally and externally with others, and what challenges have this introduced?

BB: CMHR is an interesting case because the way we started with it is that we were given a set of 2D documents and contracted to build a 3D building (model) from those documents. At first we didn't have much more of a role than being the virtual builders. We took the drawings and built what we could. What it has evolved into has become much more complex and rewarding because what BIM has allowed our firm to do is garner some trust from Smith Carter, the architect of record, and that trust has led

Communication is probably the best-kept secret of BIM.
—Brad Beck

(Continued)

to an expanded scope of work for us. It increased our responsibility on what we are contracted to do. The expanded scope can be a double-edged sword when you're out on a limb further than expected or contracted. But it makes sense for you to take on this added scope in BIM—for in order for you to have the quick process and building, everyone has to be on board. It's better overall for the project to have those working in BIM take on this added scope. Once you put together the base building you start to see the conflicts and clashes, and because we're in the model every day it's easier for us to point these things out and even to coordinate. So now we are coordinating between the architect and structural engineer, the architect and mechanical engineer. There have even been some instances where we've been asked by the architect of record to coordinate between mechanical and structural, coordinating the consultants rather than coordinating them with the architecture. As confusing as that can be, they trust us enough to ask us to do that. Whoever is doing the model needs to be part of that process because it is so inherent to what you are doing every day. As for the workflow, it has changed—in a positive direction. (See Figures 6.16 and 6.17.)

Figure 6.16   3D perspective view of main entry. *Canadian Museum for Human Rights; Smith Carter, executive architect; Antoine Predock Architect, design architect*

Figure 6.17   3D perspective of exterior curtain wall at Level 04. *Canadian Museum for Human Rights; Smith Carter, executive architect; Antoine Predock Architect, design architect*

What factor does it play that some of the people on the team, both internally and externally, aren't BIM-savvy?

BB: Overall, it has less to do with BIM itself. There are some misguided interpretations about what BIM is and what people are willing to learn about it. Some people are more willing that others to jump in, download Navisworks, and go through a Navisworks model. There's an architect I am currently working with on the CMHR team who is in his late sixties or early seventies. This is probably the last project he's going to work on before retirement, and he doesn't want to learn BIM. There's another, much younger architect at the same level who works with him that has jumped right on board. BIM provides a big-picture way of looking at everything, so when you're given a sketch to build you can pretty quickly figure out what's going to work and what's not because you're thinking in terms of three dimensions all the time. This provides the biggest advantage for people who are BIM-capable because so many architects are so used to looking at plans, sections, and elevations. There have been instances on the CMHR project where I have put together a 3D section box for a senior team member to review so they can see what's going on, and they have asked, "Can we look at this in plan or in section?" because they're not used to looking at it in 3D form.

Have you hit any significant snags? In terms of communication? Technical? Collaborative work process?

BB: The biggest snag we've had on CMHR was getting everybody, including the consultants, on board—out of that 2D AutoCAD mindset and into a 3D BIM mindset. This was difficult, especially for the MEP consultants, because they were so used to working in 2D and coordinating in the field—instead of placing ducts exactly where they're going to be placed. In the initial months the consultants were saying, "If we can't get to this we can always go back to AutoCAD and put out a set of drawings." With the model being the deliverable they've realized that they can't use CAD as a crutch.

What do you feel has been the greatest benefit so far to working in BIM?

BB: The mutual mentorship is the biggest benefit I have had from working in BIM. Sitting down together, you're both learning from each other. Another great benefit is that BIM provokes you to think in terms of construction and understanding how things get built. What that does is opens up the potential to exponentially increase the knowledge of junior staff so much faster than in the past. It's so much easier to learn from three dimensions when it is getting built than to learn from redlines on a 2D drawing. In the model you're seeing how the building will be built sooner. For example, the stacked wall feature in Revit. You used to draw two lines and that's your wall. Then you draw a wall section and put all your detail in it. With BIM, now while you're building that wall you're thinking about, OK, there's a concrete topping in this room, the bottom three inches is the stud track that will serve as the pour stop for the topping. After the first three inches the next eight and a half feet will be drywall, et cetera. So you're thinking about all those things while you're building the model. It's easier to understand what's happening when they go out there to build it than when you draw. The construction means and methods may not show up in the detail, but when you're building the model you really need to understand them. (See Figures 6.18 and 6.19.)

> *The mutual mentorship is the biggest benefit I have had from working in BIM. Sitting down together, you're both learning from each other.*
>
> —Brad Beck

(Continued)

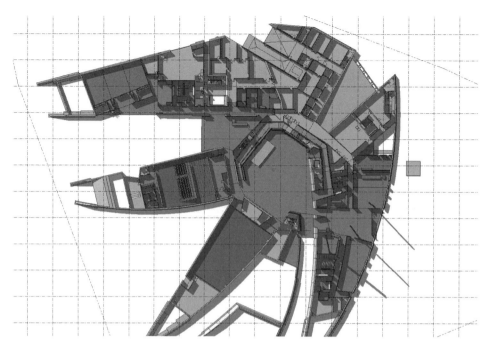

Figure 6.18   Rendered view of Level 01 plan with shadows. *Canadian Museum for Human Rights; Smith Carter, executive architect; Antoine Predock Architect, design architect*

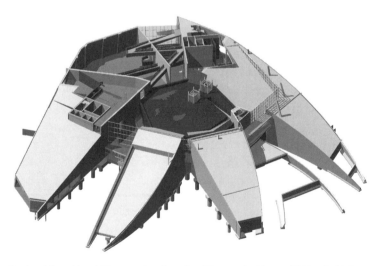

Figure 6.19   Axonometric section box taken at Level 02 mezzanine. *Canadian Museum for Human Rights; Smith Carter, executive architect; Antoine Predock Architect, design architect*

Is there anything that you feel architects should change in themselves or do differently to better utilize these virtual tools?

BB: Studying and understanding construction techniques is probably the best thing an architect can do to effectively utilize BIM now and in the future. Working with contractors as equals is another critical step architects need to take. Instead of having an adversarial relationship with a contractor, if you can call a contractor and say, "I know you need to polish the concrete, but I need to put stone down and I don't want it getting wet when you're polishing the concrete—how would you build it?" The contractor suggests a way to achieve your goal. They explain to you, "You put in the topping, and we have the stone held up a course so we can do the polishing, and then we can put that bottom course in after the polishing is done." Having that conversation is a lot better for building the model than drawing it and hoping that the contractor gets it right. Because if you just draw it, then the contractor is going to pour the topping, put in the masonry, and then come back and polish—and you're going to have two inches of concrete that doesn't get polished because it's so close to that stone. Remaining open and working with contractors is the way to go. The adversarial relationship between architect and contractor just isn't going to work for BIM and integrated design.

One premise of this book is that successful BIM implementation involves changing the attitudes and mindsets of the people who will use the technologies, which—unlike the latest software and hardware required to support the new technologies—design professionals have within their control. Agree or disagree? Any suggestions for how this can come about?

BB: While BIM requires changing the attitudes and mindsets of the people who use the technology, BIM itself is not more complicated or complex than hand drafting. BIM is architects and engineers doing what they've always said they are going to do. Design professionals have always had the control that BIM enables, but time constraints, budgets—all the things that keep documents from being as complete as they could be—have led to the giving away of some of the control to the contractor. You didn't have time to prepare a drawing, so you're relying on your specifications and your documents to communicate the design intent. What BIM allows us to do is to have a much more comprehensive design solution. That is actually what we're contracted to do. To have everything coordinated and to have a full design solution that sometimes the holes in the drawing just can't fill. BIM will allow us to take back control of those things that we missed in our drawings— especially when the model is the actual deliverable. That's the big mindset change that really isn't a change. It's understanding that we need to provide what we always said that we were going to provide. And BIM is going to help us do that. (See Figures 6.20 and 6.21.)

Had you known BIM was on the horizon before you entered architecture school, do you feel that it would have been a factor in your becoming something other than an architect?

BB: I don't think it would have changed anything; I always wanted to be an architect. My desire to become an architect has always been something much greater than software. It's great that it is here and I'm glad that I'll be able to use it, but I would be an architect if we were still hand drafting. The Howard Roarks of the industry probably don't like the process as much as I do—but I believe there's a place for everyone in the BIM environment. Howard Roark can certainly learn the software and build models himself. The collaborative process is not something that should be thought of as negative.

(Continued)

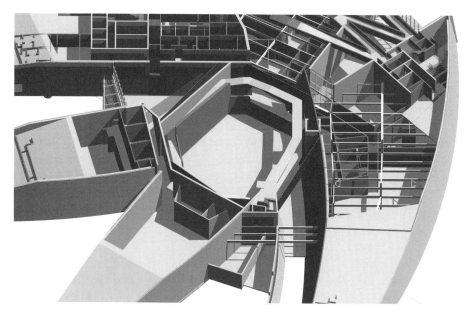

Figure 6.20   Axonometric section box of Level 02 at end of DD. *Canadian Museum for Human Rights; Smith Carter, executive architect; Antoine Predock Architect, design architect*

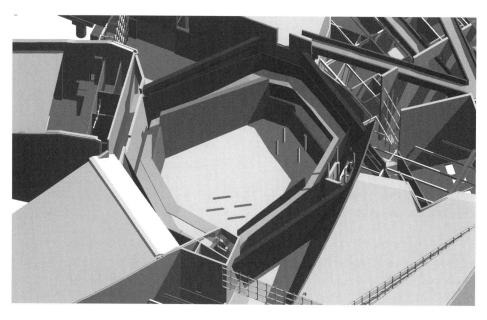

Figure 6.21   Axonometric section box of Great Hall at end of DD. *Canadian Museum for Human Rights; Smith Carter, executive architect; Antoine Predock Architect, design architect*

Some say BIM will be utilized primarily by younger, emerging professionals. Agree or disagree?

BB: I completely disagree. The knowledge required for doing a building information model is so vast that you need somebody who has experience. That goes for the global process of integrated design as well. You have to have an experienced professional that works with a younger professional that knows the software. Without the experienced professional, the software is only as good as the information that's put into it. If that person doesn't know how to build a building, then your model's not going to be correct. I believe the whole profession will evolve this way. If the experienced professionals don't want to learn the BIM software, they still need to be there as part of the process, to tell the person who is using the software how to build the virtual model. For these reasons the BIM experience will be driven by the experienced, not the emerging, professional. Firms that are eliminating senior architect positions to make way for younger BIM operators—I believe this is a horrible idea. To take somebody who has that experience and knowledge from being in the business for ten, fifteen, twenty years and eliminate that knowledge base from your firm seems like a big mistake. For every emerging professional who knows the software, you're going to need a senior staff member working on the project. (See Figures 6.22 and 6.23.)

I definitely see myself differently as an architect due to the way BIM has impacted my work. I feel a lot more confident in my ability to visualize spaces, my understanding of how buildings are put together and what processes are going to happen on site that you really need to think about.

—Brad Beck

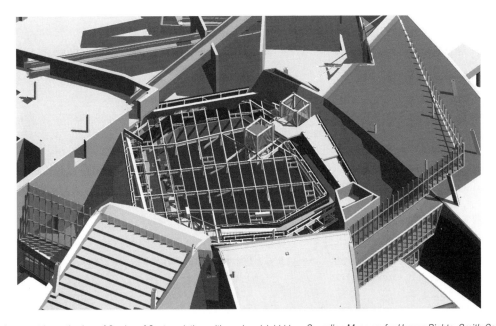

Figure 6.22   Axonometric section box of Garden of Contemplation, with garden slab hidden. *Canadian Museum for Human Rights; Smith Carter, executive architect; Antoine Predock Architect, design architect*

(Continued)

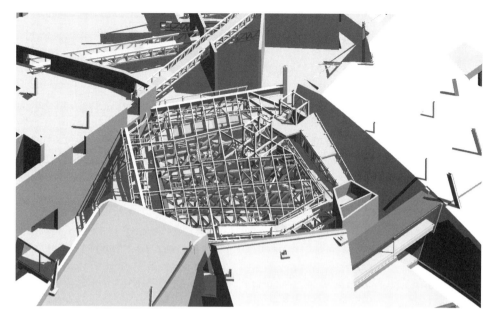

Figure 6.23   Axonometric section box of Garden of Contemplation, with garden slab hidden—structure only. *Canadian Museum for Human Rights; Smith Carter, executive architect; Antoine Predock Architect, design architect*

Does working in BIM impact how you see yourself as an architect? Do you feel you have benefited career-wise from working in BIM?

BB: I definitely see myself differently as an architect due to the way BIM has impacted my work. I feel a lot more confident in my ability to visualize spaces, my understanding of how buildings are put together and what processes are going to happen on site that you really need to think about. I find myself considering not only 3D but 4D decisions—the time it is going to take, to build the model, to actually construct something that's out at the site—I see all of this happening more fluidly than before I was working in BIM. I'm visualizing in 4D, thinking about the sequence of trades on site. I had been exposed to this prior to BIM while observing construction on other jobs, but with BIM I am able to fully grasp what that 4D element really is. With BIM I'm able to think more globally about the decisions I make—by providing an overall global perspective, what you're creating, how spaces are going to look and feel when you're in them. I'm finding that I'm gaining knowledge a whole lot faster than at any time before. And I see learning as a huge benefit, especially learning things that were never really talked about in school, things having more to do with functionality and practicality over form, design aesthetics, and other ephemera. I'm learning constructability techniques and tangible things a lot faster than I did prior to working in BIM.

Knowing what you know now, what advice would you give a recent grad just starting out in architecture?

BB: Immerse yourself in understanding how things are put together. It helps if you're working in BIM to prioritize how things are put together on site. I'd recommend that they understand not just how buildings come together but other things, how a dishwasher or refrigerator is put together. Take a radio or car apart and put it back together. This will help them to understand more

Figure 6.27   Overall rendered building section at 30% CD. *Canadian Museum for Human Rights; Smith Carter, executive architect; Antoine Predock Architect, design architect*

of all the pitfalls we're going though right now on our project's process. I can't imagine, if it was sixty years ago, how a building like this would get built in the amount of time that they're going to get it built in. Visualizing it has been so much easier with BIM. You can't limit BIM to simpler buildings, especially because it is easier to visualize a simpler building. You can almost make an argument the other way, saying that you don't need BIM for a simple building. You can understand where all your details need to go and how everything gets put together in a building where everything is orthogonal. But in a building like CMHR, you just can't get every detail you need from 2D drawings. To that point, you almost cannot do a complex building without BIM. It's possible— but very difficult. Future versions of the software will make complex forms a lot easier to build, which is a double-edged sword as well. Part of the benefit of BIM is that when you build one of these complex forms it's very difficult, but you realize that it's going to be just as difficult—if not more so—for them to actually build it. So when you're building a curved wall that's canted—as we are—and it takes you a week just to build the 3D form, it's telling you, "Hey, the guys on site are going to have a hell of a time trying to build this." The difficulty today can be seen as a benefit. And if these complex forms do become easy to build in BIM software, it might be seen as negative. It might become too easy to build virtually without realizing how difficult it is to build on site. (See Figures 6.26 and 6.27.)

Now that you've worked in multiple BIM projects, do you believe BIM has arrived and that it is the solution/future?

BB: I don't ever want to open CAD again! I don't ever want to draft in CAD again. BIM is absolutely the appropriate way for a building design solution to be delivered to the client and contractor. It's so comprehensive and there's so much information

(Continued)

that the architect is in control of that going back to drawing two-dimensionally and allowing for interpretation of that two-dimensional drawing is a mistake. You've got to build it in 3D and create a very comprehensive design solution that you can hand off to the client and contractor.

Do you feel architects are better suited to lead this effort than contractors?

BB: Architects ultimately will be the leaders of the building process. BIM is just a tool that allows us to take back the loss of leadership that we've experienced. If you asked a contractor if they even wanted to be a leader in the BIM world they would say no, stepping away from the liabilities associated with the control of that.

How would you explain then all the contractors that have embraced BIM?

BB: They've realized the benefits before architects have. Contractors see the benefits and the coordination that you get with it, and they've said, architects aren't doing this right now. We're going to do it—kicking and screaming—because we need it to coordinate. But not for the leadership role. There are things contractors can do with BIM that allow them to effi-

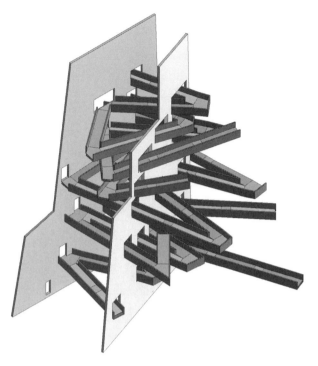

Figure 6.28   3D Axonometric of Hall of Hope showing only ramps and wedge walls at end of DD. *Canadian Museum for Human Rights; Smith Carter, executive architect; Antoine Predock Architect, design architect*

ciently manage their projects, but, overall, they would prefer that the architect be in charge of it, the architect hand them the model; get all the information from the model that the architect gave them, rather than building the model themselves. There are those who believe that BIM will have the opposite effect—initiate the phasing-out of the architect because there are contractors who can do it all. I don't agree with that. Contractors are using BIM now because they're seeing advantages that architects don't—but will. Once architects see the value and scope of BIM, they're taking it back. (See Figures 6.28 and 6.29.)

How would you describe leadership on your current team? What does it emanate from? Is there a spoken or unspoken hierarchy? Is it assigned or earned? Is it personality-driven?

BB: There's a documented hierarchy. Antoine Predock's office has a list posted on the wall indicating who's at the top all the way down to who's at the bottom. The experience is something altogether different. But then it's always different than the documented hierarchy, right? The documented hierarchy is discarded based on personality, level of trust, needs, and comfort levels—but not because of BIM. In my experience there's the guy you go to—whether or not he's the guy you're supposed to go to. I've seen that on every project I've ever worked on. Ninety percent is personality—whether you get along with the person or not.

How important is it to have a leader on a BIM-driven project team?

BB: Leadership is something you've always got to have, whether you're working in 2D, 3D, or 4D. BIM is still the tool that provides the architect with a greater leadership role in the entire process.

Does working in BIM pose leadership opportunities for emerging professionals that weren't there before BIM came into wide use?

BB: Only in this infancy stage that we're in. My firm is a great example of a firm where technology creates opportunities for emerging professionals. The three principals are younger than most of the design staff. I attribute that to their coming in when CAD was just becoming the standard. That provided them an opportunity to really show off their technical expertise and provide an asset to the firm that helped promote them quickly through the ranks. A number of emerging professionals have gotten promoted because of their grasp of the technology, and that came to an end when everybody eventually knew CAD. That opportunity was no longer there. As BIM permeates the industry, it will no longer provide that opportunity because everyone will be using it. *Right now* is the prime time to take advantage of BIM's leadership opportunity. (See Figures 6.30 and 6.31.)

With BIM there's a lot to learn. Would you say it is just as important to unlearn certain things to work effectively in BIM?

BB: You definitely need to leave CAD at the door. BIM software is so different from CAD that there's a great deal you have to unlearn—from hand drafting as well as CAD. You're not representing the building the same way. BIM is a built-to-scale 3D virtual model. Although 2D is still what you produce, as BIM grows and evolves you're going to be handing off a model. That's the ultimate goal—you don't need to do the documents. Here's your model—and everything's done. You need to unlearn the old software and the workflow and learn the new

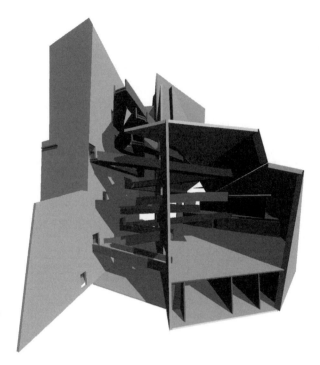

Figure 6.29   3D perspective view of Hall of Hope, showing only ramps and structure at end of DD. *Canadian Museum for Human Rights; Smith Carter, executive architect; Antoine Predock Architect, design architect*

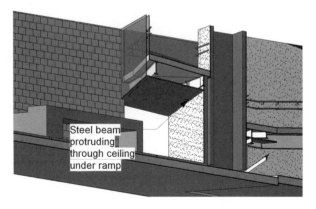

Figure 6.30   Coordination of wide flange beam and architectural finishes. *Canadian Museum for Human Rights; Smith Carter, executive architect; Antoine Predock Architect, design architect*

(Continued)

School's absolutely the place to learn BIM. Despite school curricula [being] already overburdened with required courses, BIM ought to be taught the first quarter of freshman year. That way, throughout your school career you're using the global view of how buildings get built that BIM provides.

—Brad Beck

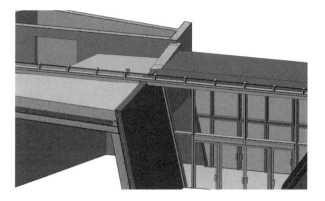

paradigm. The thing we need most to relearn in the profession is what our role in the process is. We've lost the role of master builder or chief builder—and we're now afforded the opportunity to regain this role due to BIM. Whether or not we seize on this opportunity is another story.

Figure 6.31   Axonometric section box of main entry for coordination of curtain wall and exterior finishes. *Canadian Museum for Human Rights; Smith Carter, executive architect; Antoine Predock Architect, design architect*

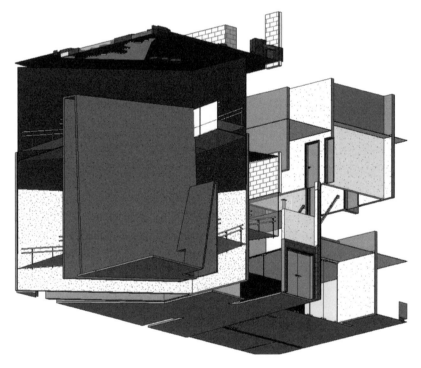

Figure 6.32   Worm's-eye view of architectural coordination in Great Hall. *Canadian Museum for Human Rights; Smith Carter, executive architect; Antoine Predock Architect, design architect*

Do you feel there's a place for learning BIM in academia, or do you think it ought to be picked up in practice or on students' own time during or after school?

BB: School's absolutely the place to learn BIM. Despite school curricula [being] already overburdened with required courses, BIM ought to be taught the first quarter of freshman year. That way, throughout your school career you're using the global view of how buildings get built that BIM provides. If you teach BIM at the very beginning, when the students are sponges and soak up everything, you don't have to go back to it after the first year because they'll already be working in it. Like I said before, you learn so much about how buildings are put together just from the software. BIM is an exceptional learning tool. It's not about the software—it's about learning construction and constructability. There are great plug-ins for most BIM software that allow you to think about how a building gets built and sequence it in time. If you build the model the way the program allows you to, you can make an animation of the construction sequence. These tools are great for academia because this information is harder to come by in the real world, when time and budgets don't allow for the building of a construction phasing model.

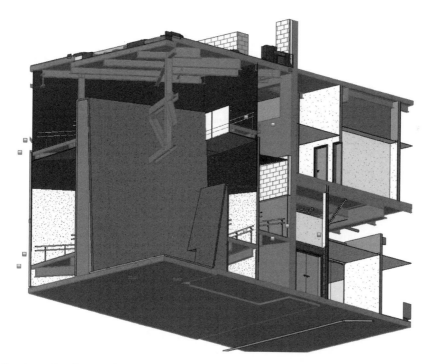

Figure 6.33 Worm's-eye view of structural coordination in Great Hall. *Canadian Museum for Human Rights; Smith Carter, executive architect; Antoine Predock Architect, design architect*

(Continued)

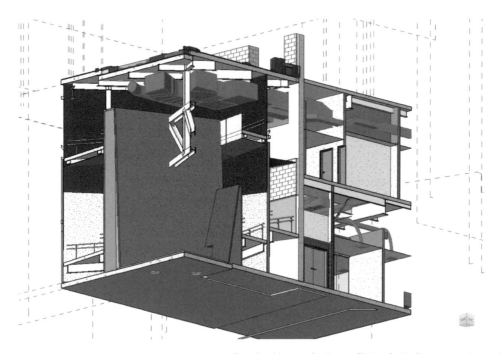

Figure 6.34   Worm's-eye view of mechanical coordination in Great Hall. *Canadian Museum for Human Rights; Smith Carter, executive architect; Antoine Predock Architect, design architect*

Would you recommend certain project size, scale, scope, new versus existing conditions for BIM? Is there an ideal firm size for BIM use? *Does size matter?*

BB: None of that matters. BIM's good for any size firm and for any size project.

What has your experience been like so far using BIM with others on the design team? Is everyone on board, or do you find one or more disciplines lagging?

BB: MEP engineers are probably lagging. They're used to designing a system for the building, not coordinating fully where everything goes. Having to figure out exactly where something's going to go—and leave it to the engineer and not the contractor in the field or to shop drawings—that requires some change on their part. Hopefully that will soon change. (See Figures 6.32, 6.33, and 6.34.)

Now that you've used it for a while, I'll ask again: BIM: just a tool, evolution (from CAD), or revolution? Which one and why?

BB: I'll combine it and say BIM is a revolutionary tool allowing architects to truly present a complete, coordinated design solution that doesn't require interpretation, while maximizing the architect's role as the leader of the design and building process.

Case Study Interview with Charles Hardy, director, Office of Project Delivery at U.S. General Services Administration (GSA) Public Buildings Service National Capital Region

In addition to his role as director, Charles is also an architect and the Regional Recovery Executive at GSA Public Buildings Service.

You play various roles with the GSA: director of construction, operational branch manager, business development advisor, project manager, and architect. Do you find one role is impacted more by the GSA's involvement in BIM than another?

Charles Hardy (CH): Not so much. All roles are touched in some way by the potential of the "I" in BIM. It is the generation, management, and use of that information that makes it valuable to all parts of an organization . . . and allows for the information to be converted into knowledge.

Before joining GSA in 1991, you worked as an architect in various firms practicing in the areas of real estate development and office design. Do you feel that GSA has given your career a second life? Do you feel that GSA's embrace of BIM has provided you with new challenges?

CH: It was time to move on. I don't necessarily look at my current position as a "second life," but rather as new challenges and opportunities. One must constantly look to be engaged and seek out growth. I believe BIM and its influence and the incorporation of it into operations provide a focus to some of the broader issues in our industry: collaboration, training and education, information management, the effective management of our facilities in a sustainable manner, the attractiveness of our industry, and many others. A challenge? You bet.

As an architect serving on boards of construction industry organizations such as CURT, CMAA, et cetera, do you ever experience any tension between design and construction cultures?

CH: There continues to be tension in the industry, but as all things, it ebbs and flows. I am firmly convinced that at no other time in recent history have we had a situation where the majority of the system wants to make it work for all. People are willing to share more information and blend roles, whether to reflect individual team member skill sets, the reality of the evolution of who does what, or because it just makes sense for the greater good of a project. We will always have those that don't share that sense of purpose. We can't manage to that. We need to focus on what is working, investigate why someone has concerns over the data accuracy, determine the validity, and act to overcome. In the end, we must understand intent, share intent, and deliver intent.

Congressman and architect Richard N. Swett, in his book *Leadership by Design*, encourages architects to engage in civic and public life. With your involvement as board member, trustee, or chair of various organizations—as well as your serving in a branch of the federal government and formerly in the U.S. Air Force Reserve—you appear to meet Swett's ideal of the citizen-architect. From your perspective, do you feel those in the profession would benefit from more of a public service attitude and/or practice?

CH: I, like many in public service, see it as a both a profession and a calling. The concept of citizen-architect or citizen-and–whatever-your-role-may-be is sound. I believe we are citizens of this great republic first and foremost, and as such need to

(Continued)

contribute to keep it strong. I have found, however, in giving of my time, whether it is in service to the organizations I support or to the military and my country, I receive much in return. I enjoy the perspective of others whose paths I may not have crossed, I enjoy the leadership models I have experienced and the many mentors I have met. When I assess my contributions to others, it pales greatly in comparison to what I have gained.

As an architect yourself, working among architects, you have managed to apply your training and education in ways that go beyond what one would consider the typical architect's role. Do you believe the demands and challenges of the new technologies—as well as the collaborative processes enabled by them—will encourage or discourage architects from getting involved beyond their specific area of competency?

CH: I think it will do nothing but encourage further exploration beyond their worlds. As BIM has opened the door for meaningful collaboration, it brings with it a desire and need for an understanding of your project partner's circumstance. It will bring architects more into planning, on through construction, into operations and maintenance, and if used effectively, keep them engaged until the disposal or repurposing of the facility they have helped bring life to. The encouragement will be a combination of desire and survival.

In your role as a member of the 3xPT Steering Group, a collaborative action between CURT, AIA, and AGC, what do you see concerning the potential for collaboration between the architecture profession and those working in the construction industry?

CH: I see great action to date, and I see a far greater potential. No longer can we each sit in our own business lines, maximizing our profits by providing the minimum acceptable service allowed under whatever contract we sign. 3xPT, and I think the industry, agrees that we will only improve by making sure we meet the project needs first, and our needs will be met as a by-product. I think this goes back to the citizen-architect comment. I think we all need to be good citizens of our projects.

When work is abundant, architects sometimes scoff at undertaking government projects. In lean times such as these you are no doubt seeing many firms that you would not have seen in more abundant times. Do architects and others do themselves a disservice by being fair-weather fans of government work?

CH: I believe so. Many come to the public sector work when private sector work is at a lull. However, that is when they get to experience what others have known for some time: it is great work, great challenges, great opportunity, and great people to work with. Firms have to determine where their business models will take them. The opportunity public sector work provides is amazing, and what I have found is that many come with stereotypes of slow-paced bureaucracies and leave with a sense they are dealing with industry leaders.

The GSA's national 3D-4D BIM program is at the industry's leading edge—whereas the GSA's expectations for a fully integrated design effort are perhaps not as stringent. Can you anticipate or indicate where the GSA plans to go with BIM and IPD/integrated design in the next five to ten years?

CH: We continue to innovate, adapt, and adopt. Looking out five to ten years is always difficult. As an owner, our interests lie in the operations and maintenance of our facilities. Our focus continues to be on how to bring that portion into the mainstream

There have been a few successes, but many more are needed. Innovation still needs to occur.
—Charles Hardy

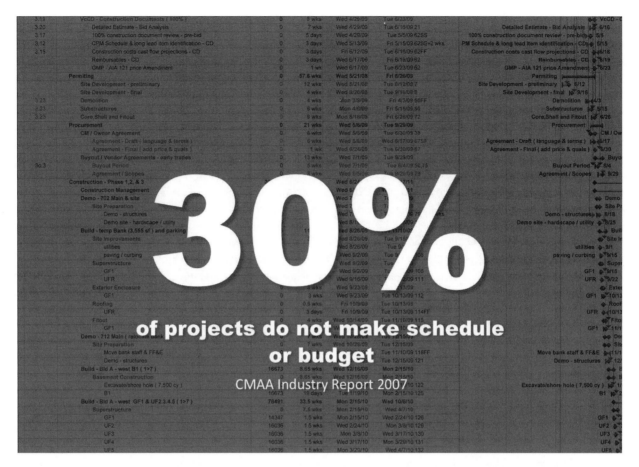

Figure 6.35   Thirty percent of projects do not make schedule or budget. *Image courtesy of Tocci Building Companies and KlingStubbins*

dialogue and practice. There have been a few successes, but many more are needed. Innovation still needs to occur. Information management needs to be more robust to, in essence, create a library system around the material so users can "check" models in and out of the system, and the models' integrity and usefulness remain. We have begun discussion on how IPD can be applied in the construct of the federal government, and we are encouraged by our initial talks. There is much to be done, but we, along with the industry, have a shared vision. (See Figure 6.35.)

Casey Jones is Director of Design Excellence and the Arts at the U.S. General Services Administration, where he is responsible for fostering excellence in federally commissioned art and architecture. Where at the GSA do design excellence and BIM overlap—or are these seen as separate entities?

CH: BIM is a tool that enables design. I personally believe that BIM starts to get people doing what they should be doing. What this means for design excellence is BIM should free up time to allow an architect to concentrate more on design, to run many

(Continued)

"what if" scenarios, and in the end, come up with a project that exceeds the expectations of the design excellence program—and more importantly, the user and, ultimately, the American people.

GSA's BIM mandate calls for BIM use in the conceptual design phase. BIM, of course, benefits the owner well beyond this phase. Taking into consideration the need to start incrementally and the need for early successes, where do you personally see the potential for utilizing BIM well beyond these initial phases?

CH: There are many uses beyond the initial phase, but the GSA mandate got folks to get going. I don't know of any projects that after the initial phase BIM was scrapped and the team reverted back to their old ways. Each team has built on it differently and innovated as it relates to their projects and their tasks at hand. The potential to use the model into the operation and maintenance of a facility is key. Then you are getting highest and best use. Also, as the circle of life in what we do continues, taking information from one project and pulling it forward as we plan the next is another area that requires further exploration.

Before GSA's BIM mandate, architects had to deliver unwanted building project budget news, such as one with the GSA federal courthouse project for Cadman Plaza East in Brooklyn, designed a decade ago by Cesar Pelli and HLW International. Has BIM, with its clash detection and rich data, essentially eradicated the necessity for firms to defend project budgets while providing value-engineering options at the same time, often required of public work in the past? Has GSA's BIM mandate reduced perceptions of excess by some and poor planning by others?

CH: Not so much BIM, as the social side of BIM. Collaboration has helped alleviate some issues and mitigate the risk on others. The GSA has been a longtime user of Construction Manager as Constructor, or CMc. We are engaging our construction contractors during design, and the information they bring to the table is welcome by both architect and owner. Phasing, logistics, material costs, labor availability are but a few things that general contractors can assist with. Information is a good thing, and more parties with greater insights typically make better information. So to answer your question, BIM-enabled collaboration and conversation has reduced those perceptions.

In mandating BIM use from its vendors, GSA originally took the lead in seeing that BIM is used widely across the profession and industry. Who in the AECO industry do you ultimately see taking the leadership role in the BIM process and why? The architect? Contractor? Owner? A third-party facilitator?

CH: This is kind of a trick question. When CURT was looking at how you optimize a project team, the answer was to let the team member best qualified to answer . . . answer. This was built on the premise that every team is not staffed with the "A" team, and that while someone may be staffed in a position, they may not have the complete renaissance skill set to deliver it all. As such, each team needs to determine who is the best planner, innovator, problem solver, speaker, et cetera, and let them fill those—and the team is stronger for it. The same holds true here. The leadership role of BIM should be borne by the team member most capable of assuming those duties. (See Figure 6.36.)

Do you feel that if you were starting out now in architecture that you would have been encouraged or discouraged, challenged or overwhelmed, by what is currently required of the emerging architect to absorb and embrace—by way of sustainability, energy analysis, integrated design, BIM, 3D visualization tools, et cetera?

CH: I think I would be greatly encouraged and challenged. When I graduated from university, there was so much more to learn and so much left unlearned. When I hear of colleges having classes with their construction management counterparts across

Figure 6.36   Thirty-seven percent of materials used in the construction industry become waste. *Image courtesy of Tocci Building Companies and KlingStubbins*

campus, I am envious. When I look at the logic of construction means and methods that BIM inherently teaches, I see the potential to educate. I see great things coming from the architectural and construction management colleges and universities.

GSA's BIM goal or "mandate" does not currently mandate IPD or integrated design. Explain GSA's goals, if any, for IPD and integrated design.

IPD is something we are looking into, but like construction management, the term is beginning to take on many meanings. GSA needs to define for our business model what integrated practice delivery, integrated project delivery, integrated design, and all the other names surrounding this mean to us.

—Charles Hardy

CH: IPD is something we are looking into, but like construction management, the term is beginning to take on many meanings. GSA needs to define for our business model what integrated practice delivery, integrated project delivery, integrated design,

(Continued)

and all the other names surrounding this mean to us. As we have looked at it to date, many of the practices of integrated design are currently being accomplished by GSA project teams across the country. The question is how you make it repeatable, reconfigurable, and predictable.

As part of the U.S. General Services Administration's 3D-4D BIM program, GSA encourages interoperability. While programs may talk to each other and transfer information back and forth, have you found that the disciplines and teams you deal with do the same? What has GSA done to encourage vendors to talk to each other and come to agreement?

CH: GSA continues to push interoperability. In our initial mandate we require the use of IFCs. In order to get the "I" in BIM operating at full speed, we need it. As we push to the evolution of BIM into the O&M phase, this becomes a much stronger need. I think industry-wide we have made great strides. We still need to keep our eyes on the prize and make sure we are providing what is needed. We support those organizations that our focusing on interoperability, and we encourage industry engagement.

Looking back on your career with the GSA, what, if anything, is your biggest frustration with the BIM initiative?

CH: Thankfully, I can say I really haven't had one.

What are some of the social—as opposed to technical or business—impacts GSA has had to contend with, such as new forms of communication, or benefitted from, such as improved communication, as a result of the inclusion and use of BIM in its process?

CH: Getting people to the table at the right time is always a challenge. And once there, getting them to openly share their information. However, we have seen great benefits from this when the team is aligned. The collaboration, dialogue, and problem solving is truly amazing. As with all information today, the greatest challenge is not to inundate people with information but to get the right information to the right person. This needs further study. Also, there remain "old school" participants that don't share information due to some myth or folklore that constrains them; others don't share under advice of counsel. Both of these situations require education and can be resolved.

Do you find that BIM can exclude some design professionals from the process due to their age, experience, or limitations with technology?

CH: No. The only thing I have found that excludes people from anything, BIM included, is their desire and drive. It's a choice. (See Figure 6.37.)

In the Great Lakes region you, architect Richard Gee, and lead project manager Michelle Wehrle are considered by the GSA to be "BIM Champions." What distinguishes a BIM Champion? In your estimation, what impact, if any, has identifying certain GSA employees this way had on their role, professional identity, and effectiveness within the organization as well as in public outreach?

CH: The BIM Champion program was put in place to identify advocates in each region for individuals inside and outside the region to contact regarding BIM. They typically are those engaged in the use of BIM and see the strong potential of its

Figure 6.37   Thirty-eight percent of carbon emissions in the United States are from buildings, not cars. *Image courtesy of Tocci Building Companies and KlingStubbins*

implementation. It has provided an easy reach-in for the public and has enabled a robust internal agency dialogue of shared practices. BIM has gone beyond evangelizing its need and use, but it still requires advocates to help folks come on board, share best and worst practices, and ultimately create other "champions."

In the video *GSA's Journey into Building Information Modeling*, addressing greater collaboration and integrated design, Stephen Hagen, with GSA's Public Building Service, asks: "How fast should we move? Is it next year that we do this? How do we challenge the construction industry?" Do you feel on some level that beyond its own goals the GSA as a catalyst is challenging the construction industry to make greater progress in integrated design and in working collaboratively?

CH: We accomplish our mission with our industry partners. It benefits us all if we are reading the same book and working off the same page. GSA is a leader in many design and construction innovations, but it takes the team to make it happen. Are we

(Continued)

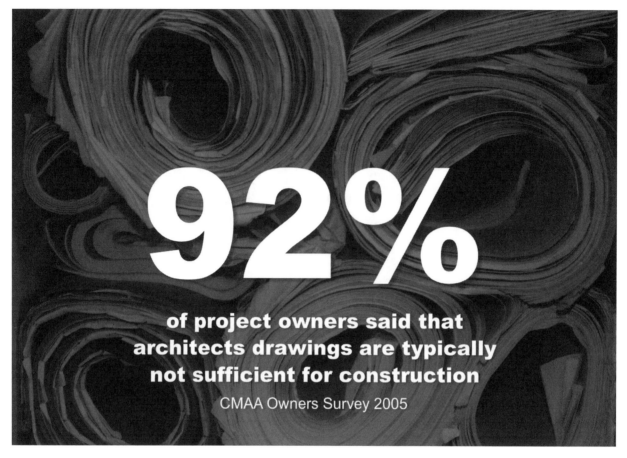

Figure 6.38   Ninety-two percent of project owners said that architects' drawings are typically not sufficient for construction. *Image courtesy of Tocci Building Companies and KlingStubbins*

a catalyst for change? I hope so. Are we challenging the construction industry, and ourselves, to improve? Definitely. Integrated design and working collaboratively are all about "the group" focused on an outcome. Whatever we can do to encourage the group that is brought together to design and construct a project to be optimized and high-performing, we will do. The more we encourage and lead the industry to have people come to the table prepared to collaborate, the more we can focus on the true task at hand. (See Figure 6.38.)

Through GSA's BIM mandate, do you feel as a building owner that GSA inspires *or* forces design excellence and better work from design professionals?

CH: I don't think you can force anyone to do anything that will be the quality that you desire. You do need to inspire. You need to get others to understand your intent, share your passion, appreciate the vision, and create shared goals.

NOTES

1. John H. Lienhard, *The Medieval Mason,* 1988, http://www.uh.edu/engines/epi1530.htm.
2. www.wikipedia.org.
3. Julie Gabrielli and Amy E. Gardner, "Architecture," May 28, 2010, http://www.wbdg.org/design/dd_architecture.php.
4. Inga Saffron, "City's Green Groundbreakers: Erdy McHenry, Architect as Master Builder," *Philadelphia Inquirer,* January 17, 2010, http://articles.philly.com/2010-01-17/news/25210169_1_design-firms-celebrity-architects-architects-focus.
5. Ibid.
6. Paul Durand, interview with the author, August 23, 2009.
7. Paul Durand, *Winter Street Architects Blog;* "Biting the BIM Bullet," August 20, 2009, http://winterstreetarchitects.wordpress.com/2009/08/20/biting-the-bim-bullet/.
8. Aaron Greven, interview with the author, August 9, 2009.
9. Ibid.
10. David Celento, "Innovate or Perish: New Technologies and Architecture's Future," *Harvard Design Magazine* 26 (Spring/Summer, 2007).
11. Andy Stapleton (Mortenson Construction), interview with the author, December 15, 2009.
12. Kimon Onuma, "BIM Ball—Evolve or Dissolve: Why Architects and the AIA are at Risk of Missing the Boat on Building Information Modeling (BIM)" (open letter, http://www.bimconstruct.org/steamroller.html, 2006).
13. Ibid.
14. Gabrielli and Gardner, "Architecture."
15. Stephen Kieran and James Timberlake, *Refabricating Architecture* (New York: McGraw-Hill Professional, 2003), 31.
16. Phil Bernstein, interview with the author, October 15, 2009.
17. Stapleton, interview.
18. Rumpf, interview.
19. Bill Reed and 7group, The Integrative Design Guide to Green Building (Hoboken, NJ: John Wiley & Sons, 2009).
20. Bernstein, interview.
21. Rumpf, interview.
22. Yanni Loukissas, interview with the author, October 15, 2009.

7 Learning BIM and Integrated Design

Figure 7.1   One hundred percent BIM. *Zach Kron, www.buildz.info*

The introduction of BIM into the workforce has education and training implications as well: factors that impact firms and practices, especially those that hire directly out of school. BIM impacts HR, hiring practices, recruitment, and ultimately the makeup of the firm, its organization if not organizational chart.

The ultimate end or goal for the architect is to lead the process and create the ultimate BIM and integrated design experience for all involved. It is not a question of learning software. It is a question of becoming familiar with the process and how this awareness is learned and acquired.

Impacts of BIM Education and Training

> The ideals instilled in architecture schools combined with the technical knowledge to realize these ideals are the two components of successful architecture.[1]
> —Kimon Onuma, "Evolve or Dissolve"

Kimon Onuma, in his open letter "Evolve or Dissolve," refers to an architect's education and training as a platform to build upon.[2] That's what education is—a foundation that supports one's goals, and upon which you construct your career.

In the past several years a growing number of schools, education programs, and courses are offering curricula in BIM studies as well as classes that make use of BIM-related software.

Students in professional and academic doctoral programs in architecture are conducting research, pushing the limits of our understanding of impacts and forces acting upon BIM and integrated design.

How do you learn BIM?

Is it BIM that you learn, or software such as Revit or ArchiCAD?

What does it mean to *learn* BIM?

By this point you should be able to differentiate BIM—the process—from software—the tools. BIM education is less about learning the software than the process in which the software is utilized. Learning BIM is not the same as learning Revit or ArchiCAD. As a rule of thumb, remember: *One trains to work in Revit or ArchiCAD; one learns to work in BIM.*

Exposure to virtual building starts early. Architects, as children, once learned about building by using Legos one brick at a time. Now kids build online, virtual brick by virtual brick.[3] Schools have the opportunity to use BIM as a design and construction teaching tool, and not only as a tool to be exploited postgraduation by practitioners. The process must be picked up along the way—it isn't something that comes naturally or that practitioners are born with.

Once out of high school, there is little incentive—other than pressure from employers of future graduates—to offer BIM education or training. NAAB student

When I look at the logic of construction means and methods that BIM inherently teaches, I see the potential to educate. I see great things coming from the architectural and construction management colleges and universities.

—Charles Hardy, interview with the author, 2010

performance criteria, for the purpose of accreditation, require graduating students to demonstrate understanding or ability in numerous areas: critical thinking skills, graphic skills, use of precedents, human behavior, and building systems integration among them. Nowhere is there a requirement for a university architecture program to teach computer software skills.

In terms of integrated design, again according to NAAB criteria, understanding collaborative skills, including the ability to recognize the varied talent found in interdisciplinary design project teams in professional practice and work in collaboration with other students as members of a design team, becomes more critical.

From an education standpoint, younger staff and emerging professionals are expected to put entire buildings together in BIM. Whereas historically these junior employees focused on individual, repetitive details—such as bathroom or column details, picking up someone else's redlines, or working exclusively in one phase, such as schematic design—with BIM, they are being asked to engage in the design and detailing of the entire virtual building model.

Where are emerging professionals learning how to put buildings together? (See Figure 7.2.)

BIM Learning and Unlearning

With BIM it is just as important to unlearn certain habits as it is to learn new skills. We've discussed

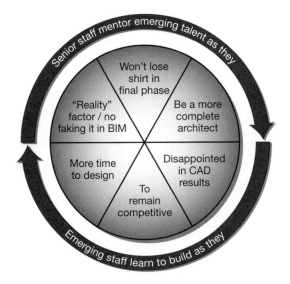

Figure 7.2   Motives, competitive advantages, and benefits for working in BIM and integrated design. How many are you capturing? How many can you claim?

how learning a program such as Revit Architecture or even ArchiCAD is more difficult for those who have been previously trained in CAD. As Phil Bernstein described in his interview, our perceptions of our roles on design and construction teams run deep, where any effort to integrate requires a conscious mindfulness: "We've been acculturated to do this stuff, sometimes for hundreds of years. And getting yourself outside that set of instincts is going to be really, really hard."[4] On the IPD side of the equation, Howard W. Ashcraft Jr. talks about unlearning contractual relationships.[5] When first starting out in BIM and integrated design, collaboration and leadership do not need to be learned. Instead, to advance in these areas, we would do well to concentrate our initial efforts on unlearning our cultural training.

What is needed is a refresher course—with intermittent prompting when we find ourselves delving into old habits. According to Andrew Pressman,

Many academic programs still produce students who expect they will spend their careers working as heroic, solitary designers. But integrated practice is sure to stimulate a rethinking of that notion. Pedagogy must focus on teaching not only how to design and detail, but also how to engage with and lead others, and how to collaborate with the professionals they are likely to work with later.[6]

Pressman continues,

"The idea that design-bid-build is being supplanted by other delivery methods has implications for development of specific skill sets for future architects and, therefore, for architectural education." This paradigm shift, according to David W. Hinson, AIA, chair of the architecture program at Auburn University, in Alabama, suggests that the construction phase will be just as collaborative as the design phases. "The importance of working in teams will extend dramatically deeper into the project timeline," says Hinson. The art of collaborating and negotiating must be integrated into courses across the curriculum, including design studio, architectural technology, and professional practice.[7]

What is the best venue for learning BIM—community, public, or private college? Vendor training programs, on site or in your office? Autodesk University, online training, tutorials, webinars, podcasts, one-on-one lessons, or b(u)y-the-book? There are even BIM summer camps, boot camps, and workshops. Resellers, consultants, and training facilities—as well as online service providers and construction groups—have stepped in to address some of the software and technical questions. But they also have their own agendas and are not seen as objective, trusted advisors to the industry when doling out advice at the same time that they are selling products or services.

The impact of BIM and integrated design on architectural education is still being assessed. While education is important to grasp the big picture and workflow, a training regimen is critical to take BIM to the next level.

BIM Training

Your investing the time, energy, and resources in reading this book goes a long way toward assuring your staying on top of the subject. The impact of BIM and integrated design on training and professional development can be significant, so whatever time you spend up front understanding the larger concepts is time well spent. Think of this book as part of your training.

Training is often cut from the budget in lean times. To remain productive and effective, a firm's contractor staff requires training in your approach to BIM. Training assures that they will utilize the program and new work process properly.

Training Decay

One of the greatest concerns about training is when it ought to occur. There are many variables to take into consideration concerning information retention from training, and timing is perhaps the most significant. Some estimate that as much as 80 percent of what one learns in training is lost within thirty days. Perhaps more significantly, up to 66 percent is lost within one day.[8] There is a great deal you can do to assure that what is learned sticks, including providing trainees with the opportunity to turn what they've learned into a habit by applying their training immediately upon training completion—for example, in the form of a pilot project in which you model and document an existing or new building. Unapplied information is lost; applied information is retained.

The best way to retain what you learn is by putting it to use. "We had some pretty poor experiences with training with ADT earlier on," says Rich Nitzsche, CIO of Perkins + Will.

> We just didn't want to make those mistakes again. With ADT we were taking a shotgun approach to training. I'm a firm believer in training decay. What we were clear on with Revit was that we were going to do just-in-time training. We took Autodesk's five-day training package and condensed it down to three days. Getting five consecutive days of anybody's time in this firm is very nearly impossible. We delivered the training ourselves. We built a mobile training package so we had a whole kit, with eight laptops, router, projector, that we shipped all over the country. Our design application managers would meet wherever this was going. It's fairly crucial that everyone's getting the same training, working with the same resources. We did a little outsourcing—when we did, we trained them on our package. Because we just didn't have enough people internally. Training is less of a struggle than it used to be, but it is still a challenge.[9]

Nitzsche found that customizing the training for the technology works best:

> We have to adjust our training because we know now more about how BIM behaves, particularly for a large team workflow. The application has changed, so that changes the training content. Instead of the one-size-fits-all deliverable, [we] try to focus on specific needs. We're trying to customize the package—a stand-alone, interiors and urban design training package.[10]

If you put time and attention into the technology, you have to do the same for your employees in terms

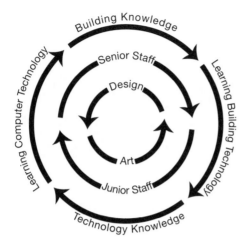

Figure 7.3 Mutual mentoring diagram.

of training. Training provides firms with a competitive advantage—and at the very least assures that they won't fall behind. Firms will want to identify the alternative ways of training and then determine whether training will be internal, by those who understand your firm's methodology; or external, by trained trainers. Having a training strategy for your team or firm is critical.[11] Plan for follow-up training and professional development to help take BIM and integrated design to the next level. (See Figure 7.3.)

One point that is often overlooked is that senior management has to become educated in the technology and process and make the decision to invest the time and resources to help the BIM process catch on and take off. The taking on of a pilot project is a critical bridge in the training process in that it connects textbook learning with hands-on application, and senior management can assure that this transition from training to project takes place. No matter the training method undertaken, what one learns in BIM training must be applied, implemented, and put into practice within thirty days, or trainees forget.

Other factors that make BIM training successful:

- A feedback loop to sharpen and improve performance

- Buy-in and support from senior management—before, during, and after training

- The attitude of the trainee—curiosity, openness, and willingness to learn and to be taught

- Explaining the big picture, relevance, and how the training fits into the goals of the firm, how the learning objectives align with your firm's strategic objectives

- A facilitator or trainer who is prepared, knowledgeable, organized, engaging, and, perhaps most important, interested and excited about the BIM process and not afraid to have fun (otherwise trainees will be less likely to learn)

- The quality of the content of the learning material

- An environment that's conducive to learning

- Identifying what's in it for the firm—but as important, what's in it for you, the trainee? What do you hope to get out of training? How badly do you want this?

Factors that contribute to the failure of BIM training include the following:

- Not understanding that training is but one possible solution to address a skills gap or to attain knowledge. Depending on your situation, training may not be the most effective intervention.

- Not being prepared, motivated, or ready to learn or to facilitate the training of others.

- Failing to allocate a realistic amount of time for behavioral changes to take place.

- Being unwilling or unable to set expectations and to measure and compare results.

- Misidentifying the right people to undertake training.

- Failing to create targeted and engaging delivery and/or content.

- Not undertaking a needs assessment: BIM training may not satisfy current needs.

Field Experience versus Mentoring

With BIM, it becomes critical that one understands how a building comes together. The opportunity to visit a job site on a regular basis or do consistent project fieldwork is not always practical or available to the BIM operator. An alternative is mentoring, in which the mid-career design professional mentors the emerging professional mentee.

Is it necessary for mid-career design professionals to learn BIM? Here there are really two questions being asked: Can they learn BIM? And should they learn BIM? The first is a question of the middle-aged brain and its capacities. The short answer is yes. The second is a business and professional question, one having to do with roles, identity, profitability, ROI, and personal growth and development. This second question is more situational—while it is a business question, and a career one, it is also, frankly, a personal decision.

The money factor does come up. At their hourly rates, especially as firms aim to work leaner and more efficiently and effectively, does it make sense to see a forty-eight-year-old working in Revit versus sitting alongside a younger BIM operator—one hand on computer technology, the other on building technology? Will mid-careerists be able to not only change but keep up? Absolutely. It all comes first and foremost down to attitude and mindset. Learning BIM involves unlearning past ways of working that are at once familiar and comfortable—but

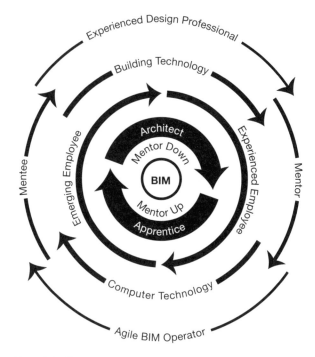

Figure 7.4   Mutual mentoring: as one mentors up and the other mentors down, there is an evening-out—a flattening of any perceived or actual hierarchy.

detrimental to your work, progress, and ultimately your indispensability.

To learn BIM, mid-career architects will need to reinvent themselves. The world, industry, and profession are not the same that we inhabited just a few years ago. So we will need to change, adjust, and adapt. When things return, we won't be returning to the way things used to be. The old formulas simply don't apply anymore. (See Figure 7.4.)

For most, learning the technology is a no-brainer, a nonquestion: Kristine Fallon Associates offers a half-day quick-start training course in BIM that will get you off and running, and resellers offer some powerful three-day workshops, not to mention tutorials, both online and old school. Several of the experts I interviewed for this book scoff at the idea that learning to master BIM is even difficult. They don't even question whether fifty-year-olds can learn it. It all really comes down to what you want, where you want to see yourself five to ten years down the road.

Two Approaches to Learning BIM

If you want to learn BIM, there are two approaches you can take at mid-career:

1. You can play the role of experienced architect and—in the classic architect/apprentice fashion—sit beside the agile BIM operator, reciprocally feeding your building technology input in exchange for their BIM technology magic.

2. You can master BIM yourself and become a master virtual builder.

Mentoring Up and Down

Reverse mentoring, mutual mentoring, or mentoring side by side (SxS) are all legitimate approaches to learning both BIM and how buildings get built. "Working styles of generations are also a factor with the new 'generation Y' leading the way using reverse mentoring or co-mentoring. For the first time in the design profession's history, there is large-scale upstream mentoring by twenty- and thirty-year-old professionals who are 'mentoring their mentors.'"[12]

The Side-by-Side Approach

The first approach has the advantage of using your current skill sets and experience to help move projects along while simultaneously advancing emerging professionals in their understanding of how buildings come together. At the same time, the emerging architect—working in BIM—has the opportunity to inform you of

- What they discover in the model

- What works and doesn't work

- Where there are gaps in the information

- Where coordination may be needed

The relationship is reciprocal and there's a clear symbiosis to it. As one mentors "up," the other mentors "down," and there is an evening-out—a flattening—of any real or perceived hierarchy. Working in BIM, privy to important information before anyone else, the emerging architect feels empowered. Working alongside the BIM operator, the senior professional is

- Assured that the building is coming together effectively

- Grateful not to have to pass along redlines wondering if they were understood and addressed correctly

- Intrinsically rewarded knowing that she has shared some hard-won lessons and experience with the next generation

Some senior firm members learn BIM—*succumb* to BIM—due to professional obligation.

Alternatively, in order to maintain control, they take a DIY approach. (See Figure 7.5.)

The DIY Approach

The DIY approach involves

- Learning the software—and the collaborative work process

- Unlearning habits you picked up along the way—including thinking in CAD

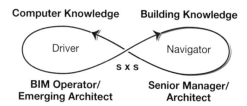

Figure 7.5   Mutual mentoring and pair programming both involve a driver and navigator working side by side (SxS.)

- Attaining an open and flexible mindset and attitude toward change

- Being easy on yourself when problems occur or trouble appears

Several studies indicate that it takes twenty-one days to break a habit, while others say it takes longer. "It takes between thirty and sixty days of doing the same thing over and over again on a daily basis to create a new habit or break an old one," says Larry Tobin, co-creator of Habit Changer. "We all walk around on a daily basis with habits that are detrimental to our productivity."[13]

But are we really calling CAD a habit in need of change, replacing it with a new habit called BIM—a two-step process whereby you call out the bad habit (CAD), identify its well-documented and acknowledged negative consequences, and create an alternative action in its place (in this case, BIM)? Or are we talking here not about habit change but about learning a whole new technology, mindset, and work process?

When I asked Jonathan Cohen his impressions of those in mid- to late career learning a new technology such as BIM and also learning to work in a completely different—fast-paced, concurrent, integrated—way than they have been used to, he responded:

I've heard this and I don't agree with it. Older people can learn new tricks. Concerning BIM,

putting a kid just out of school on BIM without knowing anything about how buildings go together doesn't make sense. Architects with experience have more to contribute to this process because they know how buildings come together. BIM is just the simulation of a building in the computer. If you don't know about buildings, then I don't know what you're modeling.[14]

Process Training

Who should get trained in BIM? Not necessarily those who excelled in CAD. Those who are selected for training in BIM should have a few attributes in common: they should be intra-/entrepreneurial, self-starters, self-motivated, and show leadership potential. The last is important because the earliest adopters will be those who teach the others. Additionally, they should know building construction and be comfortable learning, as opposed to having to prove themselves. BIM has been called a disruptive technology. Aim to minimize the disruption.

BIM tools are being taught in high schools where CAD was once taught. "Until now an architecture course would typically involve training in CAD, often AutoCAD. But in Texas now this is being changed to reflect the current job market. Students in Texas high schools will now be learning BIM and spending less time on CAD."[15]

Training and Education in Integrated Design

While most professors are against teaching software, they are open to the idea of teaching work processes and process changes brought about by integrated design. What does it mean to *learn* integrated design? We are born knowing how to collaborate—it's something we *un*learn along the way.[16] What exactly are you learning when you learn to work on integrated design teams? "When I was in architecture school I never dreamed that I would one day be talking about supply chains! As designers we have to think about the whole pipeline. We're trying to get people out of their design mindsets and think about having a broader conversation about delivering a building with the constructors."[17]

Case Study Interview with Yanni Loukissas, PhD, postdoctoral associate, Massachusetts Institute of Technology

Yanni Loukissas is a postdoctoral associate in the program in Science, Technology, and Society at MIT, where he studies human-machine-environment interaction. Yanni has served as visiting lecturer at Cornell University and brings an interdisciplinary background in architecture, computing, and ethnography to his work. He is the author of Conceptions of Design in a Culture of Simulation: Socio-technical Studies at Arup *(Routledge, 2012).*

You have called design "a system of relationships in flux." Your written work has focused on how practitioners use simulations, not only to perform various technological analyses but also to mediate their professional relationships and define new roles. What are some of the major observations that you have made about these relationships and roles?

Yanni Loukissas (YL): In *Keepers of the Geometry* I talk about changing roles and relationships. The title itself was a term used in one office that I was studying, where people are inventing new names to describe what they do and who they are within the office. There's some negotiation over what it means to be the Keeper of the Geometry. One of the things about professions that has interested me is how they negotiate for jurisdiction. I was heavily influenced by a book, *The System of Professions* by Andrew Abbott, in which he writes about the professions as existing in a larger system of relationships. He says the defining activity of professionals is competition. I would also say it is collaboration.

In any respect, it's about dealing with this system of relationships and navigating it. Professionals profess to do certain things, have a certain expertise and authority, so for someone to say that they are the Keeper of the Geometry is a kind of claim that they believe might enable them to have more control over the design, have some kind of autonomy, define themselves in a way that they think is beneficial. I am looking for ways in which people define themselves and claim their difference from others using technology to define that difference: whether they're close to the technology, whether it's a part of their role, or somehow outside of their role. For example, the principal of the same firm saw himself as set apart from the technology and was negotiating with people who were in control of it. Other people in the firm had to build their reputation and their roles around the technology and their knowledge of it. In that sense, the technology can be part of how you describe yourself and see yourself. Lewis Mumford talked about how various kinds of professions or jobs were intimately linked with technology or enabled by technology. There's a wide body of literature about this kind of stuff out there.

(Continued)

Yours might be identified as a sociotechnical approach to design by studying cultures of practice. In your work on simulation at Arup, "Conceptions of Design in a Culture of Simulation,"[18] how does their culture differ from other firm cultures? What is simulation's impact on firm culture?

YL: What I was interested in with Arup was the way in which they manage their professional roles. Where, on one hand, they try to differentiate themselves from their collaborators, their clients, building regulators—they do a lot of work to identify how they are unique, even if we don't know objectively if they are or not. They separate and distinguish themselves because they're consultants and they're being hired to perform a service, so they'd better deliver something unique. At the same time, they're also trying to make bridges and connections with other people. A lot of their work is about helping nonexperts and laypeople understand technical aspects of buildings. They're trying to do these two different things.

What I was also interested in with Arup was how they seem to take their specificity, the particularities of their relationships very seriously. And they build their simulations around those specific conditions. Although a lot of times they're using off-the-shelf software, the way that they construct the particular simulation is highly specific to an audience. And it is through that means of developing, tweaking, and specifying the simulation for a particular audience that I saw the simulations became meaningful to them. For me, that indicated this "culture of use" at Arup around simulations. Their culture is really about making simulations that are adapted and constructed around their audiences in a very particular way. Whereas before that, I had often seen simulations demonstrated as being more objective, independent of who was necessarily looking at them. Arup was highly aware of the kind of contingency of their simulations, both socially and culturally. (See Figures 7.6 and 7.7. Note: The figures accompanying this interview are for illustrative purposes and do not represent the work of the interviewee.)

Would you say that is due to what might be called Arup's culture of experimentation, that they are able to adjust their data to their audience?

YL: It's a big firm, and there are certain branches that are definitely experimental and thrive on that.

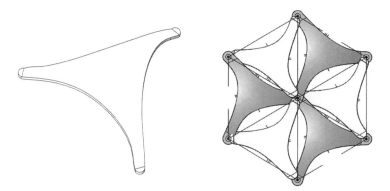

Figure 7.6   Millwork—individual component and composite—ceiling boomerang element, image of the component and hexagon pattern. When assembled, the repeating ceiling shape creates an undulating convex–concave form. *Revit Architecture Workflow: Joe Kendsersky, Autodesk Inc. Architect: KlingStubbins, Cambridge, MA*

You have written that practitioners use their skill with simulations to challenge traditional professional identities like
"architect" and "engineer." Is this deliberate, or a natural
result from working in a simulation environment?

*The interest of various professionals in claiming that they
are architects or engineers has more to do with their
being competitive, finding a niche for themselves.*
— Yanni Loukissas, PhD

YL: I don't like to say that anything is the result of the natural
use of technology, because I don't like to think that it is deter-
ministic. People are definitely influenced by technology, but they really shape their interactions with it, give it a place within their
work and their culture. The interest of various professionals in claiming that they are architects or engineers has more to do with
their being competitive, finding a niche for themselves. From one collaboration to the next, it might make more sense for them
to describe themselves as an architect, engineer, designer, or technologist—and they have to figure out what makes them most
competitive in that particular situation. That's a very conscious decision.

You have noted that drawing and digital simulation can coexist, and that today design practitioners are adopting digital
simulations without necessarily giving up all their traditional methods by sharing design options in digital models of
buildings as well sketches and physical models. You wrote, "While traditional methods of simulation have not disap-
peared, they have been swept up in a new digital culture of design."[19] How would you describe their relationship and
coexistence? Does one tolerate or ultimately improve the other?

YL: It varies, depending on how professionals wish to present themselves. Older professionals who have grown up sketching often are actively looking for ways in which sketching is unique and can be differentiated from digital modeling as a type of
expression, or ideas that a sketch can hold that simulation can't. The relationship between sketching and digital modeling is
complex and interesting—old methods and new methods—but I like to think in any context it's closely tied to professional identity. Sherry Turkle always said, "People may accept or resist a technology not for what it does but for how it makes them feel."
For some people, sketching makes them feel empowered, with control over the sketch. Reyner Banham wrote that there's a
certain generation of architects who couldn't think without a pencil in their hand. And for those same architects engaging with
digital technologies often makes them feel like novices because they don't understand it, they don't have control over it, and

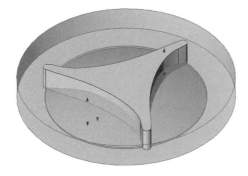 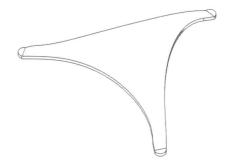

Figure 7.7   Forming the 3D ceiling component: a generic model family created using a solid extrusion and void revolve to create the concave shape. *Revit
Architecture Workflow. Revit Architecture Workflow: Joe Kendsersky, Autodesk Inc. Architect: KlingStubbins, Cambridge, MA*

(Continued)

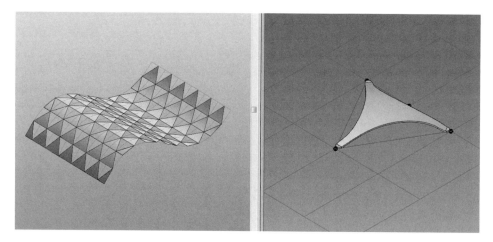

Figure 7.8   Millwork design process. The challenges were how to begin modeling the component, what template to start off with, and how to break down the entire assembly into a kit of parts. Views can be toggled back and forth to view the curtain panel pattern family and massing side by side. Revit Architecture Workflow. *Revit Architecture Workflow: Joe Kendsersky, Autodesk Inc. Architect: KlingStubbins, Cambridge, MA*

they're disempowered—even emasculated—by it. Whereas for others, the reverse is true. A lot of young architects just out of school who have mastery over digital techniques—especially when they know other people in the office aren't as good as they are—that gives them a certain kind of power, legitimacy, and control. This is all wrapped up in how people identify themselves.

How would you describe the relationship between hand drawing and BIM today? Is it a relationship of tolerance or mutual coexistence?

YL: One of the things that I've noticed is that whether people are on one side or the other, especially to an extreme where they only use computers or they only sketch—they have certain romantic notions about the other way of doing things. Often at MIT I ran into people who were wizards with computers who just wished that they could draw. One student I remember, who was in a computer graphics course, saying that he was only doing computer graphics to substitute for the fact that he could never draw very well. People aren't necessarily intolerant of the other technology. A number of people I interviewed for my dissertation had a facility with both to some extent. Nobody mentioned giving up one or the other. So today they live together in a relationship. (See Figures 7.8 and 7.9.)

With their reliance on visualization tools, do you believe that practitioners will eventually lose the ability to visualize with their mind's eye—currently one of their core competencies and attributes—much the way they've lost the ability to compute with their dependence on calculators?

YL: People are definitely training their minds to think about space in new ways. So I think it requires more subtlety than saying they have the ability to visualize or don't. To an extent, people who do 3D modeling are more facile with thinking about spatial relationships and three dimensions because they have the ability and more experience working in a 3D interactive world that gives them feedback about their assumptions in an interesting way that's much more flexible, malleable, and high speed than even working with a physical model. Which cognitive abilities they develop, and which they lose, is not clear. Certainly

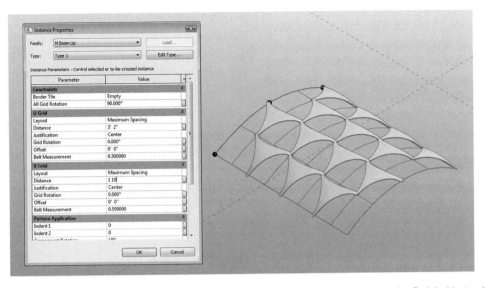

Figure 7.9   Millwork element properties dialog box. Since the ceiling components undulate, the surfaces have to overlap. Revit Architecture Workflow. *Revit Architecture Workflow: Joe Kendsersky, Autodesk Inc. Architect: KlingStubbins, Cambridge, MA*

something is lost when people don't work with physical materials and they lose a sense of how things go together, materiality, and the effects of gravity. There's also the question of embodied knowledge—I write about this in *Keepers of the Geometry*—what different people get out of working with computer models depending on how close they are to those models, whether they are building them, or whether they are just looking at them. A lot of firm principals are even more removed now—so maybe the people who are not directly building the computer models are at the most extreme disadvantage.

You appropriate or internalize those tools. I've often heard students use a term for what they do as "modeling operations." Those modeling operations they've internalized to some respect, so they don't need to be sitting in front of the computer to draw upon those ways of thinking.

— Yanni Loukissas, PhD

Because they don't get to be in the space with the physical model and understand it three-dimensionally. They also don't get to be in the virtual space of the 3D model either, really. They just see it as a flat image on the screen.

In your own teaching could you guess whether students' thinking is happening with their hands or in the model as opposed to being in their head? Those that work in simulation—are they only thinking when modeling?

YL: I don't think so. Older architects aren't only thinking when they're drawing. Certainly drawing aids thinking, and there's the feedback you get when drawing that enriches the thinking process. You appropriate or internalize those tools. I've often heard students use a term for what they do as "modeling operations." Those modeling operations they've internalized to some respect, so they don't need to be sitting in front of the computer to draw upon those ways of thinking. People often say that this

(Continued)

new generation is unable to visualize and think about complex, 3D forms, but buildings are much more complex these days. I don't know where the final evidence of that will come out because the kinds of structures that are being designed and built are much more sophisticated spatially. Where is the evidence that we're somehow getting more simplistic in our ways of thinking about space?

In a passage from your dissertation on Arup, you wrote:

> [Peter Bressington] argues that conflicts between models developed by different groups can sometimes be quite healthy. However, he cautions, the approach to these conflicts cannot be "my model is better than your model," but rather "are these models built on the same assumptions? If they are, then there is no issue." Although Bressington expresses optimism about the potential for simulations to be integrated, his words suggest that a consensus among people is necessary for this aim to be met. In other words, integration can be facilitated by technology, but it is inherently social. Integration requires a conscientious attitude on the part of practitioners.[20]

The majority of observers of this passage would no doubt emphasize issues of file sharing, coordination, and interoperability, while you have chosen to emphasize the *social* as the crux to a successful integration. Why is that? What can you tell us about the ideal attitude and mindset one needs to acquire and cultivate to work in integrated design?

YL: From my point of view it was Bressington who was emphasizing the social. That was not a foreign way of thinking about it for him. A number of people at the firm talked about the resistance certain people have to collaborating. The mindset of working collaboratively requires an ability to step outside of your own shoes and try to understand what the needs are of your collaborators. One of the things I talk about in the book are "trading zones," a term developed by Peter Galison, the Harvard professor of history of science—almost pidgin languages that are developed on the fly between people from different social or epistemological groups. Galison talks about people in collaboration having to develop intermediary languages, and it might often be the case that those languages are useful for handling and sharing information, common references. Importantly, these trading zones don't require the collaborators to give up or even reveal their own values and motivations. So people can collaborate locally but not necessarily have shared overarching goals. He writes about what's entailed and required in doing that where collaboration has certain local aspects to it—where people find ways of connecting but more broadly they might not necessarily converge in their ideas. For Arup, collaboration comes back to professional identity, whether you see yourself as a collaborator—someone who's empowered by collaboration. The way they present or position themselves has largely to do with how they develop consensus among a variety of people involved in the process. So they see themselves as collaborators, as part of their identity. Similarly, others talk about themselves as collaborators and that's the defining part of their identity. They see themselves as being very good at communicating with architects, knowing their language. It requires more than technology requires: a willingness and motivation and an ability to come together locally—but not necessarily wholly, where you're giving up all of your personal motivations.

In *Keepers of the Geometry* you talk about this being a time of technical as well as social transition for practitioners. What are you seeing in the current social transition of practice?

YL: Along with new technologies, there's been acceleration in this type of change. People see it as an opportunity to develop new roles for themselves, to reposition themselves, to discover new niche areas of specialization—like Front in New York or

SHOP Architects, all-new models of practice. People see new technology as opening new opportunities for social organization that can be built around those technologies. Not necessarily that technology drives social change, but that people see an opportunity there to get ahead or be competitive in a new way. One of the reasons I was interested in researching Arup was their history of using new technologies to expand into new domains. They've been particularly facile in that sense, whether it has to do with a new approach to adopting building regulations, trying to bypass them through the use of simulations, trading new spaces of collaboration, which can make clients feel more comfortable to reach consensus around issues. They're looking for new ways to make the new technology into a business.

Do you consider BIM a tool like CATIA, an evolution from existing software, or something transcendent and perhaps even revolutionary?

YL: Using an anthropological approach, calling something revolutionary or transcendent is taking a position, and it is a way of making sense of the technology, making it meaningful. For different people it may mean different things. For Frank Gehry's office—and for Gehry Technologies—they market CATIA as this game-changing technology. *Parametric modeling* is a term that has been thrown around as this revolutionary way of doing design. But Ivan Sutherland's first CAD system, developed in the early 1960s, Sketchpad, was a parametric system. Parametrics is the most basic ability of any computer system. There are revolutionary uses of technology and the ways people use technology to change the way they work, including the way they work with or collaborate with others. (See Figures 7.10 and 7.11.)

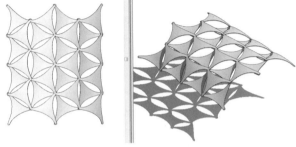

Figure 7.10   3D millwork ceiling panel studies. The overall design intent is understood. Revit Architecture Workflow. *Revit Architecture Workflow: Joe Kendsersky, Autodesk Inc. Architect: KlingStubbins, Cambridge, MA*

Is school really the best place to learn technology such as BIM? Do you want to take up class time to teach software? Or should students learn software on their own or after graduation in the workforce?

YL: Students can't wait to learn the technology until they're in the workforce. Representation is intimately tied with design thinking. Any approach to design exists within a sociotechnical context, so design can't be separated from the technology which is used to create it. Learning new technologies and investigating new opportunities and affordances in digital media is part of growing and developing as a designer. If you wait to expose students to that until after they graduate, they're already going to be partially formed as designer-thinkers and

Figure 7.11   From digital fabrication of ceiling millwork components to fabrication shop floor. *Image courtesy of Tocci Building Companies and KlingStubbins*

(Continued)

they're going to see the technology as foreign to how they think and what they do. Technology should be the focus of school in the sense that students are trained in skills. It should be more integrated into the way that design is taught and done. It's part of the context in which we do design.

Should we be concerned that students will graduate knowing how to make nice pictures but have spent time learning information technology instead of building technology?

Students can't wait to learn the technology until they're in the workforce. Representation is intimately tied with design thinking. Any approach to design exists within a sociotechnical context, so design can't be separated from the technology which is used to create it.

— Yanni Loukissas, PhD

YL: Students have to engage with materials and fabrication in addition to working on screen. That has to be part of the context in which they learn about design and understand all of its facets. Everything can't be done in school, and students aren't going to graduate fully knowing how to put a building together. Because that is such a complex process, requiring many people and trades, trying to do that might not be possible in school. Schools have defined themselves around design as something that can be separated from construction. For schools to justify their continued existence, they have to be able to identify something called design, which can be taught independently of construction and interaction with contractors. It's a kind of intellectual pursuit, something that can be handled abstractly, and realized to an extent as representation alone. There's an advantage in schools presenting design as separate from building. That's not entirely a positive thing.

Contractors and others have made great strides in adopting and implementing these digital tools, while architects in many cases have remained on the sidelines or on the fence. What advantage, if any, do you feel architects have over others in the industry when it comes to utilizing this technology and social processes? What would you tell an architect who is hesitant to adopt this work process?

YL: There have been a number of claims architects have made about the advantages these technologies provide. Frank Gehry would say that the technology brings him closer to fabricators, and fabricators closer to the process of construction. Others are interested in having simulation predict how the building is going to look or perform before it is built. People have all kinds of reasons for adopting it. For those who need convincing, what I say is that if they want to find new ways of being innovative and competitive in architecture, the best way to do that is through computation and digital technologies. Students are still interested in the old masters, replicating the way Le Corbusier worked, or Louis Kahn. What I say to them is: These practitioners, working in their own time, were taking advantage of the technologies of their time. If they were working today, it would be in a different context. You need to take advantage of the context in which you are working. It's going to be hard to compete with these old masters on their own terms. Or if you introduce new conditions, by default you'll be producing something different, using a different process—you'll be innovative just due to the fact that you are working in a new technology.

Would it be accurate to say, in your experience, that teams working in simulation have many contributors but no central leadership?

YL: Most design practices have many contributors. In the case of Arup, people often ask me: if they're the ones making the simulation, don't they control the discourse? Aren't they leading in that sense? Arup practitioners do see themselves in that way, in that they are leading the process—not necessarily the entire design process, but the process of how a particular building is going to function and perform. As design has become more fragmented and more specialized, at Arup each of these specialized realms has a leader. Prominent in my memory is this experience of being in Norman Foster's office—they had just adopted Ecotect sustainability software, and they used it to go to their consultants and say, "Now that we have this new simulation or modeling platform, we expect you to revise the way you work with us. We're going to expect more from you, a richer discourse." That's an example of architects trying to take back some level of control over the discussion by employing their own simulations.

In a recent blog post, "A House Divided Bridging Architecture's Culture War," Ann Lui wrote in the *Cornell Sun*:

> Sometimes it feels like there is a deep and growing abyss in architecture, an impassible trench that forces students to jump to one side or another or risk falling in. . . . On one side, the "new school"; on the other, "old school." . . . These two sides say only one word to you the second you decide to join the war: "Choose." And there you are . . . saying: "Pick now or forever hold your peace: Are you going to draw by hand or on the computer?" They may as well be saying to you, "Choose between AutoCad and pencils, between programming and intuition, the power of 3D printing and the warm curve of wood on the lathe. Ultimately, the issue is that there is no choice. "Old school" versus "new school," as it's waged at Cornell, is a completely false dichotomy.

She goes on to write:

> Everyone knows we can't abstain completely from computers, from Revit and Rhino, the arsenal of the "new school." But "Neither can we discard the "old school"—there is no complete rejection of history . . . The divide between "new school" and "old school" is a self-imposed illusion."[21]

Do you agree that the two schools/cultures are compatible and not mutually exclusive? Do you believe the virtual and visceral can coexist?

YL: Determining this is part of the professional debate. I don't think that there's an objective answer. Some people will take up the position that they are incompatible because that's a beneficial position for them to take strategically. This is how I approach things. I look for—what's the motivation in making those kinds of statements? Whether there's a "new school" and "old school" may not be the most important thing. The most important thing may be whether somebody has a job or not, or whether they're respected and feel like they have a voice in the department and a role. A lot of times I feel that the pursuit of professional identity and position dictates how people decide and navigate between new technologies and older ways of doing things. A lot of the older professors here who may have been in the past dismissive of digital technologies are embracing them now because they aren't seeing any other way forward for themselves. It's not a kind of absolute ideological decision. It's very socially dependent.

What role does unlearning play in school? Do you find that students need to unlearn certain habits or practices to become proficient users of these tools?

YL: A lot of what happens is unlearning. A lot of what we try to get students to do is see the context that they are working in—whether the technology, program, or the site—with new eyes. Sometimes it is helpful to approach it with a beginner's mind. To see what are the opportunities for exploiting these conditions rather than what are the preconceptions I bring to it. So it is often about unlearning.

(Continued)

Your essay *Keepers of the Geometry* opens with a question: *Why do we have to change?* With the advent of digital technology, many architects, especially older ones, are asking that very same question. Is this an important question, or is change in the profession and industry inevitable—a given?

YL: It comes back to the question of whether people think it is productive for their own roles or place in the profession for change to happen. People who are asking that often feel threatened because they may be in positions of power and for them status quo is beneficial. So they don't want a change. Whereas people who want to make a place for themselves are often the ones who are trying to change things. Change is inevitable. The idea that architecture has ever been a consistent type of practice is a myth. It has always changed. There will always be people for whom change will seem alluring and filled with opportunity to advance and position themselves better. There will always be this element of change. We cannot predict when things will change in various contexts—but change is always this element in there that's at play.

Case Study Interview with Phil Bernstein, FAIA, vice president, Autodesk

Phil Bernstein, FAIA, is a vice president at Autodesk, responsible for the company's strategies for technology serving the building industry. Formerly a principal with Pelli Clarke Pelli Architects, he teaches professional practice at Yale, where he received both his BA and his MArch. He is coeditor of Building (In) The Future: Recasting Labor in Architecture, *published in 2010 (MIT), a senior fellow of the Design Futures Council and former chair of the AIA National Contract Documents Committee.*

You have taught professional practice to graduate-level architecture students for over twenty years. What would you say are the main differences between what you advised them of when you first started out and—with BIM and IPD in their futures—what you tell them today?

Phil Bernstein (PB): I'm not sure it's a BIM and IPD argument. But I think the biggest difference is this: when I first started teaching professional practice twenty years ago, I was a project manager in a big design firm, and my course was all about "the rules." This is what architects do, this is why they do it, these are the risks, these are the rewards. These are the structures. This is why we operate the way we do—and don't break the rules since there are consequences for breaking the rules. I'd say in the modern age—especially in the last eight or nine years—especially since I have made the transition from practice to being at Autodesk, working on the things I have been working on, I teach my course much more as a dialectic now. More of a discussion of the protocols as they are understood and what sort of standard practice might result, but also a critique of that: what works and what doesn't and which constructs ought to be challenged.

The argument is that the nature of the profession is changing—there are a lot of things going on out there. BIM and IPD are manifestations of that. But there's really a broader discussion going on about the redefinition of the role of architects in the process. The proposition is really that their generation will resolve this question one way or another. And so I still teach the basic constructs of practice, but I try to do it more as a critique.

You have said, in an AIA podcast on IPD in June 2008, "Back when I was a student, everybody was trying to emulate Aldo Rossi and Michael Graves. All you needed was a drafting board, a box of Prismacolors, and an HP calculator, and you were basically done. Now students are doing theory, sustainability, they have a digital fabrication lab. They're doing globalized practice, community design. Nowhere in our curriculum is there anywhere to teach them how to run an overall process."[22] Are you concerned that students are going to lose the sense of the big picture—the long view, the cohesive tapestry—at a time when it is most critical? What potential impact could this have on their future role as leaders?

PB: I think the issue here is one of synthesis. I am a lot less interested in people understanding the pragmatic aspects of running a practice, although in my course I do introduce them to the basic building blocks of practice structure, orientation, and organization, including basic financial structures. I do so to create a more philosophical construct, so we can talk about how the practice of architecture is delivered. I think the biggest challenge we have as teachers right now is to find some way to allow our students to synthesize everything that is going on. The point I was making at the AIA conference is that there is just so much more material that there is to cover than twenty or twenty-five years ago. The footprint of getting someone up to speed

as a responsible architect is much broader and deeper than it was back in the early eighties. We're constrained by time and resources on the one hand. But there's also a synthetic problem, which is how do you create a framework in which people can integrate this?

So at least for the piece of the equation that I am responsible for, I try to create a conceptual armature that basically says these are all the big moving parts. They come together to make a building. This is your role. Remember this set of ideas because they may not hit you right in the face as soon as you graduate, but eventually you'll have to think about this. I actually believe that the people who can get through architecture school these days successfully are reasonably well equipped to face the questions. I just don't think that they have any of the answers. None of us have any of the answers. (See Figure 7.12.)

Figure 7.12   Sign reads from highway: "First IPD Project in New England." Autodesk AEC headquarters (Trapelo), Waltham, MA. *Image courtesy of Tocci Building Companies and KlingStubbins*

In school, with all one has to cover—design, representation, delivery—is there room for learning BIM and integrated design? Is school the best place to learn these processes?

PB: I do believe that, in the work that I have been doing, the fundamental means of representation in the design business is shifting from classical drafting methodologies to modeling methodologies, and that it's critically important to change the frame of reference in design school so that you are equipped to do that stuff. The challenge is: how do you teach—do training and teaching—at the same time? There's a distinction, in my view, between training [and teaching]. At Yale, for example, you don't get credit for learning a piece of software, any more

What I expect is, at least in the near term, we'll invent techniques for doing training in parallel with teaching.
—Phil Bernstein, FAIA

(Continued)

than we would give you credit for using a band saw or a water jet cutter. Those are just skills that you pick up as part of the curriculum.

I think one of the difficulties we've noticed in a number of the studios we've sponsored that are either BIM-oriented or around some other part of Autodesk's portfolio is asking students to do three things in parallel: learn a new piece of software, explore whatever the research question of the studio is—whether on sustainability, or [for example,] where we helped Greg Lynn in a studio on surface form making—*and* continue to hone their design skills. It's an awful lot to ask someone to do at the same time. So we're going to have to figure out how to solve this problem. What I expect is, at least in the near term, we'll invent techniques for doing training in parallel with teaching. What I'm hoping will happen [in terms of curriculum]—we're studying this problem in a very preliminary way at Yale right now—is that we'll invent techniques for doing training in parallel with teaching, and you'll teach building modeling as a way of teaching tectonics. You'll teach people to use a building information modeler as a mechanism for teaching how a building actually goes together. That way, you don't separate picks and clicks, menus and drop-down screens, from some other pedagogical objective that you have. If you're going to teach someone how to do a wall section, you have to teach them how to draw the thing. It's the same exact problem. That's the bad news. The good news is that the idea of building information modeling is a horizontal concept. It applies across a whole bunch of pieces of the curriculum: sustainable design, or engineering, or visualization, or daylighting. So at least if you teach it, it's a relatively efficient thing to do, instead of a one-off. (See Figure 7.13.)

Figure 7.13   Team mantra. *Image courtesy of Tocci Building Companies and KlingStubbins*

At some point in the foreseeable future—if the recent statistics from McGraw-Hill are any indication—this will be the case. Right now, most architecture students wouldn't dare graduate without being AutoCAD-capable. And we're starting to see increasing pressure on these programs to make people BIM-capable. They need it to get a job.

You have said that most of the focus in the use of digital tools has been about form making, and that the core problem set students should be addressing is "how to design better, more responsive, more environmentally appropriate, more precise buildings that meet the client's requirements." If that's going to happen, students have to refocus their attention on new tools and processes. Are architects the right entity to bring this to the table? What do you feel stands in their way? How do you suggest getting students to embrace not just the tool use and mechanisms, but the implications of these tools?

PB: We're in the middle of this discussion internally right now in the company on this whole trend in the business world that's being advocated, called *design thinking*. There's the article in the *Harvard Business Review* by IDEO's Tim Brown on the topic. It reminds me of this old jokey definition of sociology that my wife used to use when we were in college together. She was a sociology major, and people would make fun of what she did by calling it "the systematic restatement of the obvious." This design-thinking thing that the business world's gotten into feels very much that way: that design thinking is a fundamental strategy for solving problems.

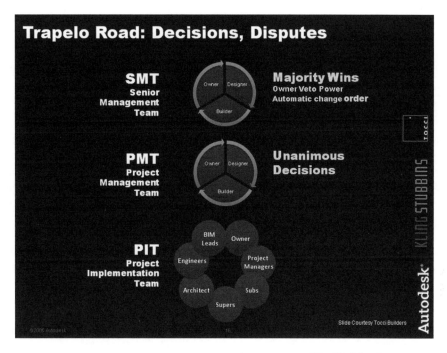

Figure 7.14   Management team structure—and how decisions are determined. *Image courtesy of Tocci Building Companies and KlingStubbins*

And the question for architects who have been trained as design thinkers is the following: What's the problem you want to work on? It's clear that the problem set of making buildings has become a much more integrated—with a lowercase "i"—dilemma. It's about understanding the implications of a building on the environment. It's about understanding the implications of a building on the operations, on its users. In the *Harvard Business Review* article, they talk about this brilliant idea they had to study nursing delivery patterns as part of a project to improve the operations of a hospital. The whole problem was very architectural. It was about layout and flows and staffing. Architects have the skill set to embrace this whole set of issues and really address the holistic problem of making buildings.

The question is: Are we interested? Because what we generally do—although we are starting to see things move off this a bit—we train everybody to be a heroic form maker. That's the objective of most design programs. And to me the problem with that approach is that it conflates the objective of creating a strong, clear-headed designer who has his or her own set of sensibilities about the larger problem of what it means to be an architect. This is part of the dialectic that we talk about in my professional practice class. "What are you going to do when you grow up?" If you want to be a shape maker, then that's one avenue. But the problem set is considerably larger than that. (See Figure 7.14.)

If the majority of architects decide that all they are interested in is forms and shapes and colors, then there are a whole bunch of other people in the process who are more than willing to step up and be the process integrators and relegate aesthetics to the

(Continued)

same tier of consultants as interior designers, graphic designers, and landscape designers. These are all people who are very important—but they don't integrate the entire problem into the problem of building.

You can tell what my own bias is here, right? I was trained as a designer and started my career as a designer. But I got much more interested in process issues fairly early in my career and advocated that a well-designed process yields a good design. But it's not my call. I've been working on the problem of creating integrated process tools so architects could play this role, but as a profession we have to make this decision. And that jury is still out. It's not a coincidence that a number of my recent students are working for contractors right now and not architects. Some of that is economic. And some of it is realizing where they can actually have some influence on the process.

You opened your AIA podcast on IPD in June 2008 with the William Gibson quote, "The future is here. It's just not widely distributed yet." Would you say that today the future is more widely distributed? And if so, would you say that for the most part the diffusion of innovative processes is shallow or deep?

PB: I think the future is more evenly distributed, but it is not so evenly distributed [as] to be the present. The adoption statistics for these new tools are pretty encouraging. Most of the AEC professionals in the U.S., for example, are aware of them and have a path to get to them. I think that we're on the front end of some evolutionary stuff. The theoretical ideas of building information modeling or even integrated project delivery—or even sustainable design—have been academic theory for thirty years, so the fact that the mainstream industry is starting to talk about them now is a very, very good sign. However, the distribution of these kinds of ideas is highly discontinuous. And if you read business network theory, it's a pretty well-understood phenomenon that pockets of innovation in a loosely integrated network—like the AEC industry—actually decrease efficiency in the short term. And we're in an industry that cannot afford much more decrease in efficiency.

So you can imagine that the efficiency opportunities of an integrated process, for example, are lost if only the architect and the mechanical engineer are on innovative tools and everybody else is not. Or the owner doesn't endorse an IPD process. So you're starting to see the beginning of Negroponte's evolution[23] but it is quite discontinuous. The quality of the dialogue has really risen enormously. Five years ago, most of the discussion in the U.S. was "What is this?" and "Why do I care?" And now the discussion is, "OK, I get it. I just need to figure out how to do it. I'm not sure how long it's going to take me. But I'm going to figure out how to do this." (See Figures 7.15 and 7.16.)

Do you believe that all levels—individuals/design professionals, firms/organizations, and the profession/industry— serve to gain from the wide use of BIM and the integrated design process enabled by it? Is there one tier that benefits the most from the advent of these processes?

PB: If you don't start at the bottom tier, which is that person sitting behind a machine trying to work through a problem—if the benefits don't accrue very directly at that level, the rest of the stuff is just theory. The direction to move has to be a top-down thing. The agreement about philosophical alignment has to happen at the supply chain level, or even at the firm level. But the benefits—the day-to-day working benefits, have to start on the desktop and flow up.

If you don't start at the bottom tier, which is that person sitting behind a machine trying to work through a problem—if the benefits don't accrue very directly at that level, the rest of the stuff is just theory.

—Phil Bernstein, FAIA

Figure 7.15   Trapelo existing conditions. Laser scan of building interior. *Image courtesy of Tocci Building Companies and KlingStubbins*

Benefits for those using BIM are legion and well known by now. In a recent interview you mentioned the clarity of the design as a benefit—specifically, "the ability to interact with the description of the building in numerous ways so people from various perspectives can understand it." I call that a co-benefit, where a benefit for one entity positively impacts others, serving to dissolve silos while ostensibly paving the way toward collaboration and integrated design. Can you think of other co-benefits for using BIM?

PB: [One] idea which I think is going to be increasingly useful is about analysis: a lot of the transactional and analytical aspects of creating a design that take up so much brainpower right now, because they are so onerous to compute by hand, are going to become increasingly automated—and therefore unlock a whole other set of possibilities for the design proposition. One that comes to mind is that we're working on something that lets people rapidly work on energy analysis with their building. That used to be so torturous, you would either not do it or you would outsource it. And the ability to actually optimize the design for its energy consumption was a highly constrained thing. It was such a pain in the ass to do it. If you can parameterize the problem and solve for *x* computationally and have some confidence that you are getting to the right answer, that clears up a whole other avenue of investigation that might be available to you. Or at a minimum gives you more cycles to work on a different set of problems. You can imagine as these platforms get more robust and analytical algorithms get more sophisticated, the whole analysis problem moves from things we understand right now—things like airflow and the modulus of elasticity—to building codes and

(Continued)

Figure 7.16   Design and construction collaboration. *Image courtesy of Tocci Building Companies and KlingStubbins*

air quality. It changes the nature of the design proposition in a pretty interesting way. It means that you will be able to generate a pretty interesting set of alternatives, rapidly narrow them such that promising avenues of investigation become much more apparent. In a way it's kind of a shift from the paradigm of a talented designer being somebody who knows where to go by intuition, to having a much more rich set of insights.

My wife reminded me that I used to describe the difference between young designers and older designers as the ability to manage an increasingly larger set of variables. When I was working for Cesar Pelli, that was one of the amazing things about him—he could keep so many things in his head and he could balance them and weigh one against the other, and he could edit out what he called the systematic generation of useless alternatives. He would prevent us from going down that avenue. A lot of the sorts of things that are transactional—does the building work from a fire code perspective, do we have the right orientation for the sun—a lot of that stuff is going to be supported by analytical algorithms, which I do believe for good designers will change the nature of the design process." (See Figures 7.17 and 7.18.)

So the results can be in the designer's head. The process can be in the computer. Because I still believe in the concept of responsible control. I still believe that there's a role for professional people. No structural engineers do their work now without computer models. But they still make sure that they know how the answers [are] coming from their computer models, [that] they're willing to sign and seal. Architects need to get to the same point.

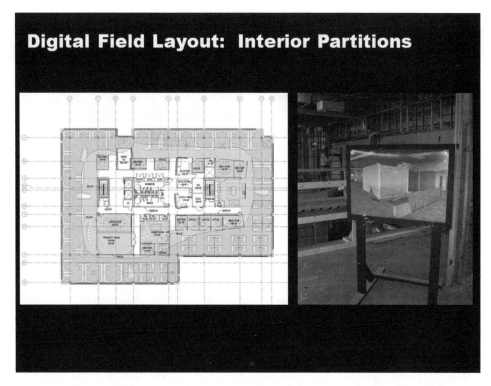

Figure 7.17   Digital field layout of interior partitions. *Image courtesy of Tocci Building Companies and KlingStubbins*

And if things like LEED and other green certification or building codes start to become standardized to the point where it's a reasonable business proposition to automate them, then that stuff just becomes automatic. Imagine getting your design to fifty percent CDs, checking it into a server on our cloud somewhere, and it came back and said "alright, your provisional LEED certification is thirty-six out of forty-eight points." And you didn't have to go through all the rigmarole that you have to go through right now.

A novel that you've identified as one of your favorites — Steinbeck's *East of Eden*—highlights the conflicts of two generations of brothers, one kind and gentle and the other rough and wild. It is a classic tale of sibling rivalry that examines opposing forces—enduring themes of light versus dark, good versus evil, hatred versus love, what we become versus what we might become. Could this serve as an analogy for the architect-contractor relationship, in terms of their conflicting/contrasting cultures and priorities?

PB: My view of this, very much colored by the work we did on our IPD project, is the unenlightened will always have these big cultural differences. I'm reading Malcolm Gladwell's *Outliers* right now, about how things other than just pure talent predispose people to success or failure. The chapter I happen to be reading at the moment explains how at the turn of the century there's this huge number of problems in the southeastern United States with families feuding and killing one another. In town after town

(Continued)

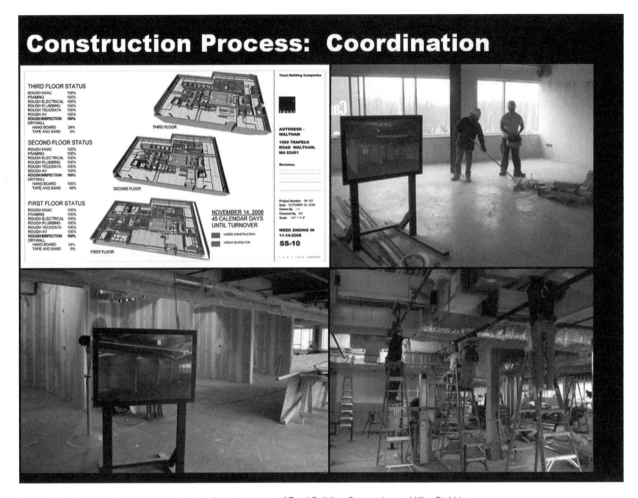

Figure 7.18   Construction process coordination. *Image courtesy of Tocci Building Companies and KlingStubbins*

after town it was Hatfield versus McCoys. And he makes the argument that that tendency to have these kind of honor-based battles can be traced back to Scottish herdsmen, these people's forebears, people who very much had attitudes about maintaining their honor, maintaining the discipline of their property, not letting anyone mess with them. The herdsmen really don't have to rely on anyone to collaborate because their cultural traditions were not about collaboration. There are going to be sectors of both the design and construction communities that believe that we're wired differently, we care about different things, we come from different backgrounds, and we can't work together. The more enlightened architects, engineers, and contractors are starting to realize that if we don't get smarter about what each other are doing and we're not actually able to work together, the building industry will never grow up. It will never get to the kinds of efficiencies and meet its possibilities. And so you're starting to see little signs that there's a desire for crossovers. There are contractors creating building information modeling teams by hiring Yale graduates. My daughter's at Northwestern, and the engineering department there is teaching an architecture course—just to get the engineers acclimated to the idea of architecture. Amongst the enlightened members of the building

Figure 7.19 Digital fabrication of ductwork. *Image courtesy of Tocci Building Companies and KlingStubbins*

community, I think if you can embrace those cultural differences and bring those different sensibilities to the table, the end product is actually improved—if you can figure out who's playing what position and how that all works. In the mid-1990s, this *East of Eden* syndrome reached its apex. And now we are trying to find another way. Because our current results just continue to suck, and speak for themselves. (See Figures 7.19, 7.20, and 7.21.)

Would you agree that for architects to lead in the future—utilizing the BIM and IPD processes—they will need to embrace their inner contractors? And vice versa?

PB: If an inner contractor is somebody who knows when to be extremely practical about things and loves to see stuff get built, then yes, absolutely. On our IPD job, one of the things I came to appreciate was our contractor's willingness to participate in the design process. Not to say, "I don't like how that works because I have a better design idea." But to engage in the proposition of design by contributing his or her insight to the particular problem that we happen to be working on, and thereby improve the result. We didn't have people sitting across the table saying, "I think it should be blue and I think it should be green." Good architects will say, "What I'm really good at is orchestrating a large, complex set of issues, examining alternatives, and synthesizing it into a result." A good contractor will make the same argument! "Well, I've got this thing I'm trying to get done. I've got lots

(*Continued*)

Figure 7.20   Photo of ceiling pipe condition. *Image courtesy of Tocci Building Companies and KlingStubbins*

of ways to go about doing it. I've got options in materials. I've got options in construction strategies. I've got options in sub-contractors. And I have to examine all those options, recombine them, and get to a result. What's so different about those two sensibilities? Is it not possible that some blurring in the line between the two disciplines might be useful? Design thinking might be useful on the construction side, and a kind of more practical, execution-oriented mindset of contractors might be more useful on the design side?

Do you believe that—in the integrated design process—the team as a whole could play the role of master builder? Would you say this has been true in your experience to date?

PB: It's master building—not master builder. Yes, it's the team. The idea that one person can be at the center of the overall process—didn't we leave that behind with Ayn Rand? Buildings are just too complicated. I couldn't even do it on my own house addition!

You have had two recent projects constructed, one in San Francisco and one in Boston—6,000 square meters of

> *The idea that one person can be at the center of the overall process—didn't we leave that behind with Ayn Rand? Buildings are just too complicated. I couldn't even do it on my own house addition!*
>
> —Phil Bernstein, FAIA

Figure 7.21   Photo of how modeled and coordinated ceiling pipe condition accommodates duct. *Image courtesy of Tocci Building Companies and KlingStubbins*

space, $13 million in project cost, on budget, LEED platinum, all Revit—the last completed, from contract signing to move-in, in eight months. Of these projects you have said team members are happy and those that worked on it are all still friends. Was the BIM and integrated design process the secret to your teams' success? What human factors would you say came into play that led to the successful outcome? To what extent does the emotional intelligence of each team member—as you understand it—help to assure this outcome?

PB: On Trapelo Road, our Boston project, it was the IPD construct that created that sense of happiness at the end. What we did was create a sense of joint responsibility for the outcome of the project, and when the project was very successful everyone shared in that success. Everybody felt that they contributed to a good design, a good budget, a good schedule, a good sustainable outcome, and there was a sense that if we all rowed the boat in the same direction, we could all get there a lot faster. Like any project, there were tensions and difficulties—lots of those kinds of challenges. But the fundamental structure of the project basically dictated that we're going to do this thing with complete information transparency, and everybody's success and failure is deeply tied to everybody else's success and failure. It just changes the mindset! The architect and contractor were collaborating very closely on every single issue of importance. Some of my favorite photographs are of Sara Vekaszy, our project architect for KlingStubbins, in the field giving directions directly to the subcontractors. We removed all the intermediate rigamarole to make that possible. It was entirely about a sociological theory about how a project could work.

(Continued)

Figure 7.22   Design process—initial ideas. *Image courtesy of Tocci Building Companies and KlingStubbins*

Figure 7.23   Trapelo interior millwork at atrium. © *Jeff Goldberg/Esto*

Of course, we picked the right people. You pick the wrong people, and the thing would probably go off the rails. I don't know if you want to describe it as emotional intelligence or not. When we picked that team for Trapelo, everybody interviewed for the job with their normal song and dance. And everybody that came in had either designed or built a jillion square feet of TI space, but no one had ever done an IPD job. We basically had three variables we could make our decision from. One, can we work with these people, because this is an IPD project? Two, can they work together? And then, three, are they savvy enough with the technology that the learning curve is going to be relatively short? (See Figure 7.22 and 7.23.)

Not all such projects end as happily. What are some of the lessons learned that you might be willing to share that can help to result in a happy outcome for others?

PB: There are a couple of things. One is being fortunate enough to pick the right people to work with—probably the single biggest consideration. Who's on the bus? Second, there has to be a willingness to jump off the cliff and try something new. Most AEC players are extremely conservative. Nobody wants to be on the leading edge of anything. I'm helping with a symposium that we're doing at Harvard Business School to help Harvard and some of the institutions in the Northeast to explore the fuzzy edges of this IPD problem because they don't know how to get their arms around it. And our project involved a certain amount

Figure 7.24   Trapelo interior millwork closeup. © *Jeff Goldberg/Esto*

of me just going around and saying, "I'm just going to jump off the cliff." I cannot in good conscience be running around the world talking about this process revolution and technology, and we're going to run another one of these jobs as a CM at risk. And everyone is saying, "Are you sure this is going to work?" And, "Do you have any way of demonstrating that this is going to work?" And I said, "No, except go read our marketing materials." Since we're talking about this, we need to have the intestinal fortitude to actually go and try it. That's not a learned thing. I don't know how to convince people to do that. We just did it ourselves. We just jumped off the edge of the cliff. I'm sure if Malcolm Gladwell looked at this thing he would tell me the six reasons why it was inevitable that I would jump off the cliff. Getting the right people and being willing to take a chance are the things as an industry we really need to start doing. (See Figures 7.24 and 7.25.)

There's a third category that we're not touching on, and that is the AEC industry in general is extremely weak about collecting information and sharing it, about what works and what doesn't. On Trapelo, it was a contractual requirement that everyone shared—we forced it! What was interesting about our project in Boston was that the Trapelo Road team, led by Tocci and Kling-Stubbins, they got together and put this very complex BIM implementation plan together: how they were going to manage the model, who was going to be in charge, how this stuff was going to be exchanged, what the rules of engagement were, who could use what when. What happened if this piece of the model got unlocked, etc. They used all the data structure. All of the Roberts Rules of using the model never got touched. They didn't have time! It wasn't benefitting anybody. Tocci would say,

(Continued)

Figure 7.25   Trapelo atrium and gallery. © *Jeff Goldberg/Esto*

"I need this information in the partition data so I can go do layouts." And the KlingStubbins folks would say, "OK, we'll just put it in." We fortunately didn't have a major failure. Nobody got killed. They didn't blow the budget. They didn't blow the schedule. Something terrible didn't happen. So we didn't have to really test the robustness of this model. That's where we'll really find out.

I'm on a bunch of these industry panels. There's a lot of talk about collecting information, doing pilot projects, et cetera. It just felt like it was taking forever. When we looked at each other and realized that we need a new building here—we said, OK, this is what we want to do.

With BIM there's a lot to learn. What would you say is just as important to unlearn?

PB: I'm going to make a neurophysiological argument here. Even on this project, where we had a completely new construct— and part of my job was to be the IPD therapist—it was extremely difficult to force myself to realize that people were playing different positions. You just automatically flow into "I'm the owner and I'm going to do what I want," or "That's the architect's responsibility," or "That's the contractor's responsibility." This stuff runs really deep. We've been acculturated to do this stuff, sometimes for hundreds of years. And getting yourself outside that set of instincts is going to be really, really hard. I spent most of my practice career working for a design architect where we just designed stuff—we didn't take much responsibility for anything else. One might argue that, except for a very limited number of practices, that construct is by definition obsolete. Unlearning—it's Pavlovian, right? People have to try something different and realize how good it feels, or how well it works, or how much money they make. Whatever it is that feels good to them. And then they'll do it again. The other issue is, frankly, generational. I'm hoping that [with] the generation of students that I've been teaching, we will change those instincts. And I think we're starting to see the beginning of it. They're less interested in the kind of heroic design model. There's a lot less star worship. Because of the amount of interesting stuff they do . . . that generation who's also very acculturated to ideas about digital fabrication, when they print with a 3D printer today, ten years from now they're going to want to print out in the field. I think that's when things will really change.

NOTES

1. Kimon Onuma, "BIM Ball—Evolve or Dissolve: Why Architects and the AIA are at Risk of Missing the Boat on Building Information Modeling (BIM)," 2006, www.bimconstruct.org/steamroller.html.

2. Onuma, "Evolve or Dissolve."

3. J. D. Biersdorfer, "Build Your Own Lego Masterpiece, Virtual Brick by Virtual Brick," *New York Times,* September 22, 2005, www.nytimes.com/2005/09/22/technology/circuits/22lego.html.

4. Phil Bernstein, interview with the author, October 15, 2009.

5. Howard W. Ashcraft Jr., "IPD is Light Years ahead of Traditional Delivery," *Building Design & Construction*, August 1, 2009, www.bdcnetwork.com/article/howard-w-ashcraft-jr-ipd-light-years-ahead-traditional-delivery.

6. Andrew Pressman, "Integrated Practice in Perspective: A New Model for the Architectural Profession," *Architectural Record,* May 2007, archrecord.construction.com/practice/projDelivery/ 0705proj-3.asp.

7. Ibid.

8. Rebecca Rupp, *Committed to Memory: How We Remember and Why We Forget* (New York: Crown, 1997).

9. Rich Nitzsche, interview with the author, February 9, 2010.

10. Ibid.

11. For a thorough guide to in-house training, see Karen Fugle, "Survival Guide Chapter 03: Essential Skills 5—Training, How to Write a Training Strategy," October 18, 2008, eatyourcad.com/.

12. "From the Editors," *DesignIntelligence,* September 15, 2007, www.di.net/news/archive/from_editors/.

13. Karen Leland, "Teach an Old Dog New Tricks: How to Break Bad Work Habits," November 16, 2009, gigaom.com/collaboration/teach-an-old-dog-new-tricks-how-to-break-bad-work-habits/.

14. Jonathan Cohen, interview with the author, February 2, 2010.

15. Karel Holloway, "Career-Oriented Courses at Texas Schools Get with the Times," *Dallas Morning News*, February 21, 2010, www.dallasnews.com/news/education/headlines/20100219-Career-oriented-courses-at-Texas-schools-5365.ece.

16. See, for example, Michael Tomasello, *Why We Cooperate* (Cambridge, MA: MIT Press, 2009).

17. Nitzsche, interview.

18. Yanni Loukissas, "Conceptions of Design in a Culture of Simulation" (dissertation, MIT, 2008).

19. Ibid, p. 35.

20. Ibid, p. 85.

21. Ann Lui, "A House Divided: Bridging Architecture's Culture War," *Cornell Sun,*September 21, 2009, dev.cornellsun.com/section/arts/content/2009/09/21/house-divided-bridging-architectures-culture-war.]

22. Phil Bernstein, "Integrated Project Delivery: Understanding the Collaborative Work of the Future in Building Design & Construction, part I," *Architecture Knowledge Review,* podcast, June 20, 2008.

23. Nicholas Negroponte, *The Architecture Machine* (Cambridge: MIT, 1970).

EPILOGUE

Conclusion: Accelerate Adoption When Early Adoption Is No Longer an Option

BIM is a tool *and* process; evolution *and* revolution; attitude *and* mindset. No matter what it is, BIM is here to stay—and if you are on the fence or have yet to adopt, you need to catch up and do so quickly.

What is missing from so many attempts to adopt is a sense of urgency: you have this on your side. You have the advantage of the tortoise that many hares have come before. You have the perspective gained by early adopters who took on the technology in its nascent state. You have the advantage of the lessons learned by these individuals, firms, and companies.

Until architects agree that all of us is better than some of us; that teamwork results in better solutions; that architecture—including the design of buildings—is improved by the inclusion of others, including contractors and clients who may have competing or otherwise completely different goals than your own—until that time arrives, BIM and integrated design will not catch on, and architects will gradually become irrelevant.

The focus throughout this book has been on people and the strategies they use to manage and cope with the transition to the new digital technology and integrated design, and the collaborative work process it enables as they initially adopt and then take the technology and process to a higher plane.

Despite articles lauding 85 percent BIM adoption rates, my own personal experience told me otherwise: that BIM was not catching on the way one would expect a new product and process should. Why was that?

It soon became apparent that social issues needed addressing—how BIM impacts and fits in with firm culture; and the impacts of integrated design on design ambitions, feelings of ownership and authorship, and professional identity.

I soon recognized that there was a need for a book that addressed BIM and integrated design from a people perspective. Upon inquiry, I found other experts in the industry backed me up on this hunch.

Don't wait for implementation day—it happens every day. We are always implementing BIM. It's a mistake to think that you implement and you're done—BIM implementation is ongoing. There's always more to learn, to master, so that you can move on to address the next advancement, the next layer or dimension higher. You reach out to others, include supplementing technologies; projects get larger and more complex; new versions of the software are released and have to be learned and then mastered; you're always striving to work more efficiently; there are always tips and tricks to learn, macros on the keyboard to memorize and utilize—and ways to share what you've learned along the way with others.

It is my hope that this book has helped to prepare you with the right attitudes, mindsets, skill sets, and aptitudes for when you adopt and implement BIM and the collaborative work process of integrated design throughout your organization. Let me know by email (randydeutsch@att.net) or by visiting http:// bimandintegrateddesign.com/, where you can leave a comment.

The assumption throughout has been that there will be no shortage of interest in BIM and integrated design for years to come, and this book has striven to meet both the depth and breadth of that interest. Potential thwarted or potential realized, your potential and the potential of BIM are both unlimited.

INDEX